Windows PowerShell:

The Personal Trainer

PowerShell 3.0 & PowerShell 4.0

William Stanek

PUBLISHED BY

Stanek & Associates
PO Box 362
East Olympia, WA 98540-0362

Cover Design: Creative Designs Ltd.
Editorial Development: Andover Publishing Solutions
Technical Review: L & L Technical Content Services

You can provide feedback related to this book by emailing the author at williamstanek@aol.com. Please use the name of the book as the subject line.

Contents at a Glance

Table of Contents

Introduction

Windows PowerShell: The Personal Trainer is the authoritative quick reference guide to Windows PowerShell and is designed to be a key resource you turn to whenever you have questions about Windows PowerShell. To this end, the book zeroes in on the key aspects of Windows PowerShell that you'll use the most.

Inside this book's pages, you'll find comprehensive overviews, step-by-step procedures, frequently used tasks, documented examples, and much more. One of the goals is to keep the content so concise that the book remains compact and easy to navigate while at the same time ensuring that the book is packed with as much information as possible—making it a valuable resource.

What's This Book About?

Windows PowerShell: The Personal Trainer covers PowerShell 3.0 and PowerShell 4.0. In this book, I teach you how PowerShell features work, why they work the way they do, and how to use them to meet your needs. One of the goals is to keep the content so concise that the book remains compact and easy to navigate while ensuring that the book is packed with as much information as possible—making it a valuable resource. In addition, this book provides hands-on, tips, and best practices for working with Windows PowerShell.

What Do I Need to Know?

To get practical and useful information into your hands without the clutter of a ton of background material, I had to assume several things. If you are reading this book, I hope that you have basic networking skills and a basic understanding of Windows, and that Windows PowerShell is already installed on your systems. I also assume that you are fairly familiar with Windows commands and procedures as well as the Windows command line. With this in mind, I don't devote entire chapters to understanding Windows architecture or installing Windows PowerShell. I do, however, provide complete details on the core features of Windows PowerShell and how you can use these features.

How Is This Book Organized?

Rome wasn't built in a day, and this book wasn't intended to be read in a day, a week, or even 21 days. Ideally, you'll read this book at your own pace, a little each day, as you work your way through the features Windows PowerShell has to offer.

Making this book easy to follow and understand was my number one goal. I really want anyone, skill level or work schedule aside, to be able to learn how to effectively use Windows PowerShell.

To make the book easy to use, this book is organized into multiple chapters. The chapters are arranged in a logical order, taking you from the essential concepts you need to know to work with Windows PowerShell to techniques for managing computers with scripts.

Windows PowerShell: The Personal Trainer is designed to be used with *Windows PowerShell for Administration: The Personal Trainer*. While this book focuses on core features, the latter book focuses on putting Windows PowerShell to work in the real world.

What Conventions Are Used in This Book?

I've used a variety of elements to help keep the text clear and easy to follow. You'll find code terms and listings in `monospace` type, except when I tell you to actually enter a command. In that case, the command appears in **bold** type. When I introduce and define a new term, I put it in *italics*.

This book also has notes, tips and other sidebar elements that provide additional details on points that need emphasis.

Other Resources

Although some books are offered as all-in-one guides, there's simply no way one book can do it all. This book is intended to be used as a concise and easy-to-use resource. It covers everything you need to perform core tasks with Windows PowerShell, but it is by no means exhaustive.

As you encounter new topics, take the time to practice what you've learned and read about. Seek additional information as necessary to get the practical experience and knowledge that you need.

I truly hope you find that *Windows PowerShell: The Personal Trainer* helps you use Windows PowerShell successfully and effectively.

Thank you,

William R. Stanek

(williamstanek@aol.com)

Chapter 1. Windows PowerShell Essentials

Chances are that if you work with Windows computers you've heard of Windows PowerShell. You may even have read other books about PowerShell and put PowerShell to work. However, you probably still have many questions about PowerShell, or you may simply be curious about what PowerShell 3.0 and PowerShell 4.0 have to offer that their predecessors didn't.

Every version of Windows has had a built-in command line that is used to run built-in commands, utilities, and scripts. Windows PowerShell extends the command line in exciting ways, opening the Windows and Windows Server operating systems in ways that were previously possible only with extensive programming.

This chapter focuses on Windows PowerShell essentials. You'll learn how to use PowerShell, how to run commands, and how to work with related features. For proficient Windows administrators, skilled support staff, and committed power users, Windows PowerShell has become increasingly indispensable. Knowing how to use PowerShell properly can save you time and effort and can mean the difference between smooth-running operations and frequent problems. Moreover, if you're responsible for multiple computers, learning the timesaving strategies that PowerShell offers is not just important, it's essential for sustaining day-to-day operations.

> **REAL WORLD** In general, you can use techniques that you learn in this book on all versions of Windows on which you can install Windows PowerShell 3.0 or PowerShell 4.0. However, when you are working across operating systems, you should always test commands, options, and scripts in a development or test environment, where the computers with which you are working are isolated from the rest of the network, before using them in live production environments.

Getting Started with Windows PowerShell

Anyone /with a background in UNIX is probably familiar with the concept of a command shell. Most UNIX-based operating systems have several full-featured command shells available, including Korn Shell (KSH), C Shell (CSH), and Bourne Shell (SH). Although Windows operating systems have always had a command-line environment, they lacked a full-featured command shell until Windows PowerShell was introduced.

Not unlike the less sophisticated Windows command prompt, the UNIX command shells operate by executing built-in commands, external commands, and command-line utilities and then returning the results in an output stream as text. The output stream can be manipulated in various ways, including redirecting it so that it can be used as input for another command. The process of redirecting one command's output to another command's input is called *piping*, and it is a widely used shell-scripting technique.

The C Shell is one of the more sophisticated UNIX shells. In many respects, C Shell is a marriage of some of the best features of the C programming language and a full-featured UNIX shell environment. Windows PowerShell takes the idea of a full-featured command shell built on a programming language a step further. It does this by implementing a scripting language based on C# and an object model based on the Microsoft .NET Framework.

Basing the scripting language for Windows PowerShell on C# ensures that the scripting language can be easily understood by current C# developers and also allows new developers to advance to C#. Using an object model based on the .NET Framework allows Windows PowerShell to pass complete objects and all their properties as output from one command to another. The ability to redirect objects is extremely powerful and allows for a much more dynamic manipulation of result sets. For example, you can get not only the name of a particular user but also the entire related user object. You can then manipulate the properties of this user object by referring to the properties you want to work with by name.

Running Windows PowerShell

Windows PowerShell 3.0 and Windows PowerShell 4.0 are enhanced and extended editions of the original implementations of PowerShell. The changes are dramatic, and they improve both the performance capabilities of PowerShell and its versatility. You can do things with PowerShell 3.0 and PowerShell 4.0 that you simply could not do with earlier versions, and you can perform standard tasks in much more efficient ways than before. The discussion that follows explores PowerShell options and configurations and also provides tips for using the command history.

PowerShell Versions and Prerequisites

Windows and Windows Server operating systems are released with a specific version of Windows PowerShell:

- Windows PowerShell 4.0 is built into Windows 8.1 and Windows Server 2012 Release 2 (R2). Also, you can install PowerShell 4.0 on computers running Windows 7 with Service Pack 1 or later, and Windows Server 2008 R2 with Service Pack 1 or later by installing Windows Management Framework 4.0.
- Windows PowerShell 3.0 is built into Windows 8 and Windows Server 2012. Also, you can install PowerShell 3.0 on computers running Windows 7 with Service Pack 1 or later, Windows Server 2008 R2 with Service Pack 1 or later, and Windows Server 2008 with Service Pack 2 or later by installing Windows Management Framework 3.0.

The prerequisites for using Windows PowerShell depend on the version you are working with:

- Windows PowerShell 4.0 requires a full installation of .NET Framework 4.5. Windows 8.1 and Windows Server 2012 R2 include Microsoft .NET Framework 4.5 by default.
- Windows PowerShell 3.0 requires a full installation of .NET Framework 4. Windows 8 and Windows Server 2012 include Microsoft .NET Framework 4.5 by default, which includes the .NET Framework 4 components.

Also, Windows PowerShell 3.0 and Windows PowerShell 4.0 require:

- WS-Management 3.0, which supports the Windows Remote Management (WinRM) service and the WS-Management (WSMan) protocol.

- Windows Management Instrumentation 3.0 (WMI), which supports PowerShell features that access managed resources through WMI.

> **REAL WORLD**   The Distributed Management Task Force (DMTF) created the Common Information Model (CIM) standard to describe the structure and behavior of managed resources. Windows Management Instrumentation (WMI) is a CIM server service that implements the CIM standard on Windows.
>
> WS-Management (WS-Man) is a protocol for managing communications between a CIM client and a CIM server. WS-Man is based on Simple Object Access Protocol (SOAP), which is implemented using the eXtensible Markup Language (XML).
>
> Windows Remote Management (WinRM) is the Microsoft implementation of the WS-Man protocol on Windows.

These components are included in Windows 8, Windows 8.1, Windows Server 2012, and Windows Server 2012 R2. For other supported operating systems, these components are installed when you install Windows Management Framework 3.0 or Windows Management Framework 4.0 as required. Different builds are available for each version of Windows, in 32-bit and 64-bit editions. See Microsoft TechNet Library Article HH847769 for complete details and links to the required components (http://technet.microsoft.com/en-us/library/hh847769.aspx).

Using the Windows PowerShell Console

Windows PowerShell has both a command-line environment and a graphical environment for running commands and scripts. The PowerShell console (powershell.exe) is a 32-bit or 64-bit environment for working with PowerShell at the command line. On 32-bit versions of Windows, you'll find the 32-bit executable in the %SystemRoot%\System32\WindowsPowerShell\v1.0 directory. On 64-bit versions of Windows, you'll find the 32-bit executable in the %SystemRoot%\SysWow64\WindowsPowerShell\v1.0 directory and the 64-bit executable in the %SystemRoot%\System32\WindowsPowerShell\v1.0 directory.

> **NOTE** %SystemRoot% refers to the SystemRoot environment variable. The Windows operating system has many environment variables, which are used to refer to user-specific and system-specific values. I'll often refer to environment variables using the standard Windows syntax %VariableName%. In Windows PowerShell, you access and work with environment variables using the Env provider. Providers are discussed in the "Using Providers" section in Chapter 3, "Managing Your Windows PowerShell Environment."

Using the Standard Console

With Windows 7, Windows Server 2008 and Windows Server 2008 R2, you can start the PowerShell console by using the Search box on the Start menu. Click Start, type **powershell** in the Search box, and then press Enter. Or, you can click Start, point to All Programs, point to Accessories, Windows PowerShell, and then choose Windows PowerShell.

If you are working with a later versions of Windows, you can start the PowerShell console by using the Apps Search box. Type **powershell** in the Apps Search box, and then press Enter. Or you can click the Windows logo, click the Apps button, and then choose Windows PowerShell.

Regardless of which version of Windows you are using, the 64-bit version of the PowerShell console is started by default on 64-bit systems. If you want to use the 32-bit PowerShell console on a 64-bit system, you must select the Windows PowerShell (x86) option.

You can start Windows PowerShell from a Windows command shell (cmd.exe) by entering the following:

```
powershell
```

Using the Elevated, Administrator Console

The standard Windows PowerShell console runs with no security context and you won't be able to perform administrative tasks. To change computer settings and perform other administrative tasks, you'll need to run the PowerShell console in elevated, administrator mode.

With Windows 7, Windows Server 2008 and Windows Server 2008 R2, you can run the PowerShell console in elevated, administrator mode by using the Search box on the Start menu. Click Start, type **powershell** in the Search box, right-click Windows PowerShell in the search results and then select Run As Administrator. Or, you can click Start, point to All Programs, point to Accessories, Windows PowerShell. Next, right-click the Windows PowerShell menu item and then select Run As Administrator.

If you are working with a later versions of Windows, you can run the PowerShell console in elevated, administrator mode by using the Apps Search box. Type **powershell** in the Apps Search box, right-click Windows PowerShell in the search results and then select Run As Administrator.

REAL WORLD By default with Windows 8.1 and Windows Server 2012 R2, Command Prompt and Command Prompt (Admin) are options on the shortcut menu that is displayed when you right-click in the lower left corner or press Windows key + X. The alternative is for the Windows PowerShell prompt and the Windows PowerShell (Admin) prompt to be displayed on this menu. To configure which options are available, on the desktop, right-click the taskbar and then select Properties. In the Taskbar And Navigation Properties dialog box, on the Navigation tab, select or clear the Replace Command Prompt With Windows PowerShell... checkbox as appropriate.

You can start an elevated, administrator Windows PowerShell console from an elevated, administrator command shell (cmd.exe) by entering the following:

```
powershell
```

Working the PowerShell Console

Figure 1-1 shows a PowerShell window. By default, the window is 120 characters wide and displays 50 lines of text. When additional text is to be displayed in the window or you enter commands and the PowerShell console's window is full, the current text is displayed in the window, and prior text is scrolled up. If you want to pause the display temporarily when a command is writing output, press Ctrl+S. Afterward, press Ctrl+S to resume or Ctrl+C to terminate execution.

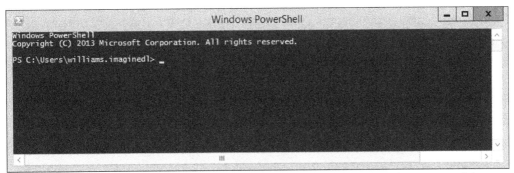

FIGURE 1-1 When you work with PowerShell, you'll frequently use the command-line environment.

In this figure, the display text is:

```
Windows PowerShell
Copyright (c) 2013 Microsoft Corporation. All rights reserved.

PS C:\Users\williams.imagined1>
```

Here, the command prompt for the PowerShell shows the current working directory preceded by PS. A blinking cursor following the command prompt indicates that PowerShell is in interactive processing mode. In interactive mode, you can type commands directly after the prompt and press Enter to execute them. For example, type **get-childitem** and then press Enter to get a listing of the current directory.

> **NOTE** When working with a standard PowerShell window, the default path is based on the current value of %UserProfile%, meaning the user profile directory for the current user. When you run PowerShell in elevated, administrator mode, the default path is %WinDir%\System32, meaning the System32 directory for the Windows installation.
>
> **MORE INFO** Get-ChildItem is used to get items in specified locations. Get-ChildItem works with the filesystem by default, but can be used with other data providers, such as the Env provider or the Cert provider, which are used to work with environment variables and digital certificates respectively. For example, you can list all environment variables on a computer by entering **get-childitem env:**.

Windows PowerShell also has a noninteractive processing mode, which is used when executing a series of commands. In noninteractive processing mode,

PowerShell reads and executes commands one by one but doesn't present a prompt to the user. Typically, commands are read from a script file, but you can start the PowerShell console in noninteractive processing mode.

To exit PowerShell, type **exit**. If you started PowerShell from a command prompt, typing **exit** will return you to the command prompt. If you want to run a separate instance of PowerShell from within PowerShell, you also can type **powershell** at the PowerShell prompt. Invoking PowerShell in this way allows you to use a separate session and initialize PowerShell with specific parameters.

Using the Windows PowerShell ISE

The official name of the graphical environment for Windows PowerShell is the Windows PowerShell Integrated Scripting Environment (ISE). Using the PowerShell application (powershell_ise.exe), you can run commands and write, run, and debug scripts in a single integrated interface. There are 32-bit and 64-bit graphical environments for working with PowerShell, and you'll find the related executables in the same location as the PowerShell console.

With Windows 7, Windows Server 2008 and Windows Server 2008 R2, you can start the PowerShell application by using the Search box on the Start menu. Click Start, type **powershell** in the Search box, and then press Enter. Or, you can click Start, point to All Programs, point to Accessories, Windows PowerShell, and then choose Windows PowerShell ISE. Or, right-click the Windows PowerShell ISE menu item and then select Run As Administrator to run the PowerShell application in elevated, administrator mode.

If you are working with a later versions of Windows, you can start the PowerShell application by using the Apps Search box. Type **powershell** in the Apps Search box, and then choose Windows PowerShell ISE. Or you can click the Windows logo, click the Apps button and then choose Windows PowerShell ISE. Or, right-click Windows PowerShell ISE and then select Run As Administrator to run the PowerShell application in elevated, administrator mode.

Regardless of which version of Windows you are using, the 64-bit version of the PowerShell ISE is started by default on 64-bit systems. If you want to use the 32-

bit application on a 64-bit system, you must select the Windows PowerShell ISE (x86) option.

You can start the PowerShell application from a command prompt (cmd.exe) by entering:

```
powershell_ise
```

Figure 1-2 shows the main window for the PowerShell application. Here, the main window displays the Script pane and the Console pane. In the Script pane, you can type the commands and text for PowerShell scripts. In the Console pane, you can enter commands at a prompt as you would using the PowerShell console and display the results of running scripts or commands.

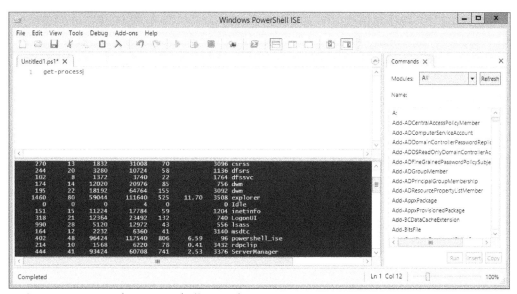

FIGURE 1-2 Use the PowerShell ISE when you are creating scripts.

As you enter text into the Script pane, the text is color coded depending on whether it is a cmdlet, function, variable, or other type of text. To run your script and display the related output in the Console pane, click the Run Script button on the toolbar or press F5. To run part of a script, select the commands to run in the Script pane and then select Run Selection or press F8.

After you enter the text of your script, you can save the script with the .ps1 extension. Click the Save option on the toolbar or press Ctrl+S. In the Save As dialog box, choose a save location, enter a name for the script and then click Save. See "Using Scripts" later in this chapter for more information on working with scripts.

Options on the View menu allow you to control the display and location of the Script pane. Select Show Script Pane to display the Script pane if it is hidden. Select the option again to hide the Script pane if it is displayed. When the Script pane is displayed, you can select Script Pane Right to display the Script pane on the right rather than at the top of the main window. Select the option again to restore the original position. You can resize the panes by clicking and dragging as well.

The default text size is fairly small. You can change the text size by using the Zoom slider in the lower-right corner of the main window. Alternatively, press Ctrl and+ to increase the text size, or press Ctrl and – to decrease the text size.

To exit the PowerShell application, press Alt+F4 or select the Exit option on the File menu. You can also exit by typing **exit** at the PowerShell prompt in the Console pane.

Configuring Windows PowerShell Console Properties

If you use the Windows PowerShell console frequently, you'll definitely want to customize its properties. For example, you can add buffers so that text scrolled out of the viewing area is accessible. You can resize the console, change its fonts, and more.

To get started, click the PowerShell prompt icon at the top of the console window or right-click the console's title bar and then select Properties. As Figure 1-3 shows, the Properties dialog box has four tabs:

- **Options** Allows you to configure cursor size, edit options, and command history. Select QuickEdit Mode if you want to use a single mouse click to paste copied text into the PowerShell window. Clear QuickEdit Mode if you want to right-click and then select Paste to insert copied text. Clear Insert Mode to overwrite text as the default editing mode. Use the command history to configure how previously used commands are buffered in memory. (You'll find more information about the command history in the next section of this chapter, "Working with the Command History.")

- **Font**   Allows you to set the font size and face used by the PowerShell prompt. Raster font sizes are set according to their pixel width and height. For example, the size 8 × 12 is 8 screen pixels wide and 12 screen pixels high. Other fonts are set by point size, such as 10-point Lucida Console. Interestingly, when you select a point size of n, the font will be n pixels high; therefore, a 10-point font is 10 screen pixels high. These fonts can be designated as a bold font type as well, which increases their screen pixel width.

- **Layout**   Allows you to set the screen buffer size, window size, and window position. Size the buffer height so that you can easily scroll back through previous listings and script output. A good setting is in the range of 2,000 to 3,000. Size the window height so that you can view more of the PowerShell window at one time. A good setting is a width of 120 and a height of 60. If you want the PowerShell window to be in a specific screen position when started, clear Let System Position Window and then specify a position, in pixels, for the upper-left corner of the PowerShell window by using Left and Top.

- **Colors**   Allows you to set the text and background colors used by the PowerShell console. Screen Text and Screen Background control the respective color settings for the window. The Popup Text and Popup Background options control the respective color settings for any pop-up dialog boxes generated when running commands at the PowerShell prompt.

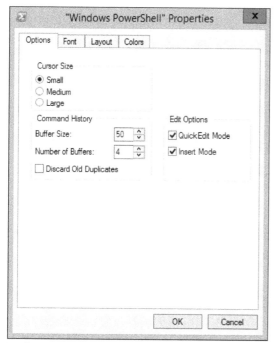

FIGURE 1-3 Configure PowerShell console properties for your environment.

When you are finished updating the window properties, click OK to save your settings to your user profile. Your settings modify only the shortcut that started the current window. Any time you start PowerShell using the applicable shortcut, PowerShell will use these settings. If, however, you start PowerShell using a different shortcut, you'll have the settings associated with that shortcut.

Working with the Command History

The command history buffer is a feature of Windows PowerShell that stores commands you've used in the current session and allows you to access them without having to retype the command text. The maximum number of commands to buffer is set through the PowerShell Properties dialog box discussed in the previous section. By default, up to 50 commands are stored.

You can change the history size by completing these steps:

1. Right-click the PowerShell console's title bar, select Properties, and then click the Options tab.

2. Use the Buffer Size field to set the maximum number of commands to store in the history, and then click OK to save your settings to your user profile.

Your settings modify only the shortcut that started the current window. Any time you start a PowerShell using the applicable shortcut, it will use these settings. If, however, you start a PowerShell using a different shortcut, you'll have the settings associated with that shortcut.

You can access commands stored in the history in the following ways:

- **Browsing with the arrow keys** Use the up arrow and down arrow keys to move up and down through the list of buffered commands. When you find the command you want to use, press Enter to execute it as entered previously, or you can modify the command text displayed by adding or changing parameters and then pressing Enter.
- **Browsing the command history pop-up window** Press F7 to display a pop-up window that contains a listing of buffered commands. Next, select a command using the arrow keys. (Alternatively, press F9, press the corresponding number on the keyboard, and then press Enter.) Execute the selected command by pressing Enter, or press Esc to close the pop-up window without executing a command.
- **Searching the command history** Enter the first few letters of the command you want to execute, and then press F8. PowerShell searches through the history for the first command that begins with the characters you entered. Press Enter to execute it, or press F8 again to search the history buffer for the next match in the command history.

As you work with the command history, keep in mind that each instance of Windows PowerShell has its own set of command buffers. Thus, buffers are valid only in the related PowerShell context.

Working with Cmdlets and Scripts

Windows PowerShell introduces the concept of a cmdlet (pronounced *commandlet*). A cmdlet is the smallest unit of functionality in Windows PowerShell. You can think of a cmdlet as a built-in command. Rather than being highly complex, most cmdlets are quite simple and have a small set of associated properties.

Using Cmdlets

You use cmdlets the same way you use any other commands and utilities. Cmdlet names are not case sensitive. This means you can use a combination of both uppercase and lowercase characters. After starting Windows PowerShell, you can enter the name of the cmdlet at the prompt, and it will run in much the same way as a command-line command.

Understanding Cmdlet Names

For ease of reference, cmdlets are named using verb-noun pairs. As Table 1-1 shows, the verb tells you what the cmdlet does in general. The noun tells you what specifically the cmdlet works with. Verbs and nouns are always separated by a hyphen with no spaces. For example, the Get-Variable cmdlet gets a named Windows PowerShell variable and returns its value. If you don't specify which variable to get as a parameter, Get-Variable returns a list of all PowerShell variables and their values. You also can get a list of all PowerShell variables and their values by entering **get-childitem variable:**.

TABLE 1-1 Common Verbs Used with Cmdlets

CMDLET VERB	USAGE
Add	Adds an instance of an item, such as a history entry or snap-in.
Clear	Removes the contents of an item, such as an event log or variable value.
ConvertFrom	Converts an item from one format to another, such as converting from a list of comma-separated values to object properties.
ConvertTo	Converts an item to a particular format, such as converting object properties to a list of comma-separated values.

Disable	Disables an enabled setting, such as disabling remote connections.
Enable	Enables a disabled setting, such as enabling remote connections.
Export	Exports an item's properties in a particular format, such as exporting console properties in XML format.
Get	Queries a specific object or a subset of a type of object, such as getting a list of running processes.
Import	Imports an item's properties from a particular format, such as importing console properties from serialized XML.
Invoke	Executes an instance of an item, such as an expression.
New	Creates a new instance of an item, such as a new variable or event.
Remove	Removes an instance of an item, such as a variable or event.
Set	Modifies specific settings of an object.
Start	Starts an instance of an item, such as a service or process.
Stop	Stops an instance of an item, such as a service or process.
Test	Tests an instance of an item for a specific state or value, such as testing a connection to see if it is valid
Write	Performs a write operation on an instance of an item, such as writing an event to the system event log.

Table 1-2 provides a list of basic utility cmdlets. Although many other cmdlets are available, these are the ones you're likely to use for performing basic tasks, such as comparing objects or getting account credentials.

TABLE 1-2 Basic Utility Cmdlets

CMDLET NAME	DESCRIPTION
Compare-Object, Group-Object, Sort-Object, Select-Object, New-Object	Cmdlets for comparing, grouping, sorting, selecting, and creating objects.
ConvertFrom-SecureString, ConvertTo-SecureString	Cmdlets for creating or exporting secure strings.
Get-Alias, New-Alias, Set-Alias, Export-Alias, Import-Alias	Cmdlets for getting, creating, setting, exporting, and importing aliases.
Get-Command, Invoke-Command, Measure-Command, Trace-Command	Cmdlets for getting information about cmdlets, invoking commands, measuring the run time of commands, and tracing commands.
Get-Credential	Gets a credential object based on a password.
Get-Date, Set-Date	Gets or sets the current date and time.
Get-ExecutionPolicy, Set-ExecutionPolicy	Gets or sets the effective execution policy for the current shell.
Get-Host	Gets information about the PowerShell host application.
Get-Location, Set-Location	Displays or sets the current working location.
Get-Process, Start-Process, Stop-Process	Gets, starts, or stops processes on a computer.
Get-PSDrive, New-PSDrive, Remove-PSDrive	Gets, creates, or removes a specified PowerShell drive.
Get-Service, New-Service, Set-Service	Gets, creates, or sets system services.

CMDLET NAME	DESCRIPTION
Get-Variable, New-Variable, Set-Variable, Remove-Variable, Clear-Variable	Cmdlets for getting, creating, setting, and removing variables as well as for clearing variable values.
Pop-Location	Obtains a pushed location from the stack.
Push-Location	Pushes a location to the stack
Read-Host, Write-Host, Clear-Host	Reads input from, writes output to, or clears the host window.
Start-Sleep	Suspends shell or script activity for the specified period.
Wait-Process	Waits for a process to be stopped before accepting input.
Write-Output	Writes an object to the pipeline.
Write-Warning	Displays a warning message.

Getting Information About Cmdlets

You can work with cmdlets by executing them directly at the PowerShell prompt or by running commands from within scripts. The cmdlets available on a particular computer depend on the PowerShell modules that are installed. You can get information about installed modules using Get-Module. For example, if you enter **get-module –listavailable**, you can get a list of all installed modules.

You can get a complete list of cmdlets available by entering **get-command**. However, the output lists both cmdlets and functions by name and definition. With cmdlets, the definition provided is the syntax, but the full syntax rarely fits on the line. More often, you simply want to know if a cmdlet exists. You can display a formatted list of cmdlets by entering the following command:

```
get-command | format-wide –column 3
```

This command shows many of the features of PowerShell that you'll use regularly at the command line. The | symbol is called a pipe. Here, you pipe the output of Get-Command to Format-Wide. Format-Wide takes the output and formats it in multiple columns. The default number of columns is two, but here we used the Column parameter to specify that we wanted to format the output into three columns, as shown in this example:

```
A:                    Add-Computer        Add-Content
Add-History           Add-Member          Add-PSSnapin
Add-Type              B:                  C:
cd..                  cd\                 Checkpoint-Computer
Clear-Content         Clear-EventLog      Clear-History
Clear-Host            Clear-Item          Clear-ItemProperty
Clear-Variable        Compare-Object      Complete-Transaction
Connect-WSMan         ConvertFrom-Csv     ConvertFrom-SecureString
```

A better way to get information about cmdlets is to use Get-Help. To get help for a particular cmdlet, you enter Get-Help followed by the cmdlet name, such as Get-Help Clear-History. If you enter **get-help *-***, you get a list of all cmdlets, which includes a synopsis that summarizes the purpose of the cmdlet—much more useful than a list of commands.

Rather than list all commands, you can list specific commands by name or by using wildcards. For example, if you know the command you are looking for begins with Get, enter **get-help get*** to view all commands that start with Get. If you know the command includes the word *computer*, you could enter **get-help *computer*** to view all commands that included this keyword. Finally, if you are looking for related commands on a specific subject, such as aliases, enter **get-help *** and then the keyword, such as **get-command *alias**.

As discussed later in the chapter in "Working with the Help Documentation," help files aren't included with the standard installation and Windows PowerShell displays automatically generated help information by default. However, when help files are available, you can examine cmdlet syntax and usage. Windows PowerShell provides three levels of Help documentation: standard, detailed, and full. If you want to view the standard Help documentation for a specific cmdlet, type **get-help** followed by the cmdlet name, such as:

```
get-help new-variable
```

The standard Help documentation provides the complete syntax for using a cmdlet, which includes details on any parameters the cmdlet supports and examples. By adding the −Detailed parameter, you can get detailed information about a cmdlet. Or you can get full technical information about a cmdlet by adding the −Full parameter. The detailed and the full documentation are both useful when you want to dig deeper, and usually either one will give you the information you are looking for.

When you work with cmdlets, you'll encounter two standard types of errors:

- **Terminating errors** Errors that halt execution
- **Nonterminating errors** Errors that cause error output to be returned but do not halt execution

With both types of errors, you'll typically see error text that can help you resolve the problem that caused it. For example, an expected file might be missing or you may not have sufficient permissions to perform a specified task.

Using Cmdlet Parameters

All cmdlet parameters are designated with an initial dash (−), such as −Name or −SourcePath. To reduce the amount of typing required, some parameters are position sensitive, so that you can sometimes pass parameters in a specific order without having to specify the parameter name. For example, in the syntax for the Get-Service cmdlet, you know the −Name parameter can be omitted because it is enclosed in brackets as shown here:

```
Get-Service [[-Name] Strings] [-ComputerName Strings]
[-DependentServices] [-Include Strings] [-Exclude Strings]
[-RequiredServices]
```

Therefore, with Get-Service, you don't have to specify the −Name parameter; you can simply type the following:

```
get-service ServiceName
```

where *ServiceName* is the name of the service you want to examine, such as:

```
get-service winrm
```

This command line returns the status of the Windows Remote Management service. Because you can use wildcards, such as *, with name values, you can also type **get-service win*** to return the status of all services whose names begin with *win*. Typically, these will include the Windows Management Instrumentation and Windows Remote Management services, as shown in this example:

```
Status     Name               DisplayName
------     ----               -----------
Stopped    WinHttpAutoProx... WinHTTP Web Proxy Auto-Discovery
Running    Winmgmt            Windows Management Instrumentation
Stopped    WinRM              Windows Remote Management
```

All cmdlets support a common set of parameters. Most cmdlets that make changes support the risk mitigation parameters: –Confirm and –WhatIf. A list of the common and risk mitigation parameters is shown in Table 1-3. Although you can use the common parameters with any cmdlet, they don't necessarily have an effect with all cmdlets. For example, if a cmdlet doesn't generate verbose output, using the –Verbose parameter has no effect.

TABLE 1-3 Common and Risk Mitigation Parameters

PARAMETER NAME	DESCRIPTION
–Confirm	Pauses execution and requires the user to acknowledge the action before continuing.
–Debug	Provides programming-level debugging information about the operation.
–ErrorAction	Controls the command behavior when an error occurs. Valid values are SilentlyContinue (suppress the error and continue), Continue (display the error and continue), Inquire (display the error and prompt to confirm before continuing), Suspend (suspends a workflow and only valid for workflows), and Stop (display the error and halt execution). The default value is Continue.

PARAMETER NAME	DESCRIPTION
–ErrorVariable	Sets the name of the variable (in addition to the standard error) in which to store errors that have occurred.
–OutBuffer	Sets the output buffer for the cmdlet.
–OutVariable	Sets the name of the variable in which to place output objects.
-PipelineVariable	Saves the results or a piped command or part of a piped command that can be passed through the pipeline.
–Verbose	Provides detailed information about the operation.
–WarningAction	Determines how a cmdlet responds to a warning message. Valid values are SilentlyContinue (suppress the warning and continue), Continue (display the warning and continue), Inquire (display the warning and prompt to confirm before continuing), and Stop (display the warning and halt execution). The default value is Continue.
–WarningVariable	Sets the name of the variable (in addition to the standard error) in which to store warnings that have occurred.
–WhatIf	Allows the user to view what would happen if a cmdlet were run with a specific set of parameters.

Using External Commands

Because Windows PowerShell runs within the context of the Windows command prompt, you can run all Windows command-line commands, utilities, and graphical applications from within the Windows PowerShell, either at the PowerShell prompt or in your scripts. However, it is important to remember that the Windows PowerShell interpreter parses all commands before passing off the command to the command-prompt environment. If the Windows PowerShell has a like-named command, keyword, alias, or function for a command, this command, and not the expected Windows command, is executed. (See the

"Initializing the Environment" and "Understanding Command Input, Parsing, and Output" sections in Chapter 2, "Getting the Most from Windows PowerShell" for more information on aliases and functions.)

Non–Windows PowerShell commands and programs must reside in a directory that is part of the PATH environment variable. If the item is found in the path, it is run. The PATH variable also controls where the Windows PowerShell looks for applications, utilities, and scripts. In Windows PowerShell, you can work with Windows environment variables by using $env. If you want to view the current settings for the PATH environment variable, you type **$env:path**. If you want to add a directory to this variable, you can use the following syntax:

```
$env:path += ";DirectoryPathToAdd"
```

Here, *DirectoryPathToAdd* is the directory path you want to add to the path, such as:

```
$env:path += ";C:\Scripts"
```

> **NOTE** In Windows PowerShell, the dollar sign ($) indicates a variable. Normally, when you work with user-created variables, you assign a specified value to a variable, such as the results of a query, and then work with the variable using its $-prefixed name. In this example, you are accessing the PATH environment variable through the Env provider and the required syntax to do this is as shown.

To have this directory added to the path every time you start Windows PowerShell, you can add the command as an entry in a PowerShell profile. A profile is a type of script used to set the working environment for PowerShell. Keep in mind that cmdlets are like built-in commands rather than stand-alone executables. Because of this, they are not affected by the PATH environment variable.

> **REAL WORLD** Computers running Windows and Windows Server have the SETX utility. With the SETX utility, you can write environment variable changes directly to the Windows registry, which makes the changes permanent rather than temporary, as the $env:path command does. You can also use SETX to obtain current registry key values and write them to a text file.

Using Scripts

Windows PowerShell scripts are text files with the .ps1 extension. You can enter any command or cmdlet that you can run at the PowerShell prompt into a script by copying the related command text to a file and saving the file with the .ps1 extension. You can then run the script in the same way you would any other command or cmdlet. However, when you are working with PowerShell scripts, the current directory might not be part of the environment path. For this reason, you might need to use "./" when you run a script in the current directory. For example, if you create a PowerShell script called run_all.ps1, and the script is in the current directory, you could run the script by entering the following command:

```
./run_all
```

> **NOTE** PowerShell is designed to accommodate users with backgrounds in UNIX or Windows operating systems. You can use a forward slash or backward slash as a directory separator. Following this, you can enter **./run_all** or **.\run_all** to reference a script in the current working directory.

Whenever you work with scripts, you need to keep in mind the current execution policy and whether signed scripts are required.

Understanding Execution Policy

The current execution policy for Windows PowerShell controls whether and how you can run configuration files and scripts. Execution policy is a built-in security feature of Windows PowerShell that is set on a per-user basis in the Windows registry. Although the default configuration depends on which operating system and edition is installed, you can quickly determine the execution policy by entering **get-executionpolicy** at the PowerShell prompt.

The available execution policies, from most secure to least secure, are:

- **Restricted** Does not load configuration files or scripts. This means all configuration files and scripts, regardless of whether they are signed or unsigned. Because a profile is a type of script, profiles are not loaded either.

- **AllSigned**   Requires all configuration files and scripts from all sources—whether local or remote—to be signed by a trusted publisher. Because of this requirement, configuration files and scripts on the local computer must be signed as configuration files, and scripts from remote computers must be signed. PowerShell prompts you before running scripts from trusted publishers.
- **RemoteSigned**   Requires all configuration files and scripts from remote sources to be signed by a trusted publisher. Configuration files and scripts on the local computer do not need to be signed. PowerShell does not prompt you before running scripts from trusted publishers.
- **Unrestricted**   Allows all configuration files and scripts to run whether they are from local or remote sources and regardless of whether they are signed or unsigned. However, if you run a configuration file or script from a remote resource, you are prompted with a warning that the file comes from a remote resource before the configuration file is loaded or the script runs.

> **REAL WORLD**   The default execution policy setting for Windows Server 2012 R2 is RemoteSigned. For earlier versions of Windows Server as well as Windows 7 and later, the default execution policy setting is Restricted.

As you can see, execution policy determines whether you can load configuration files and run scripts as well as whether scripts must be digitally signed before they will run. When an execution policy prevents loading a file or running a script, a warning is displayed explaining applicable restrictions.

You can use Set-ExecutionPolicy to change the preference for the execution policy. Changes to the policy are written to the registry. However, if the Turn On Script Execution setting in Group Policy is enabled for the computer or user, the user preference is written to the registry, but it is not effective, and Windows PowerShell displays a message explaining the conflict. You cannot use Set-ExecutionPolicy to override a group policy, even if the user preference is more restrictive than the policy setting.

To set the execution policy to require that all scripts have a trusted signature to execute, enter the following command:

```
set-executionpolicy allsigned
```

To set the execution policy so that scripts downloaded from the Web execute only if they are signed by a trusted source, enter:

```
set-executionpolicy remotesigned
```

To set the execution policy to run scripts regardless of whether they have a digital signature and work in an unrestricted environment, you can enter the following command:

```
set-executionpolicy unrestricted
```

The change occurs immediately and is applied to the local console or application session. Because the change is written to the registry, the new execution policy will be used whenever you work with PowerShell.

> **NOTE** Because only administrators are allowed to change the execution policy, you must run Windows PowerShell with the Run As Administrator option.

Understanding Script Signing

Signing scripts is much easier than you might think. To sign scripts, you can use the Set-AuthenticodeSignature cmdlet. This cmdlet creates digital signatures using a digital certificate. Digital certificates can be created by a certificate authority (CA), or you can create your own self-signed certificates. When you use certificates created by a CA, you can use the certificate on any computer that trusts the CA. When you use self-signed certificates, you can use the certificate on your local computer.

In Windows domains, you can use Active Directory Certificate Services to establish a certificate authority (CA) and create digital certificates. As most enterprises have CAs and use digital certificates to enhance security, you may already have been issued a digital certificate that you can use for code signing. To find out, enter the following command:

```
get-childitem cert:\CurrentUser\My -codesigningcert
```

Or you can examine the certificates store. The certificates store on a Windows computer stores trust information. In the certificates store, you can view information about the following:

- **Personal** Certificates stored on the local computer that are assigned to you for various uses.
- **Other People** Certificates stored on the local computer that are assigned to other people for various uses.
- **Intermediate Certification Authorities** An intermediate CA is a CA that is subordinate to a root CA and often is used to issue certificates to other CAs. Your computer will trust any certificates from these intermediate CAs.
- **Trusted Root Certification Authorities** Root CAs your computer trusts. Your computer will trust any certificates from these root CAs.
- **Trusted Publishers** Publishers whose digitally signed scripts are trusted.
- **Untrusted Publisher** Publishers whose digitally signed scripts are not trusted.

You can access the certificates store through the Internet Properties dialog box. In Control Panel, select Network And Internet and then click Internet Options. In the Internet Properties dialog box, on the Content tab, click Certificates to display the Certificates dialog box. Use the Certificates store to examine the various types of trust information and related details.

PowerShell makes certificates available through the Cert provider. As you'll learn more about in the "Using Providers" section in Chapter 3, "Managing Your Windows PowerShell Environment," the data that a provider exposes appears as a drive that you can browse much like you browse a hard drive. If you enter **cd cert:** at the PowerShell prompt, you will access the certificates store on your computer. If you then enter **dir** (which is an alias for Get-ChildItem), you'll see a list of locations you can browse. Typically, this will include CurrentUser and LocalMachine, which are the certificate stores for the currently logged-on user and the local computer, respectively, as shown in the following example and sample output:

```
cd cert:
dir

Location    : CurrentUser
```

```
StoreNames : {ACRS, SmartCardRoot, Root, Trust...}

Location   : LocalMachine
StoreNames : {TrustedPublisher, ClientAuthIssuer, Remote
Desktop,
Root...}
```

While you are working with the Cert provider, if you enter **cd currentuser** and then type **dir** again, you'll see all the substores for the current user. One of these stores is the My store, where personal certificates are stored, as shown in the following example and sample output:

```
cd currentuser
dir

Name : ACRS
Name : SmartCardRoot
Name : Root
Name : Trust
Name : AuthRoot
Name : CA
Name : UserDS
Name : Disallowed
Name : My
Name : TrustedPeople
Name : TrustedPublisher
Name : ClientAuthIssuer
```

You can see the personal certificates for code signing in the My store by entering **cd my** and then entering **dir –codesigningcert**, as shown in the following example and sample output:

```
cd my
dir -codesigningcert
Directory:
Microsoft.PowerShell.Security\Certificate::currentuser\my
Thumbprint                                Subject
----------                                -------
D382828348348388243348238423BE2828282833  CN=WRSTANEK
AED38282838383848483483848348348BAC39839  CN=WRSTANEK
```

Whether you enter Get-ChildItem –Codesigningcert or Dir –Codesigningcert, the results are the same. The command returns an array of certificates with code-signing authority. In PowerShell, you can reference individual elements in an array by their index position. The first element in an array has the index position 0, the second 1, and so on.

If you have a personal certificate for code signing issued by a CA, you can sign unsigned scripts using the following command:

```
$cert = @(Get-ChildItem cert:\CurrentUser\My
-codesigningcert)[0]

Set-AuthenticodeSignature ScriptName.ps1 $cert
```

Note that these are two separate commands and that ScriptName sets the name of the script to sign, such as:

```
$cert = @(Get-ChildItem cert:\CurrentUser\My
-codesigningcert)[0]

Set-AuthenticodeSignature run_all.ps1 $cert
```

Here, you use Get-ChildItem to access the My certificates store and get the first personal certificate for code signing and then use the certificate to sign the run_all.ps1 script. As long as the certificate is signed by an enterprise CA, you can run the signed script on any computer in the enterprise that trusts the CA.

Creating and Using Self-Signed Certificates

You can create a self-signed certificate using makecert.exe. This utility is included in the platform-specific Windows SDK, such as the Windows SDK for Windows 8.1. After you download and install the appropriate SDK, you'll find the MakeCert program in a subdirectory of the bin folder within the SDK installation folders.

Because the SDK installation folder is not added to the PATH environment variable by default, you'll need to change to the directory containing MakeCert whenever you want to work with the utility. For example, when working with Windows SDK for Windows 8.1, you'll find the 64-bit MakeCert utility in the %ProgramFiles(x86)%\Windows Kits\8.1\bin\x64 folder.

The way you use MakeCert to generate certificates will depend on the platform you are working with and the computer configuration. Generally, to create a certificate using MakeCert, you must:

1. Open an elevated, administrator command prompt (cmd.exe).
2. Change to the directory for the MakeCert utility.
3. Use the command prompt to create a local certificate authority for your computer.
4. Use the command prompt to generate a personal certificate via this certificate authority.

You create the local certificate authority by entering the following command:

```
makecert -n "CN=PowerShell Local Certificate Root" -a sha1
-eku 1.3.6.1.5.5.7.3.3 -r -sv root.pvk root.cer
-ss Root -sr localMachine
```

Here, you're running this from a command prompt with Administrator privileges in the directory where makecert is located. Note that this is a single command, and the parameters are used as follows:

- The –n parameter sets the certificate name. The name value is preceded by CN=.
- The –a parameter sets the signature algorithm as SHA1 as opposed to MD5 (the default value).
- The –eku parameter inserts the enhanced key usage object identifier: 1.3.6.1.5.5.7.3.3.
- The –r parameter specifies that you want to create a self-signed certificate.
- The –sv parameter sets the file names for the private key file and the certificate file that makecert will create.
- The –ss parameter sets the name of the store that stores the output certificate as Root for the Trusted Root Certificate Authorities store.
- The –sr parameter sets the certificate store location as the local machine, as opposed to the current user (the default value).

You generate a personal certificate via this certificate authority by entering the following command:

```
makecert -pe -n "CN=PowerShell User" -ss MY -a sha1
-eku 1.3.6.1.5.5.7.3.3 -iv root.pvk -ic root.cer
```

Note that this is a single command, and the parameters are used as follows:

- The –pe parameter marks the certificate's private key as exportable.
- The –n parameter sets the certificate name. Again, the name value is preceded by CN=.
- The –ss parameter sets the name of the store that stores the output certificate as MY, for the Personal store.
- The –a parameter sets the signature algorithm as SHA1.
- The –eku parameter inserts the enhanced key usage object identifier: 1.3.6.1.5.5.7.3.3.
- The –iv parameter specifies the name of the CA's private key file.
- The –ic parameter specifies the name of the CA's certificate file.

The first command generates two temporary files: root.pvk and root.cer. The second command uses these files to create a certificate that is stored in the Personal certificate store on the local computer.

MakeCert will prompt you for a private key password. The password ensures that no one can use or access the certificate without your consent. Create and enter a password that you can remember. You will use this password later to retrieve the certificate.

To verify that the certificate was generated correctly, use the following command to search for the certificate in the Personal certificate store on the computer:

```
get-childitem cert:\CurrentUser\My -codesigningcert
```

This command uses the Windows PowerShell Certificate provider to view information about certificates in the My personal certificate store. If the certificate was created, the output lists the certificate by its encrypted thumbprint and subject.

After you have a self-signed certificate, you can sign scripts as discussed previously. The signed script will run on the local computer. However, the signed script will not run on computers on which the execution policy requires a digital signature from a trusted authority. On these computers, Windows PowerShell reports that the script cannot be loaded and that the signature of the certificate cannot be verified.

Specifying Authentication Credentials

When you are working with cmdlets and scripts in PowerShell that modify system information, you might need to specify a credential for authentication. Whether in a script or at the prompt, the easiest way to do this is to use Get-Credential to obtain a Credential object and save the result in a variable for later use. Consider the following example:

```
$cred = get-credential
```

When PowerShell reads this command, PowerShell prompts you for a user name and password and then stores the credentials provided in the $cred variable. It is important to point out that the credentials prompt is displayed simply because you typed **Get-Credential**.

You also can specify that you want the credentials for a specific user in a specific domain. In the following example, you request the credentials for the TestUser account in the DevD domain:

```
$cred = get-credential –credential devd\testuser
```

A Credential object has UserName and Password properties that you can work with. Although the user name is stored as a regular string, the password is stored as a secure, encrypted string. Knowing this, you can reference the user name and password stored in $cred as follows:

```
$user = $cred.username
$password = $cred.password
```

Working with the Help Documentation

Earlier in the chapter in "Using Cmdlets," I introduced Get-Help. With Windows PowerShell 3.0 and later, help files aren't included with the standard installation and Windows PowerShell displays automatically generated help information by default. If you want to work with the full help documentation, you must either access the help files online or download updated help files to your computer.

Accessing Help Files

When working locally and not in a remote session, you can view help files for cmdlets online in the TechNet Library by adding the –Online parameter whenever you use Get-Help, such as:

```
get-help new-variable -online
```

If a computer doesn't have an Internet connection or you are working in a remote session, you won't be able to get online help and instead will need to rely on the default help files or help files that have been downloaded and installed on the computer. To download and install the current version of help files, enter the following command at an elevated, administrator PowerShell prompt:

```
update-help
```

When you run Update-Help without specifying additional parameters, Windows PowerShell attempts to connect to the Internet and download the help files from Microsoft's website. These actions will only be successful when the computer has a connection to the Internet and the connection isn't blocked by firewall rules or Internet privacy settings.

> **REAL WORLD** Running Update-Help from an administrator prompt is recommended as a best practice, but it is not required. By default, Update-Help downloads and installs the newest help file for modules available on a computer as well as modules in a remote session. If help files were previously installed, Update-Help only updates the help files that have been modified since they were installed. However, if you run Update-Help with standard permissions, Update-Help will not download or install help files for modules in the PowerShell installation directory, including the Windows PowerShell Core modules. Thus, to ensure help files for all available modules are installed and updated, you must run Windows PowerShell with the Run As Administrator option.

Creating a Central Help Folder

Rather than downloading and installing help files on multiple computers or when computers don't have connections to the Internet, you may want to specify a central help location for your organization and then install help files from this location as required. Installing and using help files from a central location is a two-step process:

1. You use Save-Help to download help files and save them to a specified folder or network share.
2. You use Update-Help to install help files from the central location.

With you are working with Save-Help, you specify the destination path using the –DestinationPath parameter, such as:

```
Save-Help –DestinationPath C:\HelpFiles
```

Or

```
Save-Help –DestinationPath \\Server54\PS_Help
```

As long as the destination paths exist and you have permission to write to the location, you'll be able to save the help files. In these instances, here's how Save-Help works with PowerShell 4.0 and later:

1. The PowerShell modules on the computer to which you are currently logged on as well as the modules in the current remote session determine which help files are used. When you run Save-Help, Save-Help identifies all the PowerShell modules installed on the current computer and in the current session.
2. Next, if the destination folder was previously used to save help files, Save-Help checks the version of the help files in the destination folder. If newer help files are available for the applicable PowerShell modules, Save-Help downloads the new help files and saves them in the destination folder.

> **REAL WORLD**   When you are working in a remote session, there's an important difference between the way Save-Help works with PowerShell 3.0 and PowerShell 4.0. With PowerShell 3.0, the HelpInfoUri property, which identifies the location of help files online by their URL, is not

preserved when remoting. Thus, Save-Help works only for modules installed on the local computer and does not apply to modules in the remote session. On the other hand, with PowerShell 4.0, the HelpInfoUri property is preserved when remoting. Thus, Save-Help is able to pass back the location of help files for modules that are installed on the remote computer, which in turn allows you to save help files for the modules installed on the remote computer.

Often, you'll need to pass in credentials to update help files. Use the –Credential parameter to do this. In the following example, you specify that the WilliamS account in the ImaginedL domain should be used to perform the update task:

```
Save-Help -DestinationPath \\Server54\PS_Help
-Credential ImaginedL\Williams
```

When you run the command, you are prompted for the password for the WilliamS account. The account's credentials are then used to write to the destination path.

Once you save help files to a central location, you can write the help files to any computer in your organization and in this way make the help files available locally. To do this, run Update-Help and use the –SourcePath parameter to specify the source location for the help files, such as:

```
Update-Help -SourcePath \\Server54\PS_Help
-Credential ImaginedL\Williams
```

Help files are language specific. Update-Help and Save-Help create language-specific files for all languages and locales configured on your management computer. Thus, if the Region And Language settings for your management computer specify the current locale as US English, the help commands create and work with the US English help files by default.

When you are working in an enterprise where computers are deployed using different languages, locales or both, it is important to note that a problem can occur when help files are saved with language or culture settings that are different from the language and culture settings of your management computer. For example, if help files were saved with the current locale set as US English but you are working with a computer with the current locale set as UK

English, you won't be able to retrieve the help files for that locale from the source location. An easy work around is to save help files to the central share using computers that have the appropriate languages and cultures configured.

Chapter 2. Getting the Most from Windows PowerShell

Windows PowerShell provides an effective environment for working with commands and scripts. As discussed in Chapter 1, "Windows PowerShell Essentials," you can run many types of commands at the command line, including built-in cmdlets, Windows utilities, and applications with command-line extensions. Regardless of its source, every command you'll use follows the same syntax rules. These rules state that a command consists of a command name followed by any required or optional arguments. Arguments, which include parameters, parameter values, and other command text, can also use piping to combine commands and redirection to specify the sources for inputs, outputs, and errors.

When you execute commands in PowerShell, you start a series of events that are similar to the following:

1. Multiple commands that are chained or grouped and passed on a single line are broken into individual units of execution. Values within a unit of execution are broken into a series of segments called *tokens*.

2. Each token is parsed, commands are separated from values, and values are evaluated as some kind of object type, such as String or Boolean. Variables in the command text are replaced with their actual values as appropriate during parsing.

3. The individual commands are then processed. If a command's name has a file path, PowerShell uses this path to find the command. If the command cannot be found in the specified location, PowerShell returns an error.

4. If a command's name doesn't specify a file path, PowerShell tries to resolve the command name internally. A match means that you've referenced a built-in command (including an alias to a command or a function) that can be executed immediately. If no match is found, PowerShell searches the command path for a matching command executable. If the command cannot be found in any of those locations, PowerShell returns an error. Because PowerShell does not look in the current directory by default, you must explicitly specify the current directory.

5. If the command is located, the command is executed using any specified arguments, including those that specify the inputs to use. Command output and any errors are written to the PowerShell window or to the specified destinations for output and errors.

As you can see, many factors can affect command execution, including command path settings, redirection techniques, and whether commands are chained or grouped. In this chapter, I'll describe and show examples of this breakdown of command execution to help you get the most out of PowerShell. Before diving into those discussions, however, let's look at special considerations for starting PowerShell and examine the concepts of profiles and console files.

Initializing the Environment

Windows PowerShell provides a dynamic, extensible execution environment. You can initialize the environment for PowerShell in several ways, including passing startup parameters to Powershell.exe, using a customized profile, using a console file, or any combination of the three. You can extend the environment for PowerShell in several ways as well, including by installing providers and registering snap-ins as discussed in Chapter 3, "Managing Your Windows PowerShell Environment."

Passing Startup Parameters

When you start PowerShell with standard user privileges rather than administrator privileges, you won't be able to perform many administrative tasks. To start PowerShell with administrator privileges, you must run the PowerShell console in elevated, administrator mode as discussed in Chapter 1.

When you run PowerShell from the Start screen or the Start menu, you can't pass in arguments. However, when you start PowerShell using the Search box, the Run dialog box or by entering **powershell** in an open command-shell window, you can pass arguments to PowerShell, including switches that control how PowerShell works and parameters that execute additional commands. For example, you can start PowerShell in no-logo mode (meaning the logo banner is turned off) by using the startup command **powershell -nologo**. By default, when you start PowerShell via the command shell and run a command, PowerShell initializes, runs the command and then exits. If you want PowerShell to execute a command and not terminate, type **powershell /noexit** followed by the command.

Listing 2-1 shows the basic syntax for invoking the PowerShell console. Table 2-1 lists the available startup parameters. By default, startup profiles are loaded when the PowerShell console starts. You can exit the console at any time by typing **exit** and then pressing Enter.

LISTING 2-1 PowerShell Syntax

```
powershell[.exe] [-PSConsoleFile FileName | -Version VersionNum]
  [-NoLogo] [-NoExit] [-NoProfile] [-NonInteractive] [-Sta]
  [-InputFormat {Text | XML}] [-OutputFormat {Text | XML}]
  [-WindowsStyle Style] [-EncodedCommand Base64EncodedCommand]
  [-File ScriptFilePath] [-ExecutionPolicy PolicySetting]
  [-Command CommandText]
```

TABLE 2-1 PowerShell Startup Parameters

PARAMETER	DESCRIPTION
–Command	Specifies the command text to execute as though it were typed at the PowerShell command prompt.
–EncodedCommand	Specifies the base64-encoded command text to execute.
–ExecutionPolicy	Sets the default execution policy for the console session.
–File	Sets the name of a script file to execute.
–InputFormat	Sets the format for data sent to PowerShell as either text string or serialized XML. The default format is XML. Valid values are *text* and *XML*.
-Mta	Starts PowerShell is multi-threaded mode.

PARAMETER	DESCRIPTION
–NoExit	Does not exit after running startup commands. This parameter is useful when you run PowerShell commands or scripts via the command prompt (cmd.exe).
–NoLogo	Starts the PowerShell console without displaying the copyright banner.
–Noninteractive	Starts the PowerShell console in noninteractive mode. In this mode, PowerShell does not present an interactive prompt to the user.
–NoProfile	Tells the PowerShell console not to load the current user's profile.
–OutputFormat	Sets the format for output as either text string or serialized XML. The default format is text. Valid values are *text* and *XML*.
–PSConsoleFile	Loads the specified Windows PowerShell console file. Console files end with the .psc1 extension and can be used to ensure that specific snap-in extensions are loaded and available. You can create a console file using Export-Console in Windows PowerShell.
–Sta	Starts PowerShell in single-threaded mode. This is the default.
–Version	Sets the version of Windows PowerShell to use for compatibility, such as 1.0.
–WindowStyle	Sets the window style as Normal, Minimized, Maximized, or Hidden. The default is Normal.

TIP If you want PowerShell to always start with specific parameters, you can modify the shortcut used to start PowerShell. For example, if the taskbar has a shortcut for Windows PowerShell, you can right-click this shortcut and select Properties to display the Properties dialog box for the shortcut. On the Shortcut tab, you would then edit the Target property by adding the parameters and any related parameter values required to the existing value and then clicking OK to save the changes. For example,

> after the full path to powershell.exe, you could add –NoLogo to always start PowerShell without displaying the standard banner.

Invoking Windows PowerShell

Although you'll most often work with the PowerShell console or the PowerShell application, at times you might want to invoke PowerShell to run a cmdlet from the Windows command shell (cmd.exe) environment or a batch script. To do so, you use the –Command parameter. Generally, you will also want to suppress the Windows PowerShell logo with the –NoLogo parameter and stop execution of profiles with the –NoProfile parameter. For example, at a command prompt or in a batch script, you could get a list of running processes via PowerShell with the following command:

```
powershell -nologo -noprofile -command get-process
```

When you enter this command, the Windows command shell runs PowerShell as it would any other external program, passing in the parameters and parameter values you use and then exiting PowerShell when execution completes. If you want the command shell to run a PowerShell command and remain in PowerShell after execution, you can add the –NoExit parameter as shown in the following example:

```
powershell -noexit -command get-process
```

Using –Command to Run Commands

Because –Command is the most common parameter you'll use when invoking PowerShell from a command prompt or batch script, let's take a closer look at all the ways it can be used. If you enter – as the command, the command text is read from standard input. You also can use piping and redirection techniques to manipulate the output of a command. However, keep in mind that any characters typed after the command are interpreted as command arguments. Because of this, to write a command that includes piping or redirection, you must enclose the command text in double quotation marks. The following example gets information about currently running processes and sorts it by process identifier:

```
powershell -nologo -noprofile -command "get-process |
sort-object Id"
```

> **REAL WORLD** Most commands generate output that can be redirected
> to another command as input. To do this, you use a technique called
> *piping*, whereby the output of a command is sent as the input of the next
> command. Following this, you can see the general syntax for piping is
>
> Command1 | Command2
>
> where the pipe redirects the output of Command1 to the input of
> Command2. But you can also redirect output more than once by using
> this syntax:
>
> Command1 | Command2 | Command3
>
> Generally, if a cmdlet accepts input from another cmdlet, the cmdlet will
> have an –InputObject parameter and you can pipe output to the cmdlet.

Windows PowerShell also supports script blocks. A script block is a series of
commands executed in sequence. Script blocks are enclosed in braces ({}), and
each command within a script block is separated by a semicolon. Although you
can enter script blocks enclosed in braces, you can do so directly only when
running Powershell.exe in Windows PowerShell. The results are then returned as
deserialized XML objects rather than standard objects. For example, if you are
already working at the PowerShell prompt and want to run a series of
commands through an isolated PowerShell instance, you can do so by enclosing
the commands in braces and separating commands with semicolons, as shown
in this example:

```
powershell -command {get-service; get-process}
```

Although this technique works if you are already working with the PowerShell
prompt, it doesn't work when you want to run PowerShell from a command
prompt. The workaround is to use the following format:

```
"& {CommandText}"
```

Here, the quotation marks indicate a string, and the ampersand (&) is an invoke
operator that causes the command to be executed. After you write a string that
runs a command, you will generally be able to run the command at either the

command prompt or the PowerShell prompt. For example, even though you cannot enter powershell -command {get-service; get-process} at the command prompt, you can enter the following at a command prompt:

```
powershell -command "& {get-service; get-process}"
```

Here, you pass a code block to PowerShell as a string to parse and execute. PowerShell executes Get-Service and displays the results and then executes Get-Process and displays the results. If you want one syntax that will generally succeed whether you are working with strings, multiple commands, the command prompt, or the PowerShell prompt, this syntax is the one you should use.

Using –File to Run Scripts

When you are working with the Windows command shell and want to run a PowerShell script, you also can use piping and redirection techniques to manipulate the output of a command. However, instead of using the –Command parameter, you use the –File parameter to specify the script to run. As shown in the following example, you follow the –File parameter with the path to the script to run:

```
powershell -nologo -noprofile -file c:\scripts\run_all.ps1
```

If the script is in the current directory, simply enter the script name:

```
powershell -nologo -noprofile -file run_all.ps1
```

If the path name includes blank spaces, you must enclose the path in double quotation marks, as shown in this example:

```
powershell -nologo -noprofile -file "c:\data\current
scripts\run_all.ps1"
```

> **REAL WORLD** You can specify parameters whether you start PowerShell from a taskbar shortcut or a command prompt. When starting PowerShell from the taskbar, edit the shortcut to specify parameters you want to use whenever you work with PowerShell. To do so, follow these steps:

1. On the taskbar, right-click the shortcut and then select Properties.

2. In the Properties dialog box, the Target entry on the Shortcut tab is selected by default.

3. Without pressing any other key, press the Right arrow key. This places the insertion cursor at the end of the full path to PowerShell. Insert a space, and then type your parameters and parameter values.

4. Click OK to save the settings. If you make a mistake or no longer want to use parameters, repeat this procedure and remove any parameters and values you've added.

Using Nested Consoles

Sometimes you might want to use different environment settings or parameters for a PowerShell console and then go back to your original settings without exiting the console window. To do this, you can use a technique called *nesting*. With nesting, you start a PowerShell console within another PowerShell console.

Unlike the command shell, the nested console opens with a new working environment and does not inherit its environment settings from the current console. You can work in this separate console environment and execute commands and scripts. When you type **exit** to close the instance of the nested console, you return to the previous console, and the previous environment settings are restored.

Understanding Command Input, Parsing, and Output

As you've seen from examples in this chapter and in Chapter 1, typing commands at the PowerShell prompt is a fairly straightforward process. The most basic approach is simply to type your command text and then press Enter. When you press Enter, PowerShell processes and parses the command text.

Basic Line Editing

The PowerShell console includes some basic editing capabilities for the current line. Table 2-2 lists the editing keys. Alternatively, enter **get-history** to list all the commands in the command history, or enter **clear-history** to clear the command history. Get-History lists commands by command number, and you can pass this to Invoke-History to run a specific numbered command from your command history. In this example, you run command 35:

```
invoke-history 35
```

TABLE 2-2 Basic Editing Keys

KEY	USAGE
`	Press the backward apostrophe key to insert a line break or as an escape character to make a literal character. You can also break a line at the pipe (|) character.
Alt+Space+E	Displays an editing shortcut menu with Mark, Copy, Paste, Select All, Scroll, and Find options. You can then press K for Mark, Y for Copy, P for Paste, S for Select All, L to scroll through the screen buffer, or F to search for text in the screen buffer. To copy the screen buffer to the Clipboard, press Alt+Space+E+S and then press Alt+Space+E+Y.
Alt+F7	Clears the command history.
Ctrl+C	Press Ctrl+C to break out of the subprompt or terminate execution.
Ctrl+End	Press Ctrl+End to delete all the characters in the line after the cursor.
Ctrl+Left arrow / Ctrl+Right arrow	Press Ctrl+Left arrow or Ctrl+Right arrow to move left or right one word at a time.
Ctrl+S	Press Ctrl+S to pause or resume the display of output.
Delete / Backspace	Press Delete to delete the character under the cursor, or press the Backspace key to delete the character to the left of the cursor.
Esc	Press the Esc key to clear the current line.

KEY	USAGE
F1	Moves the cursor one character to the right on the command line. At the end of the line, inserts one character from the text of your last command.
F2	Creates a new command line by copying your last command line up to the character you type.
F3	Completes the command line with the content from your last command line, starting from the current cursor position to the end of the line.
F4	Deletes characters from your current command line, starting from the current cursor position up to the character you type.
F5	Scans backward through your command history.
F7	Displays a pop-up window with your command history and allows you to select a command. Use the arrow keys to scroll through the list. Press Enter to select a command to run, or press the Right arrow key to place the text on the command line.
F8	Uses text you've entered to scan backward through your command history for commands that match the text you've typed so far on the command line.
F9	Runs a specific numbered command from your command history. Command numbers are listed when you press F7.
Home / End	Press Home or End to move to the beginning or end of the line.
Insert	Press Insert to switch between insert mode and overwrite mode.
Left / Right arrow keys	Press the Left or Right arrow key to move the cursor left or right on the current line.

KEY	USAGE
Page Up / Page Down	Press the Page Up or Page Down key to access the first or last command in the command history.
Right-click	If QuickEdit is disabled, displays an editing shortcut menu with Mark, Copy, Paste, Select All, Scroll, and Find options. To copy the screen buffer to the Clipboard, right-click, choose Select, and then press Enter.
Tab / Shift+Tab	Press the Tab key or press Shift+Tab to access the tab expansion function as discussed in "Creating and Using Functions" in Chapter 7, "Mastering Aliases and Functions."
Up / Down arrow keys	Press the Up or Down arrow key to scan forward or backward through your command history, as discussed in "Working with the Command History" in Chapter 1.
Windows key+R and then type **powershell**	Runs Windows PowerShell. However, if you've installed multiple versions of PowerShell or are using a 64-bit computer, the first version encountered runs (and this is not necessarily the one you want to use).

REAL WORLD   The way copying and pasting text works in the PowerShell console depends on whether QuickEdit mode is enabled or disabled. With QuickEdit enabled, you copy text by dragging the mouse and pressing Enter, and then paste text by clicking the mouse. When you drag the mouse to select text to copy, be careful not to pause momentarily when you start; otherwise, PowerShell will paste from the Clipboard. With QuickEdit disabled, you copy by right-clicking, selecting Mark, dragging the mouse to select the text, and then pressing Enter. You paste by right-clicking and selecting Paste. You can enable or disable QuickEdit using the Properties dialog box, as described in the "Configuring Windows PowerShell Console Properties" section of Chapter 1.

How Parsing Works

In addition to the processing modes discussed previously in "Passing Startup Parameters," PowerShell also has parsing modes. Don't confuse processing modes with parsing modes. Processing modes control the way PowerShell processes commands. Generally speaking, processing occurs either interactively or noninteractively. Parsing modes control the way PowerShell parses each value within a command line.

PowerShell breaks down command lines into units of execution and tokens. A unit of execution includes everything from the first character on a line to either a semicolon or the end of a line. A token is a value within a unit of execution. Knowing this, you can:

- Enter multiple commands on a single command line by using semicolons to separate each command.
- Mark the end of a unit of execution by pressing Enter.

The way PowerShell parses values is determined by the first token encountered when parsing a unit of execution. PowerShell parses using one of these modes:

- **Expression mode**   PowerShell uses expression mode when the first token encountered in a unit of execution *is not* the name of a cmdlet, keyword, alias, function, or external utility. PowerShell evaluates expressions as either numerical values or strings. Character string values must be contained in quotation marks, and numbers not in quotation marks are treated as numerical values (rather than as a series of characters).
- **Command mode**   PowerShell uses command mode when the first token encountered in a unit of execution is the name of a cmdlet, keyword, alias, function, or external utility. PowerShell invokes command tokens. Values after the command token are handled as expandable strings except when they start with a special character that denotes the start of a variable, array, string, or subexpression. These special characters include $, @, ', " and (, and when these characters are encountered, the value is handled using expression mode.

With these rules in mind, you can see that the following are true:

- If you enter 5+5 at the PowerShell prompt, PowerShell interprets 5+5 as an expression to evaluate and displays the result as 10.
- If you enter Write-Host 5+5 at the PowerShell prompt, PowerShell interprets 5+5 as an argument to Write-Host and displays 5+5.
- If you enter Write-Host (5+5) at the PowerShell prompt, PowerShell interprets (5+5) as an expression to evaluate and then pass to Write-Host. As a result, PowerShell displays 10.

Parsing Assigned Values

In PowerShell, variable definitions begin with the dollar sign ($) and are followed by the name of the variable you are defining. To assign a value to a variable, you use the equals sign (=) and then specify the value you want. After you create a variable, you can reference or display the value of the variable by using the variable name.

Following this, if you enter $a = 5+5 at the PowerShell prompt, PowerShell interprets 5+5 as an expression to evaluate and assigns the result to the variable a. As a result, when you write the value of $a to the PowerShell prompt by entering

```
$a
```

or by entering

```
Write-Host $a
```

the output is

```
10
```

On the other hand, let's say you define a variable named $a and assign it a string value, such as:

```
$a = "This is a string."
```

Here, the value assigned to $a is handled as a literal string, and the string is processed in expression mode. You know this because when you write the value of $a to the PowerShell prompt by entering

```
$a
```

or by entering

```
Write-Host $a
```

the output is

```
This is a string.
```

Sometimes, however, you'll want to force PowerShell to interpret a string literal expression using command mode. To see why, consider the following example:

```
$a = "Get-Process"
```

If you write the value of $a to the PowerShell prompt by entering

```
$a
```

the output is

```
Get-Process
```

This occurs because the value assigned to $a is handled as a literal string, and the string is processed in expression mode. However, you might have wanted PowerShell to actually run the Get-Process cmdlet. To do this, you need PowerShell to parse the string and determine that it contains a token that should be processed in command mode. You can accomplish this by using the & operator when you reference the $a variable, as shown in this example:

```
&$a
```

Because PowerShell processes the string in command mode, Get-Process is seen as a command token, the Get-Process cmdlet is invoked, and the output displays the currently running processes. This technique can be used with any cmdlet, keyword, alias, function, or external utility name assigned to a variable in a string. However, if you want to add values in addition to the command name, for example parameters, or use multiple commands or piping, you must enclose your command or commands in curly braces rather than quotation marks. This denotes a script block. Here is an example:

```
$a = {get-eventlog -newest 25 -logname application}
```

The value assigned to $a is handled as a special string, and the string is processed in expression mode. You know this because when you write the value of $a to the PowerShell prompt, the output is:

```
get-eventlog -newest 25 -logname system
```

You can force PowerShell to parse the contents of the script block by using:

```
&$a
```

PowerShell will then parse each token in the script block. The result will be the same as when you enter the command text.

Parsing Exceptions

When you enter part of an expression on the command line but do not complete the expression, PowerShell displays the >> subprompt, indicating that it is waiting for you to complete the expression. For example, if you type **Write-Host (** and press Enter, PowerShell displays the >> subprompt and waits for you to complete the expression. You must then complete the command line by entering any additional required text, such as **5+5)**, and then press Enter. You must then press Enter again (without typing any additional text) to exit the subprompt and return. PowerShell then interprets this input as a completed unit of execution.

If you want to intentionally split command text across multiple lines of input, you can use the backward apostrophe character (`). This technique is handy when you are copying long command lines and pasting them into a PowerShell console so that you can run them. Here's how this works:

1. Enter part of the command text, and then type `. When you press Enter, PowerShell displays the >> subprompt.
2. Enter the next part of the command text. Then either enter ` to indicate that you want to continue the command text on the next line or press Enter to mark the end of the command text.

3. When you finally mark the end of the line by pressing Enter without using the backward apostrophe (and you've closed all expressions), PowerShell parses the command text as appropriate.

An example and partial output follows:

```
get-eventlog -newest 25 `
>> -logname system
>>
```

```
Index Time    EntryType    Source              InstanceID Message
----- ----    ---------    ------              ---------- -------
258248 Feb 28 16:12   Information Service Control M...
1073748860 The description for Event ID '1073748860' in So...
258247 Feb 28 14:27   Information Service Control M...
1073748860 The description for Event ID '1073748860' in So...
```

If your command text uses the pipe (|) character, you can also break a line and continue it on the next line at the pipe character, as shown in the following example and partial output:

```
get-process |
>>   sort-object Id
>>
```

```
Handles  NPM(K)    PM(K)      WS(K) VM(M)    CPU(s)      Id
ProcessName
-------  ------    -----      ----- -----    ------      -- ------
-----
     0       0        0        24     0                    0 Idle
   710       0        0     12904    20                    4 System
    28       1      360       816     4                  516 smss
   666       6     1872      5212    94                  592 csrss
```

Output from Parsing

After parsing commands and values, PowerShell returns output. Unlike with the command shell (Cmd.exe), built-in commands that you run in PowerShell return objects in the output. An object is a collection of data points that represent an item. Objects have a specific data type, such as String, Boolean, or Numeric, and have methods and properties. Object methods allow you to perform actions on the item the object represents. Object properties store information about the item the object represents. When you work with PowerShell, you can use an object's methods and properties to take specific actions and manipulate data.

When you combine commands in a pipeline, the commands pass information to each other as objects. When the first command runs, it sends one or more objects along the pipeline to the second command. The second command receives the objects from the first command, processes the objects, and then displays output or passes new or modified objects to the next command in the pipeline. This continues until all commands in the pipeline run and the final command's output is displayed. Because you and I can't read objects, PowerShell translates the objects for output on the screen as text. You can manipulate this output in many ways.

Writing and Formatting Output

Although PowerShell reads and writes objects, the various values associated with objects are converted to text as a final part of the cmdlet execution process. When output is written to the console, this output is said to be written to the *standard output stream*. PowerShell supports other output streams as well. Before I describe these output streams, however, I'll explain how output is formatted by default.

Using Formatting Cmdlets

When you are working with external utilities and programs, those utilities and programs determine how the output is formatted. With PowerShell cmdlets, PowerShell calls designated formatting cmdlets to format the output for you. The formatter determines which properties of the output are displayed and whether they are displayed in a list or table. The formatter makes this determination based on the type of data being displayed. Strings and objects are handled and processed in different ways.

> **NOTE**   The formatting cmdlets arrange the data to be displayed but do not actually display it. The output cmdlets, discussed next, are responsible for displaying output.

Specifying Output Format

You can explicitly specify the output format by using one of the following formatting cmdlets:

- **Format-List**   Formats the output as a list of properties. All properties of the objects are formatted by default, with each property displayed on a separate line. Use –Properties to specify which properties to display by name. Enter property names in a comma-separated list. Use wildcard characters such as * to match any value as necessary.

```
Format-List [[-Property] PropertyName] [-DisplayError]
[-Expand String] [-Force] [-GroupBy Object]
[-InputObject Object] [-ShowError] [-View String]
```

- **Format-Table**   Formats the output as a table with selected properties of the objects in each column. The object type determines the default layout and the properties that are displayed. Use –AutoSize to automatically adjust the column size and number of columns based on the width of the data. Use –HideTableHeaders to omit column headings. Use –Wrap to display text that exceeds the column width on the next line.

```
Format-Table [[-Property] PropertyName] [-AutoSize]
[-DisplayError] [-Expand String] [-Force] [-GroupBy Object]
[-HideTableHeaders] [-InputObject Object] [-ShowError]
[-View String] [-Wrap]
```

- **Format-Wide**   Formats the output as a multicolumned table, but only one property of each object is displayed. Use –AutoSize to automatically adjust the column size and number of columns based on the width of the data. Use –Columns to specify the number of columns to display.

```
Format-Wide [[-Property] PropertyName] [-AutoSize]
[-Column NumColumns] [-DisplayError]
[-Expand String] [-Force] [-GroupBy Object]
[-InputObject Object] [-ShowError] [-View String]
```

- **Format-Custom**   Formats the output using a predefined alternate view. You can determine the alternate view by reviewing the *format.PS1XML files in the Windows PowerShell directory. To create your own views in new .PS1XML files, use the Update-FormatData cmdlet to add them to Windows PowerShell. Use –Depth to specify the number of columns to display.

```
Format-Custom [[-Property] PropertyName] [-Depth Num]
[-DisplayError] [-Expand String] [-Force] [-GroupBy Object]
[-InputObject Object] [-ShowError] [-View String]
```

When working with the previous formatting cmdlets, you might also want to use these cmdlets:

- **Group-Object**   Groups objects that contain the same value for specified properties. Objects are grouped in sequence, so if values aren't sorted you won't get the result you want. Use –CaseSensitive to use case-sensitive grouping rather than the default grouping, which is not case sensitive. Use –NoElement to omit the names of members of the group, such as file names if you are grouping files by extension.

  ```
  Group-Object [[-Property] PropertyName] [-AsHashTable]
  [-AsString] [-CaseSensitive] [-Culture String]
  [-InputObject Object] [-NoElement]
  ```

- **Sort-Object**   Sorts objects in ascending order based on the values of properties of the object. Use –Descending to reverse sort. Use –CaseSensitive to use case-sensitive sorting rather than the default sorting, which is not case sensitive. Use –Unique to eliminate duplicates and return only the unique members of a specified collection.

  ```
  Sort-Object [[-Property] PropertyName] [-CaseSensitive]
  [-Culture String] [-Descending] [-InputObject Object]
  [-Unique]
  ```

Using Pipelines With Formatters

To change the format of the output from any cmdlet, use the pipeline operator (|) to send the output of the command to a formatter. For example, the default format for the Get-Service cmdlet is a table that displays the value of the Status, Name, and DisplayName properties, as shown in this command and sample output:

```
get-service

Status    Name            DisplayName
------    ----            -----------
Stopped   ADWS            Active Directory Web Services
```

```
Stopped   AeLookupSvc        Application Experience
Stopped   ALG                Application Layer Gateway Service
Running   AppHostSvc         Application Host Helper Service
Stopped   AppIDSvc           Application Identity
Running   Appinfo            Application Information
Stopped   AppMgmt            Application Management
Stopped   AppReadiness       App Readiness
Stopped   AppXSvc            AppX Deployment Service (AppXSVC)
```

Format-Wide formats the output as a multicolumned table, but only one property of each object is displayed. The following command sends the output of a Get-Service cmdlet to the Format-Wide cmdlet:

```
get-service | format-wide -column 3
```

```
ADWS            AeLookupSvc         ALG

AppHostSvc      AppIDSvc            Appinfo

AppMgmt         AppReadiness        AppXSvc

aspnet_state AudioEndpointBuilder  Audiosrv
```

As a result, the service data is formatted into multiple columns for each service. The output provides the name of each configured service.

Knowing the name of a service, you can then examine services by listing the value of each configured property. For example, the following command gets detailed information on the WinRM service:

```
get-service winrm | format-list
```

```
Name                 : WinRM
DisplayName          : Windows Remote Management (WS-Management)
Status               : Stopped
DependentServices    : {}
ServicesDependedOn   : {RPCSS, HTTP}
CanPauseAndContinue  : False
CanShutdown          : False
CanStop              : False
ServiceType          : Win32ShareProcess
```

In this format, the data appears in a list instead of a table, and there is additional information about the service that the previous output formatting omitted.

Specifying Properties to Display

With any of the formatting cmdlets, you can use the –Properties parameter to specify properties to display by name. You can use wildcards such as * to match any value as necessary. For example, to display all the properties of the winlogon process, enter:

```
get-process winlogon | format-list -property *
```

```
__NounName              : Process
Name                    : winlogon
Handles                 : 168
VM                      : 56729600
WS                      : 6262784
PM                      : 1384448
NPM                     : 8288
Path                    : C:\Windows\system32\winlogon.exe
Company                 : Microsoft Corporation
CPU                     : 0.40625
FileVersion             : 6.3.9600.16384
ProductVersion          : 6.3.9600.16384
Description             : Windows Logon Application
Product                 : Microsoft Windows Operating System
Id                      : 496
PriorityClass           : High
HandleCount             : 168
WorkingSet              : 6262784
PagedMemorySize         : 1384448
PrivateMemorySize       : 1384448
VirtualMemorySize       : 56729600
```

To see all the properties of an object, send the output of a command to the Get-Member cmdlet. For example, to see all the properties of a service object, type:

```
get-service | get-member -membertype *property
```

```
   TypeName: System.ServiceProcess.ServiceController
```

```
Name                   MemberType      Definition
----                   ----------      ----------
Name                   AliasProperty   Name = ServiceName
RequiredServices       AliasProperty   RequiredServices
                                       = ServicesDependedOn
CanPauseAndContinue    Property        bool CanPauseAndContinue
                                       {get;}
CanShutdown            Property        bool CanShutdown {get;}
CanStop                Property        bool CanStop {get;}
Container              Property
System.ComponentModel.IContainer Container {get;}
DependentServices      Property    System.ServiceProcess.
                  ServiceController[] DependentServices {get;}
DisplayName            Property        string DisplayName {get;set;}
MachineName            Property        string MachineName {get;set;}
ServiceHandle          Property        System.Runtime.
              InteropServices.SafeHandle ServiceHandle {get;}
ServiceName            Property        string ServiceName {get;set;}
ServicesDependedOn     Property        System.ServiceProcess.
                  ServiceController[] ServicesDependedOn {get;}
ServiceType            Property
System.ServiceProcess.ServiceType ServiceType {get;}
Site                   Property        System.ComponentModel.ISite
                                       Site {get;set;}
Status                 Property
System.ServiceProcess.ServiceControllerStatus Status {get;}
```

Because all these properties are in the object that Get-Service retrieves for each service, you can display any or all of them by using the –Property parameter. For example, the following command uses the Format-Table command to display only the Name, Status, ServiceType, and ServicesDependedOn properties of each service:

```
get-service | format-table Name, Status, ServiceType,
ServicesDependedOn


Name        Status    ServiceType   ServicesDependedOn
----        ------    -----------   ------------------
ADWS        Stopped   Win32OwnProcess {}
AeLookupSvc Stopped   Win32ShareProcess {}
```

```
ALG          Stopped   Win32OwnProcess {}
AppHostSvc   Running   Win32ShareProcess {}
AppIDSvc     Stopped   Win32ShareProcess {RpcSs, CryptSvc, AppID}
Appinfo      Running   Win32ShareProcess {RpcSs, ProfSvc}
AppMgmt      Stopped   Win32ShareProcess {}
AppReadiness Stopped   Win32ShareProcess {}
AppXSvc      Stopped   Win32ShareProcess {rpcss}
```

Grouping and Sorting

In addition to formatting output for display, you might want to group and sort objects. All the formatting cmdlets include the –GroupBy parameter, which allows you to group output based on a specified property.

Using the –GroupBy parameter produces the same results as sending the output to the Group-Object cmdlet and then sending the output to a formatting cmdlet. However, these techniques probably won't generate the output you are looking for because these approaches generate a new header each time a new value is encountered for the specified property. For example, with the Get-Service cmdlet, you can group services by status, such as Running or Stopped, by using the following command:

```
get-service | format-list –groupby status


   Status: Stopped
Name                  : WinRM
DisplayName           : Windows Remote Management (WS-Management)
Status                : Stopped
DependentServices     : {}
ServicesDependedOn    : {RPCSS, HTTP}
CanPauseAndContinue   : False
CanShutdown           : False
CanStop               : False
ServiceType           : Win32ShareProcess


   Status: Running
Name                  : Wlansvc
DisplayName           : WLAN AutoConfig
Status                : Running
DependentServices     : {}
ServicesDependedOn    : {Eaphost, RpcSs, Ndisuio, nativewifip}
```

```
CanPauseAndContinue : False
CanShutdown         : True
CanStop             : True
ServiceType         : Win32ShareProcess
```

When you use Group-Object and group by status, you get a different result entirely:

```
get-service | group-object status
```

```
Count Name              Group
----- ----              -----
   68 Stopped           {System.ServiceProcess.ServiceControll
   89 Running           {System.ServiceProcess.ServiceControll
```

Although both outputs can be useful, neither produces the result you need if you want to see all stopped services and all started services in sequence. The workaround is to sort the objects first and then group them. You sort objects by using the Sort-Object cmdlet. Sort-Object supports sorting on a single property and sorting on multiple properties. You specify the property or properties to sort on with the –Property parameter and separate multiple properties with commas. For example, if you want to sort services by status and name, you can use the following command:

```
get-service | sort-object status, name | format-table -groupby
status
```

```
   Status: Stopped
```

```
Status    Name              DisplayName
------    ----              -----------
Stopped   ADWS              Active Directory Web Services
Stopped   AeLookupSvc       Application Experience
Stopped   ALG               Application Layer Gateway Service
Stopped   AppIDSvc          Application Identity
Stopped   AppMgmt           Application Management
Stopped   AppReadiness      App Readiness
Stopped   AppXSvc           AppX Deployment Service (AppXSVC)
```

```
   Status: Running
```

```
Status    Name            DisplayName
------    ----            -----------
Running   AppHostSvc      Application Host Helper Service
Running   Appinfo         Application Information
Running   BFE             Base Filtering Engine
Running   CertPropSvc     Certificate Propagation
Running   CryptSvc        Cryptographic Services
Running   DcomLaunch      DCOM Server Process Launcher
```

By default, properties are sorted in ascending order. You can sort in descending order with the –Descending parameter. For example, with the Get-Process cmdlet, sorting the working set in descending order can help you identify processes that are using the most resources on the computer. The command to do this is:

```
get-process | sort-object ws –descending
```

Handles	NPM(K)	PM(K)	WS(K)	VM(M)	CPU(s)	Id	ProcessName
1434	93	268752	285920	681	51.39	1972	powershell
527	48	123184	142892	788	8.77	2648	ServerManager
980	103	113112	140340	1335	22.30	3020	mmc
1376	76	58204	111476	568	29.78	2844	explorer
371	25	89964	105580	580	1.97	3460	wsmprovhost
561	45	104328	102364	748	12.73	3540	ServerManager
1252	69	36092	88760	434	9.50	3344	explorer
528	69	62712	78176	796	8.52	940	mmc
532	22	64688	66092	602	0.77	1800	powershell
476	22	64488	64008	602	0.64	2576	powershell
199	20	13896	60528	148	0.69	1980	dwm
199	25	27500	60420	157	4.44	748	dwm
652	27	37452	45184	157	2.63	1960	svchost
1681	51	19984	34804	139	23.44	796	svchost

In the output, you'll likely see multiple occurrences of some processes, such as powershell or svchost. If you enter the following command:

```
get-process | sort-object name –unique
```

Handles	NPM(K)	PM(K)	WS(K)	VM(M)	CPU(s)	Id	ProcessName
199	20	13896	60528	148	0.69	1980	dwm
1376	76	58204	111476	568	29.78	2844	explorer
980	103	113112	140340	1335	22.30	3020	mmc
1434	93	268752	285920	681	51.39	1972	powershell
527	48	123184	142892	788	8.77	2648	ServerManager
652	27	37452	45184	157	2.63	1960	svchost
371	25	89964	105580	580	1.97	3460	wsmprovhost

In the output, you'll see only the first occurrence of each process. However, this doesn't give you a complete picture of how many processes are running and what resources are being used by those processes.

Writing to Output Streams

Windows PowerShell supports several Write cmdlets for writing to different output streams. The first thing to know about these cmdlets is that they don't actually render the output. They simply pipeline (send) the output to a specified output stream. Although some output streams modify formatting of the output, the job of actually rendering and finalizing output belongs to the Output cmdlets discussed in the next section.

The available output streams include the following:

- Standard output stream
- Verbose message stream
- Warning message stream
- Debugging message stream
- Error stream

Explicitly Writing Output

You can explicitly write output using one of the following output cmdlets:

- **Write-Host** Writes to the standard output stream and allows you to set the background color and foreground color for text. By default, any text you write is terminated with a newline character. Use –NoNewLine to write text without inserting a newline character. Use –Separator to specify a string to output between objects you are displaying. Use –Object to specify the object or string literal to display.

```
Write-Host [[-Object] Object] [-BackgroundColor Color]
[-ForegroundColor Color] [-NoNewline] [-Separator Object]
```

- **Write-Output**   Sends a specified object down the pipeline to the next command or for display in the console. Because Write-Output accepts an input object, you can pipeline objects to it, and it in turn will pipeline objects to the next command or the console as appropriate.

```
Write-Output [[-InputObject] Object] [-NoEnumerate]
```

The main reason to use Write-Host is to take advantage of the formatting options it provides, which include alternative text and background colors. You use the –BackgroundColor parameter to set the background color for output text and the –ForegroundColor parameter to set the text color. The available colors are:

- Black, DarkBlue, DarkGreen, DarkCyan
- DarkRed, DarkMagenta, DarkYellow, Gray
- DarkGray, Blue, Green, Cyan
- Red, Magenta, Yellow, White

In the following example, you specify that you want black text on a yellow background:

```
write-host –backgroundcolor yellow –foregroundcolor black "This
is text!"
```

```
This is text!
```

> **NOTE**   The Write-Host cmdlet writes output to the application that is hosting PowerShell. Typically, this is the PowerShell console (powershell.exe) or the PowerShell application (powershell_ise.exe). Other applications can host the PowerShell engine, and those applications may handle Write-Host output in a different way. This means that you'll want

> to use Write-Host only when you know which host application will be used and how the host application will handle Write-Host output.

The Write-Output cmdlet also writes to the standard output stream. Unlike Write-Host, which does not accept input objects, Write-Output accepts objects as input. However, the purpose of Write-Output is simply to send a specified object to the next command in the pipeline. If the command is the last in the pipeline, the object is displayed on the console.

One situation in which to use Write-Output is when you want to be explicit about what you are writing to output. For example:

```
get-process | write-output
```

Here, you pipeline the output of Get-Process to Write-Output to show you are writing output.

When you are using variables, Write-Output is also helpful for being explicit about output you are writing. Consider the following example:

```
$p = get-process; $p
```

Here you create the $p variable, store Process objects in it, and then write those objects to the output. To be explicit about the write operation, you can change the previous line of code to read as follows:

```
$p = get-process; write-output $p
```

Using Other Output Streams

When you want to work with output streams other than the standard output stream, use the following Write cmdlets:

- **Write-Debug** Writes debug messages to the console from a script or command. By default, debug messages are not displayed in the console and do not cause execution to halt. You can display debug messages using the –Debug parameter (which is common to all cmdlets) or the $DebugPreference variable. The –Debug parameter overrides the value of the $DebugPreference variable for the current command.

```
Write-Debug [-message] DebugMessage
```

- **Write-Error**   Writes error messages to the console from a script or command. By default, error messages are displayed in the console but do not cause execution to halt. Using the –ErrorAction parameter (which is common to all cmdlets) or the $ErrorActionPreference variable, you can modify the behavior. The –ErrorAction parameter overrides the value of the $ErrorActionPreference variable for the current command.

```
Write-Error [-Message] String [-ErrorId String]
[-TargetObject Object] [AddtlParams]


Write-Error -ErrorRecord ErrorRecord [AddtlParams]


Write-Error -Exception Exception [-Category String]
[-TargetObject Object] [AddtlParams]


AddtlParams=
[-CategoryTargetName String] [-CategoryTargetType String]
[-CategoryReason String] [-CategoryActivity String]
[-RecommendedAction String]
```

- **Write-Warning**   Writes warning messages to the console from a script or command. By default, warning messages are displayed in the console but do not cause execution to halt. You can modify the behavior using either the –WarningAction parameter (which is common to all cmdlets) or the $WarningPreference variable. The –WarningAction parameter overrides the value of the $WarningPreference variable for the current command.

```
Write-Warning [-message] WarningMessage
```

- **Write-Verbose**   Writes verbose messages to the console from a script or command. By default, verbose messages are not displayed in the console and do not cause execution to halt. You can display verbose messages using the –Verbose parameter (which is common to all cmdlets) or the $VerbosePreference variable. The –Verbose parameter overrides the value of the $VerbosePreference variable for the current command.

```
Write-Verbose [-message] VerboseMessage
```

Write-Debug, Write-Error, Write-Warning, and Write-Verbose can each be managed using either a common parameter or a preference variable. In every case, the common parameters accept a value of $true or $false, and the preference variable accepts one of the following values:

- Stop
- Inquire
- Continue
- SilentlyContinue

For example, the $DebugPreference variable determines how PowerShell handles debugging messages. You can specify:

- $DebugPreference=Stop to display debug messages and stop executing.
- $DebugPreference=Inquire to display debug messages that ask whether you want to continue.
- $DebugPreference=Continue to display debug messages and continue with execution.
- $DebugPreference=SilentlyContinue to not display debug messages and continue execution without interruption.

The –Debug parameter overrides the value of the $DebugPreference variable for the current command. You can specify **–Debug $true** or **–Debug** to turn on debugging, or you can specify **–Debug $false** to suppress the display of debugging messages when the value of $DebugPreference is not SilentlyContinue.

> **MORE INFO**   A parameter that accepts a $true or $false value is referred to as a switch parameter. Generally, with any switch parameter, you can simply specify the parameter name to indicate that you want to set the parameter to $true. However, if you don't want a parameter or option to be used, you must explicitly set the parameter or option to $false.

Rendering and Finalizing the Output

Whether you enter a single cmdlet, send output to other cmdlets using piping, or format output explicitly, the final part of parsing and displaying output is a hidden background call to an output cmdlet. By default, as the last part of the execution process, PowerShell calls the default output cmdlet, which is typically the Out-Host cmdlet.

You can explicitly specify the output cmdlet to use by sending the output to one of the following output cmdlets:

- **Out-File** Sends the output to a file. You must specify the path to the output file to use. If the output file exists, you can use the –Force parameter to overwrite it or the –Append parameter to add the output to the file. You can use Out-File instead of the standard redirection techniques discussed in the next section.

  ```
  Out-File [-FilePath] String [[-Encoding] String]
  [AddtlParams]
  ```

  ```
  Out-File [[-Encoding] String] -LiteralPath String
  [AddtlParams]
  ```

  ```
  AddtlParams=
  [-Append] [-Force] [-InputObject SObject] [-NoClobber]
  [-Width NumChars]
  ```

- **Out-GridView** Sends the output to a grid view window and displays the output in an interactive table. The grid view window supports sorting, grouping, copying, and filtering.

  ```
  Out-GridView [-InputObject Object] [-Title WindowTitle]
  [-Wait | -PassThru | -OutputMode Mode]
  ```

- **Out-Host** Sends the output to the command line. Add the –Paging parameter to display one page of output at a time (similar to using the More command in the command shell).

  ```
  Out-Host [-InputObject Object] [-Paging]
  ```

- **Out-Null** Sends the output to the null port. This deletes the output without displaying it, which is useful for output that you don't need.

  ```
  Out-Null [-InputObject Object]
  ```

- **Out-Printer** Sends the output to the default printer or to a named printer. Use the –Name parameter to specify the UNC path to the printer to use, such as –Name "\\PrintServer85\LaserP45".

```
Out-Printer [[-Name] String] [-InputObject Object]
```

- **Out-String** Converts the output of all objects to a single string and then sends the result to the console. Use the –Stream parameter to send the strings for each object separately. Use the –Width parameter to specify the number of characters to display in each line of output. Any additional characters are truncated. The default width is 80 characters.

```
Out-String [-InputObject Object] [-Width NumChars] [-Stream]
```

All these cmdlets accept input objects, which means you can pipeline objects to them. The following example writes events from the application log to the C:\logs\app\current.txt file:

```
get-eventlog –newest 10 –logname application | out-file
-filepath c:\logs\app\current.txt
```

All these cmdlets also accept objects as input. The following example displays the currently running processes in a grid view window:

```
$p = get-process; $p | out-gridview
```

Figure 2-1 shows the command output in grid view. Here, you store the results of Get-Process in the $p variable. Next, you use a pipeline character to send the $p variable to Out-GridView.

You also could have achieved the same result by sending the output of Get-Process directly to Out-GridView, as shown in this example:

```
get-process | out-gridview
```

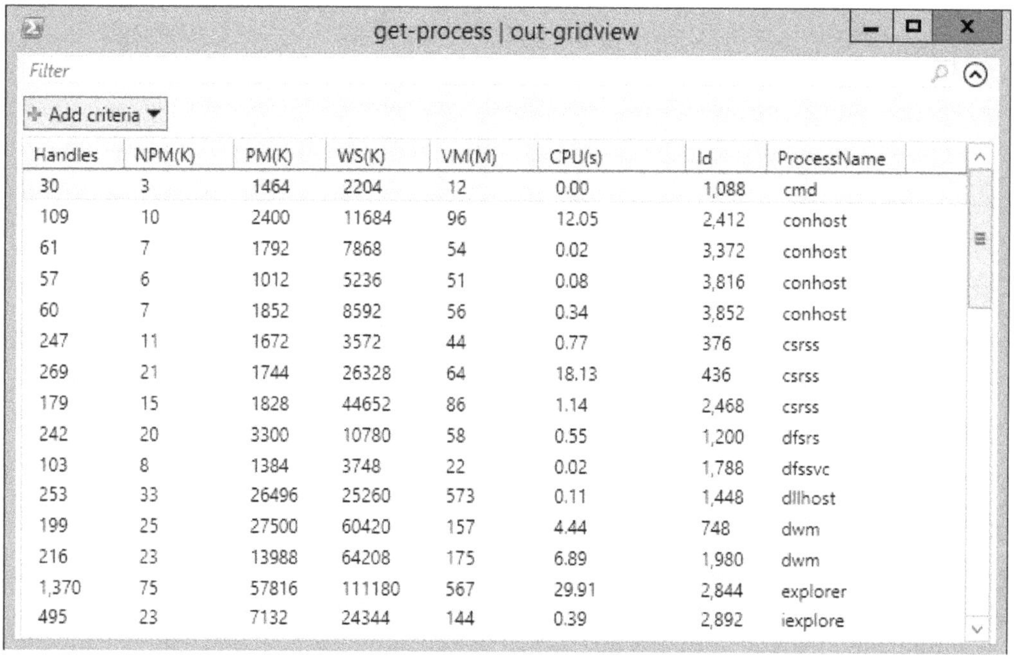

get-process | out-gridview

Handles	NPM(K)	PM(K)	WS(K)	VM(M)	CPU(s)	Id	ProcessName
30	3	1464	2204	12	0.00	1,088	cmd
109	10	2400	11684	96	12.05	2,412	conhost
61	7	1792	7868	54	0.02	3,372	conhost
57	6	1012	5236	51	0.08	3,816	conhost
60	7	1852	8592	56	0.34	3,852	conhost
247	11	1672	3572	44	0.77	376	csrss
269	21	1744	26328	64	18.13	436	csrss
179	15	1828	44652	86	1.14	2,468	csrss
242	20	3300	10780	58	0.55	1,200	dfsrs
103	8	1384	3748	22	0.02	1,788	dfssvc
253	33	26496	25260	573	0.11	1,448	dllhost
199	25	27500	60420	157	4.44	748	dwm
216	23	13988	64208	175	6.89	1,980	dwm
1,370	75	57816	111180	567	29.91	2,844	explorer
495	23	7132	24344	144	0.39	2,892	iexplore

Figure 2-1 Command output is displayed in the grid view.

More on Redirecting Input, Output, and Error

By default, commands take input from the parameters specified when they are called by PowerShell and then send their output, including errors, to the standard console window. Sometimes, however, you'll want to take input from another source or send output to a file or another output device, such as a printer. You might also want to redirect errors to a file rather than have them displayed in the console window. In addition to using the Output cmdlets discussed previously, you can perform these and other redirection tasks by using the techniques introduced in Table 2-3 and discussed in the examples that follow.

TABLE 2-3 Redirection Techniques for Input, Output, and Errors

REDIRECTION TECHNIQUE	DESCRIPTION
command1 | command2	Sends the output of the first command to be the input of the second command.

REDIRECTION TECHNIQUE	DESCRIPTION
command > [path]filename	Sends output to the named file, creating the file if necessary or overwriting it if it already exists.
command >> [path]filename	Appends output to the named file if it exists or creates the file and then writes to it.
command 2> [path]filename	Creates the named file and sends any error output to it. If the file exists, it is overwritten.
command 2>> [path]filename	Appends errors to the named file if it exists or creates the file and then writes errors to it.
command 2>&1	Sends error output to the same destination as standard output.

Piping is the primary redirection technique, and you'll find examples of piping throughout this chapter. Another command redirection technique is to send output to a file. You can do this with the Out-File cmdlet. You also can use > to create or overwrite a named file, or >> to create or append data to a named file. For example, if you want to write the current status of running processes to a file, you can use the following command:

```
get-process > processes.txt
```

Unfortunately, if there is a file in the current directory with the same file name, this command overwrites the file and creates a new one. If you want to append this information to an existing file rather than overwrite an existing file, change the command text to read as follows:

```
get-process >> processes.txt
```

By default, errors from commands are written as output on the command line. As discussed previously, you can manage the error stream using Write-Error, the –ErrorAction parameter (which is common to all cmdlets), or the $ErrorActionPreference variable. Another way to redirect standard error is to tell

PowerShell that errors should go to the same destination as standard output. To do this, type the 2>&1 redirection symbol as shown in this example:

```
chkdsk /r > diskerrors.txt 2>&1
```

Here, you send standard output and standard error to a file named Diskerrors.txt. If you want to track only errors, you can redirect only the standard error. In this example, standard output is displayed at the command line and standard error is sent to the file Diskerrors.txt:

```
chkdsk /r 2> diskerrors.txt
```

If the error file exists, it is overwritten automatically. To append to an existing file rather than overwrite it, you can use the append technique shown in the following example:

```
chkdsk /r 2>> diskerrors.txt
```

Chapter 3. Managing Your Windows PowerShell Environment

When you start Windows PowerShell, the working environment is loaded automatically. Many features of the working environment come from profiles, which are a type of script that run when you start PowerShell. However, the working environment is also determined by imported modules, snap-ins, providers, command paths, file extensions, and file associations. You'll learn about these features of PowerShell in this chapter.

Additionally, when you work remotely, your working environment is different from when you work locally. For this reason, you'll use different techniques when you work remotely than when you are working on your local computer. Not only does PowerShell support remote execution of commands, but PowerShell also supports remote sessions and remote background jobs. You'll learn about these features of PowerShell in Chapter 4, "Using Sessions and Remoting" and in Chapter 5, "Using Background Jobs and Scheduled Jobs."

Using Profiles

PowerShell scripts and profiles end with the .ps1 file extension. Generally speaking, profiles are always loaded when you work with Windows PowerShell, but there are specific exceptions. For example, when testing a script, you might want to invoke PowerShell without loading a profile and then run the script. Doing so will help ensure that you've coded the script properly and haven't used any profile-specific settings.

You use profiles to store frequently used elements, including:

- **Aliases** An alias is an alternate name for a command, function, script, file, executable, or other command element. After you create an alias, you can use the alias as a keystroke shortcut or friendly name to invoke the related command element. For example, gsv is an alias for Get-Service. Instead of entering **get-service winrm** to get information about the WinRM service, you could enter **gsv winrm**. To list all available aliases, enter **get-alias** at the PowerShell prompt.

```
Get-Alias [[-Name] Strings] [-Exclude Strings]
[-Scope String]


Get-Alias [[-Definition] Strings] [-Exclude Strings]
[-Scope String]
```

- **Functions**   A function is a named set of PowerShell commands. When you call a function by its name, the set of commands runs just as though you had typed each command at the command line. For example, you could create a function to examine critical processes and services on a computer and generate a report. By adding the function to a profile, you would then be able to run the function at any time by entering the function name at the PowerShell prompt. To list all available functions, enter **get-childitem function:** at the PowerShell prompt.

```
Get-ChildItem [[-Path] Strings] [[-Filter] Strings]
[AddtlParams]


Get-ChildItem [[-Filter] String] -LiteralPath Strings
[AddtlParams]


Get-ChildItem [-Attributes FileAttributes] [-Directory]
[-File] [-Force] [-Hidden] [-ReadOnly] [-System]
[-UseTransaction [{$True|$False}]]


AddtlParams=
[-Exclude Strings] [-Force] [-Include Strings] [-Name]
[-Recurse] [-UseTransaction [{$True|$False}]]
```

- **Variables**   A variable is a placeholder for a value. In addition to environment variables from the operating system, PowerShell supports automatic, preference, and user-created variables. To reference a variable at the prompt or in scripts, you must precede the variable's name with a dollar sign ($). For example, to reference the home variable, you must enter **$home**. To list all available variables, enter **get-variable** at the PowerShell prompt.

```
Get-Variable [[-Name] Strings] [-Exclude Strings] [-Include
Strings] [-Scope String] [-ValueOnly]
```

NOTE Your scripts and command text can use any of the available variables. Automatic variables are fixed and are used to store state information. Preference variables are changeable and are used to store working values for PowerShell configuration settings. By default, variables you create exist only in the current session and are lost when you exit or close the session. To maintain user-created variables, you must store them in a profile. For detailed information on variables, see "Working with Variables and Values" in Chapter 6, "Navigating Core PowerShell Structures."

TIP You can view the value of an automatic or a preference variable simply by entering its name at the PowerShell prompt. For example, to see the current value of the $home variable, enter **$home** at the PowerShell prompt. Environment variables are accessed in a slightly different way. You must reference $env: and then the name of the variable. For example, to display the value of the %ComputerName% variable, you must enter **$env:computername**.

Creating Profiles

You can create a profile by using a standard text editor. Simply enter the commands that define the aliases, functions, variables, or other elements you want to use, and then save the file with the appropriate file name in the appropriate location on your computer. That's it. This means you can use the following technique to create a profile:

1. In Notepad or any other text editor, enter the command text for the aliases, functions, variables, and any other command elements you want to use.
2. Save the file with the appropriate file name and file extension for a profile, such as Profile.ps1.
3. Copy the profile file to the appropriate location, such as a folder named $pshome.

When you are working with the PowerShell console and the PowerShell application, there are six types of profiles you need to know about. Table 3-1 summarizes these profiles. $home and $pshome are automatic variables. The

$home variable stores the current user's home directory. The $pshome variable stores the installation directory for PowerShell.

TABLE 3-1 Common PowerShell Profiles

PROFILE TYPE	DESCRIPTION
Current User, PowerShell Console	A profile specific to the user account for the current user context and applicable only to the PowerShell console. Directory: $home\[My]Documents\WindowsPowerShell Name: profile.ps1
Current User, PowerShell ISE	A profile specific to the user account for the current user context and applicable only to the PowerShell application. Directory: $home\[My]Documents\WindowsPowerShell Name: Microsoft.PowerShellISE_profile.ps1
Current User, All Hosts	A profile specific to the current user context and applicable to both the PowerShell console and the PowerShell application. Directory: $home\[My]Documents Name: profile.ps1
All Users, PowerShell Console	A profile applicable to all users but specific to the PowerShell console. Directory: $pshome Name: Microsoft.PowerShell_profile.ps1
All Users, PowerShell ISE	A profile applicable to all users but specific to the PowerShell application. Directory: $pshome Name: Microsoft.PowerShellISE_profile.ps1
All Users, All Hosts	A profile applicable to all users for both the PowerShell console and the PowerShell application. Directory: $pshome Name: profile.ps1

When PowerShell starts, PowerShell looks for profiles in the specified locations and runs the profiles in the following order:

1. The All Users, All Hosts profile
2. Either the All Users, PowerShell or All Users, PowerShell ISE profile as appropriate
3. The Current User, All Hosts profile
4. Either the Current User, PowerShell or Current User, PowerShell ISE profile as appropriate

The order of the profiles' execution determines the precedence order for any conflicts. Whenever there is a conflict, the last value written wins. Following this, an alias defined in the Current User, PowerShell profile or the Current User, PowerShell ISE profile has precedence over any conflicting entries in any other profile.

> **TIP**   As PowerShell downloads help files for a module no more than once per day, you can add Update-Help to your profile without worrying about PowerShell repeatedly downloading help files for a particular module. Note also that if your organization has a central save location for help files, updates are only available when new help files are downloaded and saved to that location.

Understanding Execution Order

Whenever you work with Windows PowerShell and PowerShell profiles, don't overlook the importance of execution order and the PATH environment variable. It is important to keep in mind where the commands you are using come from. PowerShell searches for commands in the following order:

1. **Aliases**   PowerShell looks for alternate built-in or profile-defined aliases for the associated command name. If an alias is found, the command to which the alias is mapped is run.
2. **Functions**   PowerShell looks for built-in or profile-defined functions with the command name. If a function is found, the function is executed.

3. **Cmdlets or language keywords**   PowerShell looks for built-in cmdlets or language keywords with the command name. If a cmdlet or language keyword is found, the appropriate action is taken.

4. **Scripts**   PowerShell looks for scripts with the .ps1 extension. If a PowerShell script is found, the script is executed.

5. **External commands and files**   PowerShell looks for external commands, non-PowerShell scripts, and utilities with the command name. If an external command or utility is found in a directory specified by the PATH environment variable, the appropriate action is taken. If you enter a file name, PowerShell uses file associations to determine whether a helper application is available to open the file.

Because of the execution order, contrary to what you might think, when you type **dir** and then press Enter to get a listing of the current directory, you are not running the dir command that is built into the Windows command shell (cmd.exe). Instead, when you type **dir** at the PowerShell prompt, you are actually running a PowerShell command. This command is called Get-ChildItem. Why does this occur? Although PowerShell does pass commands through to the Windows command shell, it does so only when a PowerShell command or an alias to a PowerShell command is not available. Because dir is a registered alias of Get-ChildItem, you are actually running Get-ChildItem when you enter **dir**.

Working with the Command Path

The Windows operating system uses the command path to locate executables. The types of files that Windows considers to be executables are determined by the file extensions for executables. You can also map file extensions to specific applications by using file associations.

Managing the Command Path

You can view the current command path for executables by displaying the value of the PATH environment variable. To do this, open a PowerShell console, type **$env:path** on a line by itself, and then press Enter. The results should look similar to the following:

```
C:\Windows\System32;C:\Windows;C:\Windows\System32\Wbem;
C:\Windows\System32\WindowsPowerShell\v1.0\
```

> **NOTE** Observe the use of the semicolon (;) to separate individual paths.
> PowerShell uses the semicolon to determine where one file path ends and
> another begins.

The command path is set during logon using system and user environment
variables, namely the %PATH% variable. The order in which directories are listed
in the path indicates the search order PowerShell uses when it searches for
executables. In the previous example, PowerShell searches in this order:

1. C:\Windows\System32
2. C:\Windows
3. C:\Windows\System32\Wbem
4. C:\Windows\System32\PowerShell\v1.0

You can permanently change the command path in the system environment by
using the SETX command. For example, if you use specific directories for scripts
or applications, you may want to update the path information. You can do this
by using the SETX command to add a specific path to the existing path, such as
setx PATH "%PATH%;C:\Scripts".

> **NOTE** Observe the use of the quotation marks and the semicolon. The
> quotation marks are necessary to ensure that the value
> %PATH%;C:\Scripts is read as the second argument for the SETX
> command. As mentioned previously, the semicolon is used to specify
> where one file path ends and another begins. Because the command path
> is set when you open the PowerShell console, you must exit the console
> and open a new console to load the new path. If you'd rather not exit the
> console, you can update the PATH environment variable for the console
> as discussed in "Using External Commands" in Chapter 1, "Windows
> PowerShell Essentials."

In this example, the directory C:\Scripts is appended to the existing command
path, and the sample path listed previously would be modified to read as
follows:

```
C:\Windows\System32;C:\Windows;C:\Windows\System32\Wbem;C:\Windo
ws\System32\PowerShell\v1.0;C:\Scripts
```

Don't forget about the search order that Windows uses. Because the paths are searched in order, the C:\Scripts directory will be the last one searched. This can sometimes slow execution of your scripts. To help Windows find your scripts faster, you may want C:\Scripts to be the first directory searched. In this case, you could set the command path by using the following command:

```
setx PATH "C:\Scripts;%PATH%"
```

Be careful when setting the command path. It is easy to overwrite all path information accidentally. For example, if you don't specify the %PATH% environment variable when setting the path, you will delete all other path information. One way to ensure that you can easily re-create the command path is to keep a copy of the command path in a file. To write the current command path to a file, type **$env:path > orig_path.txt**. Keep in mind that if you are using a standard console rather than an administrator console, you won't be able to write to secure system locations. In this case, you can write to a subdirectory to which you have access or your personal profile. To write the command path to the PowerShell console, type **$env:path**. Now you have a listing or a file that contains a listing of the original command path.

Managing File Extensions and File Associations

File extensions are what allow you to execute external commands by typing just their command name at the PowerShell prompt. Two types of file extensions are used:

- **File extensions for executables**   Executable files are defined with the %PATHEXT% environment variable. You can view the current settings by typing **$env:pathext** at the command line. The default setting is .COM;.EXE;.BAT;.CMD;.VBS;.VBE;.JS;.JSE;.WSF;.WSH;.MSC;.CPL. With this setting, the command line knows which files are executables and which files are not, so you don't have to specify the file extension at the command line.
- **File extensions for applications**   File extensions for applications are referred to as *file associations*. File associations are what enable you to pass

arguments to executables and to open documents, spreadsheets, or other application files by double-clicking file icons. Each known extension on a system has a file association that you can view by typing **cmd /c assoc** followed by the extension, such as **cmd /c assoc .exe**. Each file association in turn specifies the file type for the file extension. This information can be viewed using the FTYPE command followed by the file association, such as **cmd /c ftype exefile**.

> **NOTE**   Observe that you call ASSOC and FTYPE via the command shell. The reason is that they are internal commands for the command shell.

With executables, the order of file extensions sets the search order used by the command line on a per-directory basis. Thus, if a particular directory in the command path has multiple executables that match the command name provided, a .com file would be executed before a .exe file and so on.

Every known file extension on a system has a corresponding file association and file type—even extensions for executables. In most cases, the file type is the extension text without the period, followed by the keyword *file*, such as cmdfile, exefile, or batfile. The file association specifies that the first parameter passed is the command name and that other parameters should be passed on to the application.

You can look up the file type and file association for known extensions by using the ASSOC and FTYPE commands. To find the association, type **cmd /c assoc** followed by the file extension that includes the period. The output of the ASSOC command is the file type. So if you type **cmd /c ftype *association*** (where *association* is the output of the ASSOC command), you'll see the file type mapping. For example, if you type **cmd /c assoc .exe** to see the file associations for .exe executables, you then type **cmd /c ftype exefile** to see the file type mapping.

You'll see the file association is set to

```
exefile="%1" %*
```

Thus, when you run an .exe file, Windows knows the first value is the command that you want to run and anything else you've provided is a parameter to pass along.

> **TIP** File associations and types are maintained in the Windows registry and can be set using the ASSOC and FTYPE commands, respectively. To create the file association, type **cmd /c assoc** followed by the extension setting, such as **cmd /c assoc .pl=perlfile**. To create the file type, set the file type mapping, including how to use parameters supplied with the command name, such as cmd /c ftype **perlfile=C:\Perl\Bin\Perl.exe "%1" %***.

Navigating Windows PowerShell Extensions

In Windows PowerShell, cmdlet and function modules provide the basic functionality. Modules come in two forms: those written using managed code assemblies and based on C# and the .NET framework and those written using non-managed code assemblies, such as those written in C++.

Windows PowerShell can be extended in several different ways. Typically, extensions are in the form of PowerShell snap-ins that add PowerShell providers to the working environment. The data that a provider exposes appears in a drive that you can browse.

Working with Windows PowerShell Extensions

Cmdlets that you'll use to work with Windows PowerShell snap-ins, providers, and drives include:

- **Add-PSSnapin** Adds one or more registered snap-ins to the current session. After you add a snap-in, you can use the cmdlets and providers that the snap-in supports in the current session.

  ```
  Add-PSSnapin [-Name] Strings [-PassThru]
  ```

- **Export-Console** Exports the names of PowerShell snap-ins in the current session to a PowerShell console file (.psc1). You can add the snap-ins in the console file to future sessions by using the –PSConsoleFile parameter of PowerShell.exe.

```
Export-Console [[-Path] String] [-NoClobber] [-Force]
```

- **Get-Module** Gets information modules. The first syntax shown in the following example gets information about imported modules that are on the computer and available in the current session. The second syntax shown gets information about available modules that you can use.

```
Get-Module [[-FullyQualifiedName] Strings] [[-Name] Strings]
[-All] [-Refresh] [-ListAvailable]


Get-Module [[-Name] Strings] [-CimNamespace String]
[-CimResourceUri ResourceUri] [-ListAvailable] [-Refresh]
-CimSession CimSession


Get-Module [[-FullyQualifiedName] Strings] [[-Name] Strings]
[-ListAvailable] [-Refresh] -PSSession PSSession
```

- **Get-PSProvider** Gets information about all or specified providers that are installed on the computer and available in the current session. Providers are listed by name, capability, and drive.

```
Get-PSProvider [[-PSProvider] Strings]
```

- **Get-PSSnapin** Gets objects representing snap-ins that were added to the current session or registered on the system. Snap-ins are listed in detection order. You can register snap-ins using the InstallUtil tool included with Microsoft .NET Framework 2.0.

```
Get-PSSnapin [[-Name] Strings] [-Registered]
```

- **Import-Module** Imports one or more available modules into the current session. After you add a module, you can use the cmdlets and functions that the module supports in the current session.

```
Import-Module [-Name] Strings [AddtlParams] [AddtlParams2]
Import-Module [-Assembly] Assemblies [AddtlParams]
Import-Module [-ModuleInfo] ModGUIDs [AddtlParams]


AddtlParams=
[-Alias Strings] [-ArgumentList Objects] [-AsCustomObject]
```

```
[-Cmdlet Strings] [-DisableNameChecking] [-Force]
[-Function Strings] [-Global] [-NoClobber] [-PassThru]
[-Prefix String] [-Scope String] [-Variable Strings]
[-Version Version]

AddtlParams2=
[-MinimumVersion Version] [-RequiredVersion Version]
[[-CimSession CimSession] | [-PSSession PSSession]]
```

- **New-Module** Creates a module based on script blocks, functions, and cmdlets that you specify. Also available are New-ModuleManifest and Test-ModuleManifest.

```
New-Module [-ScriptBlock] ScriptBlock [-ArgumentList Objects]
[-AsCustomObject] [-Cmdlet Strings] [-Function Strings]
[-ReturnResult]

New-Module [-Name] String [-ScriptBlock] ScriptBlock
[-ArgumentList Objects] [-AsCustomObject] [-Cmdlet Strings]
[-Function Strings] [-ReturnResult]
```

- **Remove-Module** Removes a module that you added to the current session.

```
Remove-Module [-Name] Strings [-Force]
Remove-Module [-ModuleInfo] ModGUIDs [-Force]
```

- **Remove-PSSnapin** Removes a PowerShell snap-in that you added to the current session. You cannot remove snap-ins that are installed with Windows PowerShell.

```
Remove-PSSnapin [-Name] Strings [-PassThru]
```

Using Snap-ins

Windows PowerShell snap-ins are .NET programs that are compiled into DLL files. Snap-ins can include providers and cmdlets. PowerShell providers are .NET programs that provide access to specialized data stores so that you can access the data stores from the command line. Before using a provider, you must install the related snap-in and add it to your Windows PowerShell session.

Snap-in Essentials

When you add a snap-in, the providers and cmdlets that it contains are immediately available for use in the current session. To ensure that a snap-in is available in all future sessions, add the snap-in via your profile. You can also use the Export-Console cmdlet to save the names of snap-ins to a console file. If you start a console by using the console file, the named snap-ins are available.

To save the snap-ins from a session in a console file (.psc1), use the Export-Console cmdlet. For example, to save the snap-ins in the current session configuration to the MyConsole.psc1 file in the current directory, enter the following command:

```
export-console MyConsole
```

The following command starts PowerShell with the MyConsole.psc1 console file:

```
powershell.exe -psconsolefile MyConsole.psc1
```

You can list the available snap-ins by entering **get-pssnapin**. To find the snap-in for each Windows PowerShell provider, enter the following command:

```
get-psprovider | format-list name, pssnapin
```

To list the cmdlets in a snap-in, enter

```
get-command -module SnapinName
```

where SnapinName is the name of the snap-in you want to examine.

PowerShell Core Commands

Beginning with PowerShell 3.0, the core commands are packaged in modules rather than snap-ins. The only exception is Microsoft.PowerShell.Core, a snap-in that contains providers and cmdlets used to manage the basic features of Windows PowerShell. Microsoft.PowerShell.Core includes the Alias, Environment, FileSystem, Function, Registry, and Variable providers and basic cmdlets like Add-History, Add-PSSnapin, Get-Command, Get-Help and New-Module.

> **NOTE** A key difference between modules and snap-ins is that while modules can add all types of commands to the working environment, including cmdlets, functions, providers, variables, aliases, and PowerShell drives, snap-ins can only add cmdlets and providers.

Microsoft.PowerShell.Core is registered in the operating system and added to the default session whenever you start Windows PowerShell. To use snap-ins that you create or obtain from other sources, you must register them and add them to your console session. To find registered snap-ins (other than the built-in snap-ins) on your system or to verify that an additional snap-in is registered, enter the following command:

```
get-pssnapin -registered
```

Adding and Removing Snap-ins

You can add a registered snap-in to the current session by using Add-PSSnapin. The basic syntax is to follow Add-PSSnapin with the name of the snap-in to add. For example, if you want to add the ADRMS.PS.Admin snap-in, you would enter **add-pssnapin adrms.ps.admin**.

Once you add the snap-in, its providers and cmdlets are available in the console session. If you add the necessary Add-PSSnapin commands to a relevant profile, you can be sure that modules you want to use are always loaded.

To remove a Windows PowerShell snap-in from the current session, use Remove-PSSnapin to remove the snap-in from the session. The basic syntax is to follow Remove-PSSnapin with the name of the snap-in to remove, such as Remove-PSSnapin ADRMS.PS.ADMIN. Although the removed snap-in is still loaded, the providers and cmdlets that it supports are no longer available.

Checking for Snap-in Availability

When you are performing administrative tasks or creating scripts for later use, you'll may want to ensure that a particular PowerShell snap-in is available before you try to use its features. The easiest way to do this is to attempt to perform the action or run a script only if the snap-in is available. Consider the following example:

```
if (get-pssnapin -name ADRMS.PS.Admin -erroraction
silentlycontinue)
 {

  Code to execute if the snap-in is available.

} else {

  Code to execute if the snap-in is not available.

}
```

Here, when the ADRMS.PS.Admin snap-in is available, the statement in parentheses evaluates to True, and any code in the related script block is executed. When the ADRMS.PS.Admin snap-in is not available, the statement in parentheses evaluates to False, and any code in the Else statement is executed. Note also that I set the –ErrorAction parameter to SilentlyContinue so that error messages aren't written to the output if the snap-in is not found.

> **TIP** The same technique can be used with providers and modules.

Using Providers

The data that a provider exposes appears in a drive that you can browse much like you browse a hard drive, allowing you to view, search though, and manage related data. To list all providers that are available, type **Get-PSProvider**. Table 3-2 lists the built-in providers. Note the drives associated with each provider.

TABLE 3-2 Built-In PowerShell Providers

PROVIDER	DATA ACCESSED & DRIVE
Alias	Windows PowerShell aliases {Alias}
Certificate	X509 certificates for digital signatures

	{Cert}
Environment	Windows environment variables {Env}
FileSystem	File system drives, directories, and files {C, D, E, ...}
Function	Windows PowerShell functions {Function}
Registry	Windows registry {HKLM, HKCU}
Variable	Windows PowerShell variables {Variable}
WSMan	WS-Management {WSMan}

PowerShell includes a set of cmdlets that are specifically designed to manage the items in the data stores that are exposed by providers. You use these cmdlets in the same ways to manage all the different types of data that the providers make available to you. Table 3-3 provides an overview of these cmdlets.

TABLE 3-3 Cmdlets for Working with Data Stores

CMDLET	DESCRIPTION
Get-PSDrive	Gets all or specified PowerShell drives in the current console. This includes logical drives on the computer, drives mapped to network shares, and drives exposed by Windows PowerShell providers. Get-PSDrive does not get Windows mapped drives that are added or created after you open PowerShell. However, you can map drives using New-PSDrive, and those drives will be available. Get-PSDrive [[-Name] *Strings*] [-PSProvider *Strings*] [-Scope *String*] [-UseTransaction] Get-PSDrive [[-LiteralName] *Strings*] [-PSProvider *Strings*] [-Scope *String*] [-UseTransaction]
New-PSDrive	Creates a PowerShell drive that is mapped to a location in a data store, which can include a shared network folder, a local directory, or a registry key. The drive is available only in the current PowerShell console. New-PSDrive [-Name] *String* [-PSProvider] *String* [-Root] *String* [-Credential *Credential*] [-Description *String*] [-Scope *String*] [-UseTransaction]
Remove-PSDrive	Removes a PowerShell drive that you added to the current console session. You cannot delete Windows drives or mapped network drives created by using other methods. Remove-PSDrive [[-Name] *Strings* [-Force] [-PSProvider *Strings*] [-Scope *String*] [-UseTransaction] Remove-PSDrive [[-LiteralName] *Strings* [-Force] [-PSProvider *Strings*] [-Scope *String*] [-UseTransaction]
Get-ChildItem	Gets the items and child items in one or more specified locations. Get-ChildItem [[-Path] *Strings*] [[-Filter] *String*] [AddtlParams] Get-ChildItem [[-Filter] *String*] [-LiteralPath] *Strings* [AddtlParams] Get-ChildItem [-Attributes *FileAttribs*] [-Directory] [-File] [-Force] [-Hidden] [-ReadOnly] [-System] [-UseTransaction] AddtlParams= [-Exclude *Strings*] [-Force] [-Include *Strings*] [-Name] [-Recurse] [-UseTransaction]
Get-Item	Gets the item at the specified location. Get-Item [[-LiteralPath]	

CMDLET	DESCRIPTION
	[-Path]] *Strings* [AddtlParams] AddtlParams= [-Credential *Credential*] [-Exclude *Strings*] [-Filter *String*] [-Force] [-Include *Strings*] [-UseTransaction]
New-Item	Creates a new item. New-Item [-Path] *Strings* [AddtlParams] New-Item -Name *String* [AddtlParams] AddtlParams= [-Credential *Credential*] [-Force] [-ItemType *String*] [-Value *Object*] [-UseTransaction]
Set-Item	Changes the value of an item to the value specified in the command. Set-Item [-Path] *Strings* [[-Value] *Object*] [AddtlParams] Set-Item [[-Value] *Object*] –LiteralPath *Strings* [AddtlParams] AddtlParams= [-Credential *Credential*] [-Exclude *Strings*] [-Filter *String*] [-Force] [-Include *Strings*] [-PassThru] [-UseTransaction]
Remove-Item	Deletes the specified item. Remove-Item [-Path] *Strings* [AddtlParams] Remove-Item –LiteralPath *Strings* [AddtlParams] AddtlParams= [-Credential *Credential*] [-Exclude *Strings*] [-Filter *String*] [-Force] [-Include *Strings*] [-Recurse] [-UseTransaction]
Move-Item	Moves an item from one location to another. Move-Item [-Path] *Strings* [[-Destination] *String*] [AddtlParams] Move-Item [[-Destination] *String*] –LiteralPath *Strings* [AddtlParams] AddtlParams= [-Credential *Credential*] [-Exclude *Strings*] [-Filter *String*] [-Force] [-Include *Strings*] [-PassThru] [-UseTransaction]
Rename-Item	Renames an item in a Windows PowerShell provider namespace.

CMDLET	DESCRIPTION
	Rename-Item [-Path] *String* [-NewName] *String* [AddtlParams] Rename-Item [-NewName] *String* -LiteralPath *String* [AddtlParams] AddtlParams= [-Credential *Credential*] [-Force] [-PassThru] [-UseTransaction]
Copy-Item	Copies an item from one location to another within a namespace. Copy-Item [-Path] *Strings* [[-Destination] *String*] [AddtlParams] Copy-Item [[-Destination] *String*] –LiteralPath *Strings* [AddtlParams] AddtlParams= [-Container] [-Credential *Credential*] [-Exclude *Strings*] [-Filter *String*] [-Force] [-Include *Strings*] [-PassThru] [-Recurse] [-UseTransaction]
Clear-Item	Deletes the contents of an item but does not delete the item. Clear-Item [-Path] *Strings* [AddtlParams] Clear-Item –LiteralPath *Strings* [AddtlParams] AddtlParams= [-Credential *Credential*] [-Exclude *Strings*] [-Filter *String*] [-Force] [-Include *Strings*] [-UseTransaction]
Invoke-Item	Performs the default action on the specified item. Invoke-Item [-Path] *Strings* [AddtlParams] Invoke-Item –LiteralPath *Strings* [AddtlParams] AddtlParams= [-Credential *Credential*] [-Exclude *Strings*] [-Filter *String*] [-Include *Strings*] [-UseTransaction]
Clear-ItemProperty	Deletes the value of a property but does not delete the property. Clear-ItemProperty [-Path] *Strings* [-Name] *String* [AddtlParams] Clear-ItemProperty [-Name] *String* –LiteralPath *Strings* [AddtlParams] AddtlParams= [-Credential *Credential*] [-Exclude *Strings*] [-Filter *String*] [-Force] [-Include *Strings*] [-PassThru] [-UseTransaction]
Copy-ItemProperty	Copies a property and value from a specified location to another location.

CMDLET	DESCRIPTION
	Copy-ItemProperty [-Path] *Strings* [-Destination] *String* [-Name] *String* [AddtlParams]
	Copy-ItemProperty [-Destination] *String* [-Name] *String* –LiteralPath *Strings* [AddtlParams]
	AddtlParams= [-Credential *Credential*] [-Exclude *Strings*] [-Filter *String*] [-Force] [-Include *Strings*] [-PassThru] [-UseTransaction]
Get-ItemProperty	Gets the properties of a specified item. Get-ItemProperty [-Path] *Strings* [[-Name] *Strings*] [AddtlParams] Get-ItemProperty [[-Name] *String*] –LiteralPath *Strings* [AddtlParams] AddtlParams= [-Credential *Credential*] [-Exclude *Strings*] [-Filter *String*] [-Include *Strings*] [-UseTransaction]
Move-ItemProperty	Moves a property from one location to another. Move-ItemProperty [-Path] *Strings* [-Destination] *String* [-Name] *Strings* [AddtlParams] Move-ItemProperty [-Destination] *String* [-Name] *Strings* –LiteralPath *Strings* [AddtlParams] AddtlParams= [-Credential *Credential*] [-Exclude *Strings*] [-Filter *String*] [-Force] [-Include *Strings*] [-PassThru] [-UseTransaction]
New-ItemProperty	Creates a property for an item and sets its value. New-ItemProperty [-Path] *Strings* [-Name] *String* [AddtlParams] New-ItemProperty [-Name] *String* –LiteralPath *Strings* [AddtlParams] AddtlParams= [-Credential *Credential*] [-Exclude *Strings*] [-Filter *String*] [-Force] [-Include *Strings*] [-Value *Object*] [-UseTransaction]
Remove-ItemProperty	Deletes the specified property and its value from an item. Remove-ItemProperty [-Path] *Strings* [-Name] *Strings* [AddtlParams] Remove-ItemProperty [-Name] *Strings* –LiteralPath *Strings* [AddtlParams]

CMDLET	DESCRIPTION
	AddtlParams= [-Credential *Credential*] [-Exclude *Strings*] [-Filter *String*] [-Force] [-Include *Strings*] [-UseTransaction]
Rename- ItemProperty	Renames the specified property of an item. Rename-ItemProperty [-Path] *String* [-Name] *String* [-NewName] *String* [AddtlParams] Rename -ItemProperty [-Name] *String* [-NewName] *String* –LiteralPath *String* [AddtlParams] AddtlParams= [-Credential *Credential*] [-Exclude *Strings*] [-Filter *String*] [-Force] [-Include *Strings*] [-PassThru] [-UseTransaction]
Set-ItemProperty	Creates or changes the value of the specified property of an item. Set-ItemProperty [-Path] *Strings* [-Name] *String* [-Value] *Object* [AddtlParams] Set-ItemProperty [-Path] *Strings* -InputObject *Object* [AddtlParams] Set-ItemProperty -InputObject *Object* -LiteralPath *Strings* [AddtlParams] Set-ItemProperty [-Name] *String* [-Value] *Object* -LiteralPath *Strings* [AddtlParams] AddtlParams= [-Credential *Credential*] [-Exclude *Strings*] [-Filter *String*] [-Force] [-Include *Strings*] [-PassThru] [-UseTransaction]

Navigating Provider Drives

Providers deliver consistent access to data. In addition to the built-in cmdlets, providers can:

- Have custom cmdlets that are designed especially for related data.
- Add "dynamic parameters" to the built-in cmdlets that are available only when using the cmdlet with the provider data.

The drive associated with each provider is listed in the default display of Get-PSProvider, but you can get more information about a provider drive by using the Get-PSDrive cmdlet. For example, the Registry provider makes the HKEY_LOCAL_MACHINE root key available as the HKLM drive. To find all the properties of the HKLM drive, enter the following command:

```
get-psdrive hklm | format-list *
```

You can view and navigate through the data in a provider drive just as you would data in a file system drive. To view the contents of a provider drive, use the Get-Item or Get-ChildItem cmdlet. Type the drive name followed by a colon (:). For example, to view the contents of the Function drive, type:

```
get-childitem function:
```

You can view and manage the data in any drive from another drive by including the drive name in the path. For example, to view the HKLM\Software registry key in the HKLM drive from another drive, type:

```
get-childitem hklm:\software
```

To get into the drive, use the Set-Location cmdlet. Remember the colon when specifying the drive path. For example, to change your location to the root of the Function drive, type **set-location function:**. Then, to view the contents of the Function drive, type **get-childitem**.

You can navigate through a provider drive just as you would a hard drive. If the data is arranged in a hierarchy of items within items, use a backslash (\) to indicate a child item. The basic syntax is:

```
Set-location drive:\location\child-location\...
```

For example, to change your location to the HKLM\Software registry key, use a Set-Location command, such as:

```
set-location hklm:\software
```

You can also use relative references to locations. A dot (.) represents the current location. For example, if you are in the C:\Windows\System32 directory and you want to list its files and folders, you can use the following command:

```
get-childitem .\
```

Managing Providers

PowerShell providers are packaged as snap-ins. When PowerShell loads providers, the providers can add dynamic parameters that are available only when the cmdlet is used with that provider. For example, the Certificate drive adds the –CodeSigningCert parameter to the Get-Item and Get-ChildItem cmdlets. You can use this parameter only when you use Get-Item or Get-ChildItem in the Cert drive.

Although you cannot uninstall a provider, you can remove the Windows PowerShell snap-in for the provider from the current session. To remove a provider, use the Remove-PSSnapin cmdlet. This cmdlet does not unload or uninstall providers. It removes all the contents of the snap-in, including providers and cmdlets. This makes the related providers and cmdlets unavailable in the current session.

Another way to remove features made available based on snap-ins is to use the Remove-PSDrive cmdlet to remove a particular drive from the current session. When you remove a drive, the data on the drive is not affected, but the drive is no longer available in the current session.

Often, you'll want to ensure that a particular PowerShell provider or PSDrive is available before you try to work with its features. The easiest way to do this is to attempt to perform the action or run a script only if the provider or PSDrive is available. Consider the following example:

```
If (get-psprovider -psprovider wsman -erroraction
silentlycontinue)
 { Code to execute if the provider is available.

} else { Code to execute if the provider is not available.

}
```

Here, when the WSMan provider is available, the statement in parentheses evaluates to True, and any code in the related script block is executed. When the WSMan provider is not available, the statement in parentheses evaluates to

False, and any code in the Else statement is executed. Note also that I set the –ErrorAction parameter to SilentlyContinue so that error messages aren't written to the output if the provider is not found.

Working with Provider Drives

When you are using provider drives, you might also want to manage content, configure locations, and work with paths. Table 3-4 provides an overview of cmdlets that you can use to perform related tasks.

TABLE 3-4 Cmdlets for Working with Provider Drives

CMDLET	DESCRIPTION
Add-Content	Adds content to the specified item, such as adding words to a file. Add-Content [-Path] *Strings* [-Value] *Objects* [AddtlParams] Add-Content [-Value] *Objects* -LiteralPath *Strings* [AddtlParams] Add-Content [-Encoding {Unknown | String | Unicode | Byte | BigEndianUnicode | UTF8 | UTF7 | UTF32 | Ascii | Default | Oem}] [-Force] [-Stream *String*] [-UseTransaction] AddtlParams= [-Credential *Credential*] [-Exclude *Strings*] [-Filter *String*] [-Force] [-Include *Strings*] [-PassThru] [-UseTransaction]
Clear-Content	Deletes the contents of an item, such as deleting the text from a file, but does not delete the item. Clear-Content [-Path] *Strings* [AddtlParams] Clear-Content -LiteralPath *Strings* [AddtlParams] AddtlParams= [-Credential *Credential*] [-Exclude *Strings*] [-Filter *String*] [-Force] [-Include *Strings*] [-UseTransaction]
Get-Content	Gets the content of the item at the specified location. Get-Content [-Path] *Strings* [AddtlParams] Get-Content -LiteralPath *Strings* [AddtlParams] Get-Content [-Delimiter *String*] [-Encoding {Unknown | String | Unicode | Byte | BigEndianUnicode | UTF8 | UTF7 | UTF32 | Ascii | Default | Oem}] [-Force] [-Raw] [-Stream *String*] [-Wait] [-UseTransaction]

CMDLET	DESCRIPTION
	AddtlParams= [-Credential *Credential*] [-Exclude *Strings*] [-Filter *String*] [-Force] [-Include *Strings*] [-ReadCount *Count*] [-TotalCount *Count*] [-UseTransaction]
Set-Content	Writes content to an item or replaces the content in an item with new content. Set-Content [-Path] *Strings* [-Value] *Objects* [AddtlParams] Set-Content [-Value] *Objects* -LiteralPath *Strings* [AddtlParams] Set-Content [-Encoding {Unknown | String | Unicode | Byte | BigEndianUnicode | UTF8 | UTF7 | UTF32 | Ascii | Default | Oem}] [-Force] [-Raw] [-Stream *String*] [-Wait] [-UseTransaction] AddtlParams= [-Credential *Credential*] [-Exclude *Strings*] [-Filter *String*] [-Force] [-Include *Strings*] [-PassThru] [-UseTransaction]
Get-Location	Gets information about the current working location. Get-Location [-PSDrive *Strings*] [-PSProvider *Strings*] [-UseTransaction] Get-Location [-Stack] [-StackName *Strings*] [-UseTransaction]
Set-Location	Sets the current working location to a specified location. Set-Location [[-Path] *String*] [-PassThru] [-UseTransaction] Set-Location [-PassThru] -LiteralPath *String* [-UseTransaction] Set-Location [-PassThru] [-StackName *String*] [-UseTransaction]
Push-Location	Adds the current location to the top of a list of locations. ("stack"). Push-Location [[-Path] *String*] [-PassThru] [-StackName *String*] [-UseTransaction] Push-Location [-LiteralPath] *String*] [-PassThru] [-StackName *String*] [-UseTransaction]
Pop-Location	Changes the current location to the location most recently pushed onto the stack. Pop-Location [-PassThru] [-StackName *String*] [-UseTransaction]

CMDLET	DESCRIPTION
Join-Path	Combines a path and a child-path into a single path. The provider supplies the path delimiters. Join-Path [-Path] *Strings* [-ChildPath] *String* [-Credential *Credential*] [-Resolve] [-UseTransaction]
Convert-Path	Converts a path from a Windows PowerShell path to a Windows PowerShell provider path. Convert-Path [-Path] *Strings* [-UseTransaction] Convert-Path -LiteralPath *Strings* [-UseTransaction]
Split-Path	Returns the specified part of a path. Split-Path -LiteralPath *Strings* [-Credential *Credential*] [-Resolve] [-UseTransaction] Split-Path [-Path] *Strings* [AddtlParams] AddtlParams= [-Credential *Credential*] [-IsAbsolute | -Leaf | -Parent | -NoQualifier | -Qualifier] [-Resolve] [-UseTransaction]
Test-Path	Determines whether all elements of a path exist. Test-Path [-Path] *Strings* [AddtlParams] Test-Path –LiteralPath *Strings* [AddtlParams] Test-Path [-NewerThan *DateTime*] [-OlderThan *DateTime*] AddtlParams= [-Credential *Credential*] [-Exclude *Strings*] [-Filter *String*] [-Include *Strings*] [-IsValid] [-PathType {<Any> | <Container> | <Leaf>}] [-UseTransaction]
Resolve-Path	Resolves the wildcard characters in a path and displays the path's contents. Resolve-Path [-Path] *Strings* [-Credential *Credential*] [AddtlParams] Resolve-Path –LiteralPath *Strings* [AddtlParams] AddtlParams= [-Credential *Credential*] [-Relative] [-UseTransaction]

Setting the Working Location

The currently selected provider drive determines what data store you are working with. The default data store is the file system, and the default path within the file system is the profile directory for the currently logged-on user (in most cases).

The current working location is the location that Windows PowerShell uses if you do not supply an explicit path to the item or location that is affected by the command. Typically, this is a directory on a hard drive accessed through the FileSystem provider. All commands are processed from this working location unless another path is explicitly provided.

PowerShell keeps track of the current working location for each drive even when the drive is not the current drive. This allows you to access items from the current working location by referring only to the drive of another location. For example, suppose that your current working location is C:\Scripts\PowerShell. Then you use the following command to change your current working location to the HKLM drive:

```
Set-Location HKLM:
```

Although your current location is now the HKLM drive, you can still access items in the C:\Scripts\PowerShell directory by using the C drive, as shown in the following example:

```
Get-ChildItem C:
```

PowerShell retains the information that your current working location for the C drive is the C:\Scripts\PowerShell directory, so it retrieves items from that directory. The results would be the same if you ran the following command:

```
Get-ChildItem C:\Scripts\PowerShell
```

You can use the Get-Location command to determine the current working location, and you can use the Set-Location command to set the current working location. For example, the following command sets the current working location to the Scripts directory of the C drive:

```
Set-Location c:\scripts
```

After you set the current working location, you can still access items from other drives simply by including the drive name (followed by a colon) in the command, as shown in the following example:

```
Get-ChildItem HKLM:\software
```

This example retrieves a list of items in the Software container of the HKEY Local Machine hive in the registry.

You use special characters to represent the current working location and its parent location. To represent the current working location, you use a single period. To represent the parent of the current working location, you use two periods. For example, the following command specifies the PowerShell subdirectory in the current working location:

```
Get-ChildItem .\PowerShell
```

If the current working location is C:\Scripts, this command returns a list of all the items in C:\Scripts\PowerShell. However, if you use two periods, the parent directory of the current working location is used, as shown in the following example:

```
Get-ChildItem ..\Data
```

In this case, PowerShell treats the two periods as the C drive, so the command retrieves all the items in the C:\Data directory.

A path beginning with a slash identifies a path from the root of the current drive. For example, if your current working location is C:\Scripts\PowerShell, the root of your drive is C. Therefore, the following command lists all items in the C:\Data directory:

```
Get-ChildItem \Data
```

If you do not specify a path beginning with a drive name, slash, or period when supplying the name of a container or item, the container or item is assumed to be located in the current working location. For example, if your current working

location is C:\Scripts, the following command returns all the items in the
C:\Scripts\PowerShell directory:

```
Get-ChildItem PowerShell
```

If you specify a file name rather than a directory name, PowerShell returns
details about that file, as long as the file is available in the current working
location. If the file is not available, PowerShell returns an error.

Using Modules

Windows PowerShell modules are self-contained, reusable units of execution
that can include:

- Script functions that are made available through .PSM1 files.
- .NET assemblies that are compiled into .DLL files and made available
  through .PSD1 files.
- PowerShell snap-ins that are made available in .DLL files.
- Custom views and data types that are described in .PS1XML files.

Module Essentials

Most modules have related snap-ins, .NET assemblies, custom views, and
custom data types. In the .PSD1 files that define the included assemblies, you'll
find an associative array that defines the properties of the module, as is shown
in the example that follows and summarized in Table 3-5.

```
@{
    GUID = '41486F7D-842F-40F1-ACE4-8405F9C2ED9B'
    Author="Microsoft Corporation"
    CompanyName="Microsoft Corporation"
    Copyright="© Microsoft Corporation. All rights reserved."
    ModuleVersion = '2.0.0.0'
    PowerShellVersion = '3.0'
    FormatsToProcess = 'Storage.format.ps1xml'
    TypesToProcess = 'Storage.types.ps1xml'
    NestedModules = @('Disk.cdxml', 'DiskImage.cdxml',
'Partition.cdxml', 'VirtualDisk.cdxml', 'PhysicalDisk.cdxml',
'StorageEnclosure.cdxml', 'StorageNode.cdxml',
'StoragePool.cdxml', 'ResiliencySetting.cdxml',
'StorageProvider.cdxml', 'StorageSubSystem.cdxml',
```

```
'Volume.cdxml', 'StorageSetting.cdxml',
'MaskingSet.cdxml','InitiatorId.cdxml','InitiatorPort.cdxml','Ta
rgetPort.cdxml','TargetPortal.cdxml','StorageCmdlets.cdxml',
'OffloadDataTransferSetting.cdxml', 'StorageJob.cdxml',
'StorageTier.cdxml', 'FileIntegrity.cdxml',
'StorageReliabilityCounter.cdxml', 'FileStorageTier.cdxml' )
```

TABLE 3-5 Common Properties of Modules

PROPERTY	DESCRIPTION
Author, CompanyName, Copyright	Provides information about the creator of the module and copyright.
CLRVersion	The common language runtime (CLR) version of the .NET Framework required by the module.
CmdletsToExport	Cmdlets the module supports.
Description	The descriptive name of the module.
FormatsToProcess	A list of FORMAT.PS1XML files loaded by the module to create custom views for the module's cmdlets.
GUID	The globally unique identifier (GUID) of the module.
ModuleVersion	The version and revision number of the module.
NestedModules	A list of snap-ins, .NET assemblies, or both loaded by the module.
PowerShellVersion	The version of PowerShell required by the module. The version specified or a later version must be installed for the module to work.
RequiredAssemblies	A list of .NET assemblies that must be loaded for the module to work.

TypesToProcess	A list of TYPES.PS1XML files loaded by the module to create custom data types for the module's cmdlets.

Working with Modules

Although PowerShell includes a New-Module cmdlet for creating dynamic modules from script blocks, you'll more commonly use Get-Module, Import-Module, and Remove-Module to work with existing modules. You can list the available modules by entering **get-module -listavailable**. However, this will give you the full definition of each module in list format. A better way to find available modules is to look for them by name, path, and description:

```
get-module -listavailable | format-list name, path, description
```

You can also look for them only by name and description:

```
get-module -listavailable | format-table name, description
```

If you want to determine the availability of a specific module, enter the following command:

```
get-module -listavailable [-name] ModuleNames
```

where ModuleNames is a comma-separated list of modules to check. You can enter module names with or without the associated file extension and use wildcards such as. Note that when you use the –ListAvailable parameter, the –Name parameter is position sensitive, allowing you to specify modules using either

```
get-module -listavailable -name ModuleNames
```

or

```
get-module -listavailable ModuleNames
```

Here is an example:

```
get-module -listavailable -name networkloadbalancingclusters
```

Obtaining and Installing Modules

The core set of modules available in PowerShell depends on the versions of Windows you are running as well as the components that are installed. The components for available modules are registered in the operating system as necessary but are not added to your PowerShell sessions by default (in most instances). Additionally, modules that define functions and include .PSM1 files require an execution policy to be set so that signed scripts can run.

Only installed modules are available for use. Windows and Windows Server include some pre-installed modules. Most other modules are installed as part of system configuration. For example, when you add roles or features in Server Manager, Server Manager installs any PowerShell modules related to these roles or features. Installing the Remote Server Administration Tools feature on your management computer also will install the PowerShell modules for tools you select for installation.

You don't necessarily need to install modules on your management computer to use them. When you connect to a remote computer from your management computer, modules installed on the remote computer typically are implicitly imported into the session. This allows you to use the modules to manage the remote computer.

> **NOTE** If your organization has in-house developed modules, you may want to install modules on particular computers to work with these modules. Here, modules typically are stored in folders and you can copy these folders from one computer to another to install a module. The key is to ensure you copy the folder and its contents to a location specified by the $env:PSModulePath variable. $env:PSModulePath determines the path that PowerShell searches for modules.

Importing Modules

Beginning with PowerShell 3.0, installed modules are imported automatically the first time you use a command in a module. Because of this, you don't need to explicitly import modules as was required previously. For example, PowerShell imports the Micrsoft.PowerShell.Utility module when you run the

Get-Alias cmdlet, making all the cmdlets in this module available without having to import the module again.

Modules are also imported:

- When you get help for a command using Get-Help.
- When you get a command using Get-Command.

Because the wildcard character (*) performs a search rather than actual use of a command, modules are not imported when you use * with Get-Help and Get-Command. Other important caveats to keep in mind:

- Only modules stored in the location specified by $env:PSModulePath are imported automatically. Modules in other locations are not imported automatically.
- Only modules delivered as folders are imported automatically. Modules that consist of a file, such as a .DLL or .PSM1 file, are not imported automatically.
- Commands that use providers may not cause the related module to be imported. If so, the provider won't be available.
- The $PSModuleAutoloadingPreference variable can be configured to enable, disable and configure automatic importing of modules. If automatic importing of modules is disabled, you must always explicitly import modules.

You can explicitly import an available module into the current session by using the Import-Module cmdlet. The basic syntax is to follow Import-Module with the name of the module to import. For example, to import the WebAdminstration module, type **import-module webadministration**. After you import a module, its providers, cmdlets, functions and other features are available in the console session.

> **NOTE** There are several reasons for explicitly importing modules rather than having PowerShell implicitly import modules. One reason is simply to ensure the module you want to work with is available in the current session. Also, if you want to ensure a module's commands don't replace existing commands, you may want to use the –Prefix or –NoClobber

parameters of Import-Module. The –Prefix parameters adds a unique prefix to the noun names of all imported commands. The –NoClobber parameter prevents the module from adding commands that would replace existing commands in the session.

If you add the necessary Import-Module commands to a relevant profile, you can be sure that modules you want to use are always loaded when available. To find imported modules or to verify that an additional module is imported, enter the following command:

```
get-module | format-table name, description
```

Any module listed in the output is imported and available.

To remove a module from the current session, use the Remove-Module cmdlet. The basic syntax is to follow Remove-Module with the name of the module to remove. For example, to remove the WebAdministration module from the current session, type **remove-module webadministration**. The module is still loaded, but the providers, cmdlets, and other features that it supports are no longer available.

You will often want to be sure that a particular module has been imported before you try to use its features. In the following example, when the WebAdministration module is available, the statement in parentheses evaluates to True, and any code in the related script block is executed:

```
if (get-module -name WebAdministration -erroraction
silentlycontinue)
 {

  Code to execute if the module is available.

} else {

  Code to execute if the module is not available.

}
```

As shown previously, you could add an Else clause to define alternative actions. As before, I set the –ErrorAction parameter to SilentlyContinue so that error messages aren't written to the output if the module has not been imported.

Chapter 4. Using Sessions and Remoting

Windows PowerShell supports remote execution of commands and remote sessions. When you work remotely, you type commands in Windows PowerShell on your management computer but execute the commands on one or more remote computers.

Enabling Remote Commands

Remote access in Windows PowerShell 3.0 and Windows PowerShell 4.0 is made available through:

- PowerShell sessions which use the PowerShell remoting features.
- Common Information Model (CIM) sessions which use PowerShell remoting features by default (but also can use DCOM).
- PowerShell Web Access which allows you to connect to a web gateway application running on IIS, which in turns executes your remote commands.

NOTE To work remotely, your computer and the remote computer must be properly configured. Individual cmdlets provide access to remote computers as well. Here, you use the –ComputerName parameter of these cmdlets, the cmdlets connect to the remote machine over Distributed COM (DCOM), and return the results to the local machine. For example, when you use the –ComputerName parameter of Get-Process to examine processes on remote computers, Get-Process communicates with the remote computers using DCOM and not the standard PowerShell remoting features. The exception is for session-related commands, as well as Invoke-Command, which always use either an implicitly created session or an explicitly created session. With sessions, PowerShell remoting works as discussed in this section.

REAL WORLD PowerShell Web Access is a feature of Windows Server 2012 and later. Although you'll hear that PowerShell Web Access allows you to connect to a remote computer through a web browser, technically, that isn't accurate. With PowerShell Web Access, you establish a connection to a remote server using the URI address of its HTTP or HTTPS endpoint. These connections are made over the standard TCP ports for web traffic, which by default are port 80 for HTTP and port 443 for HTTPS, but they are not established using a web browser.

Remoting Fundamentals

When you use the –ComputerName parameter of many cmdlets, the cmdlets connect to the remote machine over Distributed COM (DCOM). As DCOM uses RPC calls on dynamic ports, you may not be able to manage remote computers through firewalls. For example, when trying to work remotely through a firewall that isn't configured to allow DCOM traffic, you will get an "RPC server is not available" error and won't be able to connect. Although an administrator could configure a firewall to allow this traffic, this typically requires using a less secure configuration.

In contrast, the standard PowerShell remoting features use the WS-Management (WSMan) protocol and the Windows Remote Management (WinRM) service. When you use WSMan, PowerShell remoting connects your local PowerShell session with a PowerShell session on a remote computer. Commands you enter in the local session are sent to the remote computer, executed locally on the remote computer, and then the results are returned to your local PowerShell session. As everything runs within the same framework, you can be certain that you can consistently work with remote computers as long as you know how to establish remote sessions using PowerShell.

PowerShell remoting has significant advantages over using standard applications for remote management. One advantage is that a single TCP port is used for all standard communications and a single TCP port is used for all secure communications, which by default are ports 5985 and 5986 respectively. Thus, when you are connecting to remote computers through firewalls, only these TCP ports need to be open to establish connections. Another significant advantage is that from a single console you can simultaneously work with multiple remote computers. To do this, you simply establish a session with the computers you want to work with and then execute commands within the context of that session.

Configuring Remoting

WinRM must be configured appropriately on any computer that you want to manage remotely. You can verify the availability of WinRM and configure PowerShell for remoting via WinRM by following these steps:

1. Start Windows PowerShell as an administrator by right-clicking the Windows PowerShell shortcut and selecting Run As Administrator.

2. The WinRM service is configured for manual startup by default. You must change the startup type to Automatic and start the service on each computer you want to work with. At the PowerShell prompt, you can verify that the WinRM service is running using the following command:

```
get-service winrm
```

As shown in the following example, the value of the Status property in the output should be Running:

```
Status    Name              DisplayName
------    ----              -----------
Running   WinRM             Windows Remote Management
```

3. To configure Windows PowerShell for remoting via WinRM, type the following command:

```
Enable-PSRemoting -force
```

You can use Test-WsMan to verify that a remote computer is configured correctly and determine the version of WSMan available.

Connecting Between Domains and in Workgroups

In many cases, you will be able to work with remote computers in other domains. However, if the remote computer is not in a trusted domain, the remote computer might not be able to authenticate your credentials. To enable authentication, you need to add the remote computer to the list of trusted hosts for the local computer in WinRM.

You have several options for modifying the list of trusted hosts. The first option is to use the WinRM command-line utility and replace the existing list of trusted hosts with the value you specify using the following syntax

```
winrm s winrm/config/client '@{TrustedHosts="RemoteComputer"}'
```

where RemoteComputer is the name or IP address of the remote computer, such as

```
winrm s winrm/config/client '@{TrustedHosts="CorpServer56"}'
```

Or

```
winrm s winrm/config/client '@{TrustedHosts="192.168.10.80"}'
```

To confirm that the computer was added to the TrustHosts list, display the WinRM client configuration details by entering: **winrm g winrm/config/client**.

Another way to specify a remote host to trust is to use Set-Item and the WSMan: provider to modify the TrustedHosts list. Unlike the WinRM utility, which replaces the trusted hosts list, the WSMan: provider adds the value you specify to the existing list, making it easier for you to specify multiple trusted hosts. The basic syntax is:

```
Set-Item -Path WSMan:\localhost\Client\TrustedHosts -Value
'RemoteComputer'
```

where RemoteComputer is the name of the remote computer, such as

```
Set-Item -Path WSMan:\localhost\Client\TrustedHosts -Value
'MailServer12'
```

> **NOTE**   Typically, you are prompted to confirm that you want to modify the TrustedHosts lists. Confirm that you do by pressing Y. To bypass this message, use the –Force parameter. Note also that you can set values in this way because the WSMan: provider adds the value to the existing value by setting –Concatenate to $true automatically.

If you're wondering which hosts are trusted, you can list trusted hosts by entering:

```
Get-Item -Path WSMan:\localhost\Client\TrustedHosts |fl name,
value
```

When you are working with computers in workgroups, accessing a domain computer from a workgroup or vice versa, you must either use HTTPS as the transport or add the remote machine to the TrustedHosts configuration settings. If you cannot connect to a remote host, verify that the service on the remote host is running and is accepting requests by running the following command on the remote host:

```
winrm quickconfig
```

This command analyzes and configures the WinRM service. If the WinRM service is set up correctly, you'll see output similar to the following:

```
WinRM service is already running on this machine.
WinRM is already set up for remote management on this computer.
```

If the WinRM service is not set up correctly, you see output similar to the following and need to respond affirmatively to several prompts. When this process completes, WinRM should be set up correctly.

```
WinRM Quick Configuration
Running command "Set-WSManQuickConfig" to enable remote
management of this computer by using the Windows Remote
Management (WinRM) service.
 This includes:
1. Starting or restarting (if already started) the WinRM service
2. Setting the WinRM service startup type to Automatic
3. Creating a listener to accept requests on any IP address
4. Enabling Windows Firewall inbound rule exceptions for WS-
Management traffic (for http only).

Do you want to continue?
[Y] Yes  [A] Yes to All  [N] No  [L] No to All  [S] Suspend  [?]
Help (default is "Y"): Y
WinRM has been updated to receive requests.
WinRM service type changed successfully.

WinRM has been updated for remote management.
Created a WinRM listener on HTTP://* to accept WS-Man requests
to any IP on this machine.
WinRM firewall exception enabled.

Confirm
Are you sure you want to perform this action?
```

```
Performing the operation "Set-PSSessionConfiguration" on target
"Name: microsoft.powershell SDDL:
O:NSG:BAD:P(A;;GA;;;BA)(A;;GA;;;RM)S:P(AU;FA;GA;;;WD)(AU;SA;GXGW
;;;WD). This lets selected users remotely run Windows
PowerShell commands on this computer.".
[Y] Yes   [A] Yes to All   [N] No   [L] No to All   [S] Suspend   [?]
Help (default is "Y"): Y
```

Creating HTTPS and Other Listeners

By default, WinRM QuickConfig creates an HTTP listener on a remote host, but does not create an HTTPS listener. If you want to make HTTPS connections to the remote host, you'll do the following:

1. Obtain an SSL certificate for the remote computer and make sure the certificate has common name (CN) entry that matches the identifier you are using.
2. Install the remote computer's SSL certificate in the certificate store for the management computer you are using (and not the user's certificate store).
3. On the remote computer, use New-WSManInstance to add an HTTPS listener for WSMan.

To create an HTTPS listener for WSMan, you need the thumbprint value of the remote computer's SSL certificate. One way to obtain this value is to access the Cert: provider and list the certificate thumbprints, as shown in this example:

```
Get-ChildItem -Path cert:\LocalMachine -Recurse |
select Subject, FriendlyName, Thumbprint | fl
```

After you obtain the certificate thumbprint, you can use New-WSManInstance to create the HTTPS listener on the remote computer, such as:

```
$thumbprint = "XXX-XXXX-XX-XXXX-XX"
New-WSManInstance -ResourceURI winrm/config/Listener
-SelectorSet @{Transport='HTTPS', Address="IP:192.168.10.34"}
-ValueSet @{Hostname="Server12.Imaginedlands.com",
CertificateThumbprint=$thumbprint}
```

Here, you create an HTTPS listener for Server12. As mentioned previously, WinRM listens on port 5985 for HTTP and port 5986 for HTTPS. Although you can configure alternate listening ports, you must delete the current listening port before creating a new listening port, as shown in this example:

```
winrm delete winrm/config/listener?Address=*+Transport=HTTP
```

```
winrm create winrm/config/listener?Address=*+Transport=HTTP
@{Port="5999"}
```

> **NOTE** As the port change applies to all computers and sessions the computer runs, you should only change the listening port if required by IT policy or firewall settings.

Generally, to use PowerShell remoting features, you must start Windows PowerShell as an administrator by right-clicking the Windows PowerShell shortcut and selecting Run As Administrator. When starting PowerShell from another program, such as the command prompt (cmd.exe), you must start that program as an administrator.

Executing Remote Commands

You can use Windows PowerShell remoting to run cmdlets and external programs on remote computers. For example, you can run any built-in cmdlets and external programs accessible in the PATH environment variable ($env:path). However, because PowerShell runs as a network service or local service, you cannot use PowerShell to open the user interface for any program on a remote computer. If you try to start a program with a graphical interface, the program process starts but the command cannot complete, and the PowerShell prompt does not return until the program is finished or you press Ctrl+C.

Understanding Remote Execution

When you submit a remote command, the command is transmitted across the network to the Windows PowerShell client on the designated remote computer, and runs in the Windows PowerShell client on the remote computer. The command results are sent back to the local computer and appear in the Windows PowerShell session on the local computer. Note that all of the local input to a remote command is collected before being sent to the remote computer, but the output is returned to the local computer as it is generated.

Whenever you use PowerShell remoting features, keep the following in mind:

- You must start Windows PowerShell as an administrator by right-clicking the Windows PowerShell shortcut and selecting Run As Administrator. When starting PowerShell from another program, such as the command prompt (cmd.exe), you must start that program as an administrator.
- The current user must be a member of the Administrators group on the remote computer or be able to provide the credentials of an administrator. When you connect to a remote computer, PowerShell uses your user name and password credentials to log on to the remote computer. The credentials are encrypted.
- When you work remotely, you use multiple instances of Windows PowerShell: a local instance and one or more remote instances. Generally, in the local instance, the policies and profiles on the local computer are in effect. On a remote instance, the policies and profiles on the remote computer are in effect. This means cmdlets, aliases, functions, preferences, and other elements in the local profile are not necessarily available to remote commands. To ensure you can use cmdlets, aliases, functions, preferences, and other elements in the local profile with remote commands, you must copy the local profiles to each remote computer.
- Although you can execute commands on remote computers, any files, directories, and additional resources that are needed to execute a command must exist on the remote computer. Additionally, your user account must have permission to connect to the remote computer, permission to run Windows PowerShell, and permission to access files, directories, and other resources on the remote computer.
- The functionality available through your remote session depends on the version of PowerShell on the remote computer. For example, if you connect to a remote computer that has PowerShell 3.0 installed, you cannot use the features of PowerShell 4.0, even if PowerShell 4.0 is available on your local machine.

Standard Commands for Remoting

Except when you are using CIM sessions, the cmdlets you'll use for remoting include:

- **Connect-PSSession**   Reconnects to one or more PowerShell sessions that were disconnected. You can use Connect-PSSession to connect to any valid disconnected session, including those that were started in other sessions or on other computers, those that were disconnected intentionally, such as by using the Disconnect-PSSession cmdlet, and that were disconnected unintentionally, such as by a network interruption when running the Invoke-Command cmdlet. Session objects are instantiated when you create a session in the PowerShell console or the PowerShell application. A session object is created for each remote computer to which you connect. As long as the session objects are valid and you have appropriate credentials, you can use these objects to reconnect to the sessions.
- **Disconnect-PSSession**   Disconnects a PowerShell session. You can only disconnect from open non-interactive sessions, meaning you can disconnect from sessions started with New-PSSession but cannot disconnect from sessions started with Enter-PSSession. Additionally, you cannot disconnect from closed or broken sessions.
- **Enter-PSSession**   Starts an interactive session with a single remote computer. During the session, you can run commands just as if you were typing directly on the remote computer. You can have only one interactive session at a time. Typically, you use the –ComputerName parameter to specify the name of the remote computer. However, you can also use a session that you created previously by using New-PSSession for the interactive session.
- **Exit-PSSession**   Ends an interactive session and disconnects from the remote computer. You can also type **exit** to end an interactive session. The effect is the same as using Exit-PSSession.
- **Export-PSSession**   Gets cmdlets, functions, aliases, and other command types from an open session and saves them in a Windows PowerShell script module file (.psm1). When you want to use the commands from the script module, use the Add-Module cmdlet to add the commands to the local session so that they can be used. To export commands, first use New-

PSSession to connect to the session that has the commands that you want to export. Then use Export-PSSession to export the commands. By default, Export-PSSession exports all commands except for commands that already exist in the session. However, you can use the –PSSnapin, –CommandName, and –CommandType parameters to specify the commands to export.

- **Get-PSSession**   Gets the PowerShell sessions (PSSessions) that were created in the current session. Without parameters, this cmdlet returns all available PSSessions. You can use the parameters of Get-PSSession to get the sessions that are connected to particular computers or identify sessions by their names, IDs, or instance IDs. For computers, type the NetBIOS name, IP address, or fully qualified domain name. To specify the local computer, enter the computer name, localhost, or a dot (.). For IDs, type an integer value that uniquely identifies the PSSession in the current session. PSSessions can be assigned friendly names with the –Name parameter. You can reference the friendly names using wildcards. To find the names and IDs of PSSessions, use Get-PSSession without parameters. An instance ID is a GUID that uniquely identifies a PSSession, even when you have multiple sessions running in PowerShell. The instance ID is stored in the RemoteRunspaceID property of the RemoteRunspaceInfo object that represents a PSSession. To find the InstanceID of the PSSessions in the current session, enter **get-pssession | Format-Table Name, ComputerName, RemoteRunspaceId**.

- **Import-PSSession**   Imports cmdlets, aliases, functions, and other command types from an open session into the current session on your management computer. You can import any command that Get-Command can find in the other session. To import commands, first use New-PSSession to connect to the session from which you will import. Then use Import-PSSession to import commands. By default, Import-PSSession imports all commands except for commands that exist in the current session. To overwrite existing commands, use the –AllowClobber parameter. PowerShell adds the imported commands to a temporary module that exists only in your session, and it returns an object that represents the module. Although you can use imported commands just as you would use any command in the session, the imported part of the command actually runs in the session from which it was imported. Because imported commands might take longer to run than local commands, Import-

PSSession adds an –AsJob parameter to every imported command. This parameter allows you to run the command as a PowerShell background job.

- **Invoke-Command** Runs commands on a local computer or one or more remote computers, and returns all output from the commands, including errors. Use the –ComputerName parameter to run a single command on a remote computer. To run a series of related commands that share data, create a PowerShell session (PSSession) on a remote computer, and then use the –Session parameter of Invoke-Command to run the command in the PSSession or use the –InDisconnectedSession parameter to run commands without maintaining persistent connections to the remote sessions.

- **New-PSSession** Creates a PowerShell session (PSSession) on a local or remote computer. When you create a PSSession, Windows PowerShell establishes a persistent connection to the remote computer, and you can use the PSSession to interact directly with the computer.

- **Receive-PSSession** Gets the results of commands running in PowerShell sessions that were disconnected. Receive-PSSession connects to the session, resumes any commands that were suspended, and gets the results of commands running in the session. You can use a Receive-PSSession in addition to or in place of a Connect-PSSession command. Receive-PSSession can connect to any disconnected or reconnected session, including those that were started in other sessions or on other computers, those that were disconnected intentionally, such as by using the Disconnect-PSSession cmdlet, and that were disconnected unintentionally, such as by a network interruption when running the Invoke-Command cmdlet. If you use the Receive-PSSession cmdlet to connect to a session in which no commands are running or suspended, Receive-PSSession connects to the session, but returns no output or errors.

- **Remove-PSSession** Closes one or more PowerShell sessions and frees the resources the sessions were using. It is a best practice to remove sessions when you are finished using them.

Invoking Remote Commands

One way to run commands on remote computers is to use the Invoke-Command cmdlet. With this cmdlet, you can do the following:

- Run commands in an implicitly-created PowerShell session, in an explicitly-created PowerShell session, in a disconnected session, or as a background job.
- Use the –ComputerName parameter to specify the remote computers to work with by DNS name, NetBIOS name, or IP address.
- When working with multiple remote computers, separate each computer name or IP address with a comma.
- Enclose your command or commands to execute in curly braces, which denotes a script block, and use the –ScriptBlock parameter to specify the command or commands to run.

For example, you can type the following command as a single line to run a Get-Process command remotely:

```
invoke-command -computername Server43, Server27, Server82
-scriptblock {get-process}
```

Here, you are opening temporary sessions to Server43, Server27 and Server82, and running the Get-Process command. The results from the command execution on each remote computer are returned as results to the local computer. If the temporary session is interrupted, such as by a network or power outage, PowerShell creates a background job for the disconnected session, which makes it easier to reconnect, resume execution and get the results.

> **MORE INFO**   Although you are using an implicitly created session, the session works much like a standard PowerShell session. As discussed in "Understanding Remote Execution and Object Serialization," this means PowerShell connects over WSMan, the results are serialized using XML, and passed over WSMan back to the local machine where the results are deserialized.
>
> By default, Invoke-Command runs under your user name and credentials. Use the –Credential parameter to specify alternate credentials using the

UserName or Domain\UserName syntax. You will be prompted for a password.

REAL WORLD When you connect to a remote computer that is running Windows or Windows Server, the default starting location is the home directory of the current user, which is stored in the %HomePath% environment variable ($env:homepath) and the Windows PowerShell $home variable.

When you use Invoke-Command, the cmdlet returns an object that includes the name of the computer that generated the data. The remote computer name is stored in the PSComputerName property. Typically, the PSComputerName property is displayed by default. You can use the –HideComputerName parameter to hide the PSComputerName property.

If the PSComputerName property isn't displayed and you want to see the source computer name, use the Format-Table cmdlet to add the PSComputerName property to the output as shown in the following example:

```
$procs = invoke-command -script {get-process | sort-object
-property Name} -computername Server56, Server42, Server27

&$procs | format-table Name, Handles, WS, CPU, PSComputerName
-auto
```

Name	Handles	WS	CPU	PSComputerName
acrotray	52	3948544	0	Server56
AlertService	139	7532544		Server56
csrss	594	20463616		Server56
csrss	655	5283840		Server56
CtHelper	96	6705152	0.078125	Server56
acrotray	43	3948234	0	Server42
AlertService	136	7532244		Server42
csrss	528	20463755		Server42
csrss	644	5283567		Server42
CtHelper	95	6705576	0.067885	Server42
acrotray	55	3967544	0	Server27
AlertService	141	7566662		Server27
csrss	590	20434342		Server27

```
csrss                    654   5242340              Server27
CtHelper                  92   6705231   0.055522   Server27
```

> **NOTE**   It's important to point out that because the object is serialized and deserialized, the object's methods aren't available. Although this happens across any WSMan connection, this doesn't happen when DCOM is used.

PowerShell includes a per-command throttling feature that lets you limit the number of concurrent remote connections that are established for a command. Generally, the default is 32 or 50 concurrent connections, depending on the cmdlet. You can use the –ThrottleLimit parameter to set a custom throttle limit for a command. Keep in mind the throttling feature is applied to each command, not to the entire session or to the computer. If you are running a command concurrently in several sessions, the number of concurrent connections is the sum of the concurrent connections in all sessions.

Keep in mind that although PowerShell can manage hundreds of concurrent remote connections, the number of remote commands that you can send might be limited by the resources of your computer and its ability to establish and maintain multiple network connections. To add more protection for remoting, you can use the –UseSSL parameter of Invoke-Command. As with commands that are run locally, you can pause or terminate a remote command by pressing Ctrl+S or Ctrl+C.

> **REAL WORLD**   PowerShell remoting is available even when the local computer is not in a domain. For testing and development, you can use the remoting features to connect to and create sessions on the same computer. PowerShell remoting works the same as when you are connecting to a remote computer.
>
> To run remote commands on a computer in a workgroup, you might need to change Windows security settings on the management and target computers. On the target computer, meaning to which you want to connect, you must allow remote access to the computer using Enable-PSRemoting –Force. On your management computer, meaning the computer you are working from, you must either run Enable-PSRemoting or do the following: ensure the WinRM service is started and enable the local account token filter policy by ensuring the

LocalAccountTokenFilterPolicy registry entry in
HKLM\SOFTWARE\Microsoft\Windows\CurrentVersion\Policies\System
has its value set to 1.

You can determine whether the WinRM service is running by entering
Get-Service WinRM. You can check the version of WinRM that's installed
by entering **Test-WSMan –Auth default**. Enter **Get-PSSessionConfiguration** to check the remoting configuration for
PowerShell.

Establishing PowerShell Sessions

Windows PowerShell supports both local and remote sessions. A *session* is a
runspace that establishes a common working environment for commands.
Commands in a session can share data. After you create a session, you can work
with it interactively by using Enter-PSSession or you can invoke commands
against the session by using Invoke-Command. When you are finished using a
session, you can disconnect from it and reconnect later or you can exit the
session to free up the resources used by the session.

Invoking Sessions

Using the New-PSSession cmdlet, you can establish a session to create a
persistent connection to a computer you want to work with. Unless you use the
–ComputerName parameter and use it to specify the name of one or more
remote computers, PowerShell assumes you are creating a session for the local
computer. With New-PSSession, you must use the –Session parameter with
Invoke-Command to run the command in the named session. For example, you
can establish a session by typing the following command:

```
$s = New-PSSession –ComputerName Server24
```

Here, *$s* is a variable that stores the session object. PowerShell knows you are
creating a remote session because you've used the –ComputerName parameter.
PowerShell creates a persistent connection with the specified computer. Use
Invoke-Command with the –Session parameter to run the command in the
named session as shown in this example:

```
invoke-command -session $s -scriptblock {get-process}
```

Here, you use Invoke-Command to run Get-Process in the $s session. Because this session is connected to a remote computer, the command runs on the remote computer.

When you create a session, you can control the session via the session object that is returned. If you want to get information about remote sessions on a particular remote computer, you can use Get-PSSession. For example, you could enter **get-pssession –ComputerName Server24 | fl**. You'd then see detailed information about remote sessions on this computer and their status, such as:

```
ComputerName           : CorpServer134
ConfigurationName      : Microsoft.PowerShell
InstanceId             :
Id                     : 2
Name                   : IT
Availability           : Available
ApplicationPrivateData : {DebugMode, DebugStop, PSVersionTable,
DebugBreakpointCount}
Runspace               : System.Management.Automation.RemoteRunspace
State                  : Opened
IdleTimeout            : 7200000
OutputBufferingMode    : Block
DisconnectedOn         :
ExpiresOn              :
```

As you can see from the output, the session is assigned the session ID of 2. This ID also can be used to work with or get information about the session. For example, if you enter **get-pssession –id 2 | fl** you'd get the same information.

> **NOTE**   Sessions also can be controlled via a name assigned when invoking the session. Use the –Name parameter to set the name. If you don't specify a name for the session, a default name typically is assigned, based on the ID of the session. For example, if the session ID is 11, the automatically assigned name typically is Session11.

The output of Get-PSSession provides additional information that is useful for working with sessions, including:

- **ConfigurationName**   Specifies the type of session, which is important for differentiating PowerShell sessions and CIM sessions. PowerShell sessions are listed as Microsoft.PowerShell.
- **Availability**   Specifies the availability of the session with respect to the current PowerShell window. A session listed as Available was created in the current window. A session listed with another value wasn't created in the current window. Generally, None means the session is not available and Busy means the session is active in another window or on another computer.
- **State**   Specifies the state of the session. A session listed as Opened was created in the current window and is active. A session listed as Broken was unintentionally disconnected. A session listed as Disconnected was intentionally disconnected.

Although the examples so far work with one computer, you can just as easily establish a session with multiple computers. Simply establish the session and name all the computers in a comma-separated list, such as:

```
$s = New-PSSession -ComputerName Server24, Server37, Server92
```

By default, your current credentials are used to establish connections. However, you might also need to specify a user account that has permissions to perform remote administration using the –Credential parameter.

You can provide alternative credentials in one of two ways. You can:

- Pass in a Credential object to provide the information required for authentication. A Credential object has UserName and Password properties. Although the user name is stored as a regular string, the password is stored as a secure, encrypted string.
- Specify the user account that has permission to perform the action. After you specify a user name, PowerShell displays a prompt for the user's password. When prompted, enter the password and then click OK.

> **REAL WORLD**   With credentials, the user name can be provided in several formats. If you are working in a domain and the appropriate domain is already shown in the credentials dialog box, you don't have to specify the domain as part of the user name. However, if you are working

in a domain and the domain isn't set, you should provide the required domain and user information using the Domain\UserName format, such as ImaginedL\WilliamS for the user WilliamS working in the ImaginedL domain. Additionally, if you want to work with a local computer account rather than a domain account, you can specify a local computer account using the ComputerName\UserName format, such as PC29\TomG for the local user TomG on PC29.

To see how the –Credential parameter can be used, consider the following example:

```
$t = New-PSSession –ComputerName Server24, Server45, Server36
–Credential Cpandl\WilliamS
```

Here, you establish a session with Server24, Server45, and Server36 and specify your domain and user name. As a result, when you use Invoke-Command to run commands in the $t session, the commands run on each remote computer with those credentials. Note that although this is a single session, each runspace on each computer is separate.

Extending this idea, you can also just as easily get the list of remote computers from a text file. In this example, servers.txt contains a comma-separated list of computers:

```
$ses = get-content c:\test\servers.txt | new-pssession
–credential cpandl\williams
```

Here, the contents of the Servers.txt file are piped to New-PSSession. As a result, the $ses session is established with all computers listed in the file. Typically, the names are provided in a comma-separate list, such as:

```
Server14, Server87, Server21
```

Sometimes, you'll want to execute an application or external utility on a remote computer as shown in the following example:

```
$comp = get-content c:\computers.txt
$s = new-pssession -computername $comp
invoke-command -session $s { powercfg.exe –energy }
```

Here, C:\Computers.txt is the path to the file containing the list of remote computers to check. On each computer, you run PowerCfg with the –Energy parameter. This generates an Energy-Report.html file in the default directory for the user account used to access the computer. The energy report provides details on power configuration settings and issues that are causing power management not to work correctly. If you'd rather not have to retrieve the report from each computer, you can write the report to a share and base the report name on the computer name, as shown in the following example:

```
$comp = get-content c:\computers.txt
$s = new-pssession -computername $comp
invoke-command -session $s { powercfg.exe –energy –output
"\\fileserver72\reports\$env:computername.html"}
```

Here, you write the report to the \\fileserver72\reports share and name the file using the value of the ComputerName environment variable. Note that when you work with PowerShell and are referencing applications and external utilities, you must specify the .exe file extension with the program name.

When you are running commands on many remote computers, you might not want to wait for the commands to return before performing other tasks. To avoid having to wait, use Invoke-Command with the –AsJob parameter to create a background job in each of the runspaces:

```
invoke-command –session $s -scriptblock {get-process moddr |
stop-process -force } -AsJob
```

Here, you use Invoke-Command to get and stop a named process via the $s session. Because the command is run as a background job, the prompt returns immediately without waiting for the command to run on each computer.

Although being able to establish a session on many computers is handy, sometimes you might want to work interactively with a single remote computer. To do this, you can use the Enter-PSSession cmdlet to start an interactive session with a remote computer. At the Windows Powershell prompt, type **Enter-PSSession *ComputerName***, where *ComputerName* is the name of the remote computer. The command prompt changes to show that you are connected to the remote computer, as shown in the following example:

```
[Server49]: PS C:\Users\wrstanek.cpandl\Documents>
```

Now the commands that you type run on the remote computer just as if you had typed them directly on the remote computer. For enhanced security through encryption of transmissions, the Enter-PSSession cmdlet also supports the –Credential and –UseSSL parameters. You can end the interactive session using the command Exit-PSSession or by typing **exit**.

Understanding Remote Execution and Object Serialization

When you are working with remote computers, you need to keep in mind the following:

- How commands are executed
- How objects are serialized

Whether you use Invoke-Command or Enter-PSSession with remote computers, Windows PowerShell establishes a temporary connection, uses the connection to run the current command, and then closes the connection each time you run a command. This is an efficient method for running a single command or several unrelated commands, even on a large number of remote computers.

The New-PSSession cmdlet provides an alternative by establishing a session with a persistent connection. With New-PSSession, Windows PowerShell establishes a persistent connection and uses the connection to run any commands you enter. Because you can run multiple commands in a single, persistent runspace, the commands can share data, including the values of variables, the definitions of aliases, and the contents of functions. New-PSSession also supports the –UseSSL parameter.

When you use Windows PowerShell locally, you work with live .NET Framework objects, and these objects are associated with actual programs or components. When you invoke the methods or change the properties of live objects, the changes affect the actual program or component. And, when the properties of a program or component change, the properties of the object that represent them change too.

Because live objects cannot be transmitted over the network, Windows PowerShell serializes the objects sent in remote commands. This means it converts each object into a series of Constraint Language in XML (CLiXML) data elements for transmission. When Windows PowerShell receives a serialized file, it converts the XML into a deserialized object type. Although the deserialized object is an accurate record of the properties of the program or component at execution time, it is no longer directly associated with the originating component, and the methods are removed because they are no longer effective. Also, the serialized objects returned by the Invoke-Command cmdlet have additional properties that help you determine the origin of the command.

> **NOTE** You can use Export-Clixml to create XML-based representations of objects and store them in a file. The objects stored in the file are serialized. To import a CLiXML file and create deserialized objects, you can use Import-CLixml.

Disconnecting Sessions

With PowerShell 3.0 and later, sessions can be disconnected and reconnected. Although a power loss or temporary network outage can unintentionally disconnect you from a session, you disconnect from a session intentionally by using Disconnect-PSSession. Alternatively, you can run Invoke-Command with the –InDisconnectedSession parameter to run commands in a disconnected state.

When you disconnect from a session, any command or scripts that are running in the session continue running, and you can later reconnect to the session to pick up where you left off. You also can reconnect to a session if you were disconnected unintentionally.

Because you can only disconnect from open non-interactive sessions, you can disconnect from sessions started with New-PSSession, but cannot disconnect from sessions started with Enter-PSSession. Also, you cannot disconnect from closed or broken sessions, or sessions started in other PowerShell windows or by other users.

You can disconnect a session using its object, its ID or its name. In the following example, you create a session, work with the remote computer and then disconnect from the session:

```
$s = new-pssession -computername corpserver74
invoke-command -session $s { get-process }

. . .

disconnect-pssession -session $s
```

You can only disconnect sessions that are in the Opened state. To disconnect all open sessions at the same time, enter the following command:

```
Get-PSSession | Disconnect-PSSession
```

As you can't disconnect sessions that are already disconnected or broken, PowerShell will display errors if any sessions are in these states. To avoid these errors, you can use a filter to specify that you only want to disconnect Opened sessions. Here is an example:

```
get-pssession | where {$_.state -eq "Opened"} |
disconnect-pssession
```

Here, Get-PSSession lists all current sessions and then you filter the output using the Where-Object cmdlet so that only sessions with the State property set to Opened are passed through the pipeline and disconnected.

Sessions are considered to be idle when they are disconnected, even if commands are running. By default, sessions can be idle for 7200000 milliseconds (2 hours) before they are closed. Use –IdleTimeoutSec to specify a different timeout, up to 12 hours. In the following example, the time out is set to 8 hours (60 seconds x 60 x 8):

```
disconnect-pssession -session $s -idletimeout 60*60*8
```

> **REAL WORLD** The output buffering mode determines whether commands continue to run while a session is disconnected. The default output buffering mode for disconnected sessions is Block, which means command execution is suspended when the output buffer fills and doesn't resume again until the session is reconnected. Alternatively, you can set

> the output buffering mode to Drop, which ensures that commands keep executing when the output buffer fills. However, with Drop, as new output is saved, the oldest output is discarded by default. To prevent this, redirect the command output to a file.

Reconnecting Sessions

To connect to any disconnected session, including those that were started in other sessions or on other computers, those that were disconnected intentionally, and those that were disconnected unintentionally, you have several choices. You can use either Connect-PSSession or Receive-PSSession.

The difference between connecting to a session and receiving a session is subtle but important. When you connect to a session, you reconnect to the session and are able to begin working with the remote computer or computers to which the session connects. When you receive a connection, you reconnect to the session, resume any commands that were suspended, and get the results of commands running in the session.

Whether you are reconnecting to a session using Connect-PSSession or Receive-PSSession, you need to identify the session to which you want to connect. If you are using the same computer and the same PowerShell window, you can enter **Get-PSSession** to list sessions by ID and name and then reconnect to sessions, as shown in the following examples:

```
connect-pssession -session $s
connect-pssession -id 2
connect-pssession -name CheckServerTasks
```

If you are using a different computer or PowerShell window, you'll need to use the –ComputerName parameter with Get-PSSession to list sessions on remote computers and then reconnect to sessions. Consider the following example and sample output:

```
Get-PSSession -ComputerName Server24, Server45, Server36
-Credential Cpandl\WilliamS


Id Name    ComputerName   State  ConfigurationName  Availability
-- ----    -----------    -----  -----------------  -----------
```

```
2  Task     Server24 Disconnected Microsoft.PowerShell     None
3 Session12 Server45 Opened      Microsoft.PowerShell Available
4  Clnr     Server36 Broken      Microsoft.PowerShell     None
5  SChks    Server36 Disconnected Microsoft.PowerShell     Busy
```

Here, you find that each of the servers has active sessions. Although the session IDs are generated on a one up basis on the local computer, the session names are the actual names assigned either automatically or by users when the sessions were created. Note also that ComputerName identifies the remote computer and State specifies the state of the session as being Opened, Disconnected or Broken. Opened connections are already active in the current window.

You can reconnect disconnected and broken sessions, provided the sessions aren't active (busy). However, be sure to connect using the name assigned rather than the locally generated ID. For example, you could use the following command to reconnect to the Task session on Server24:

```
connect-pssession -computername server24 -name task
```

However, you could not use the locally generated session ID to connect to the Task session. Why? Because the session ID is locally generated and does not match the session ID on Server74.

PowerShell also allows you to reconnect multiple sessions simultaneously. Consider the following example and sample output:

```
Get-PSSession -ComputerName Server74, Server38, Server45
-Credential Cpandl\WilliamS

Id Name      ComputerName  State  ConfigurationName  Availability
-- ----      ------------  -----  -----------------  ------------
8 Session14 Server74 Disconnected Microsoft.PowerShell     None
9 Session18 Server38 Broken       Microsoft.PowerShell     None
10 SChks    Server45  Disconnected Microsoft.PowerShell     None
```

Here, you have sessions on three different servers that are available to be connected. If you wanted to reconnect the sessions to continue working with the servers, the easiest way to do this would be to enter:

```
Get-PSSession -ComputerName Server74, Server38, Server45
-Credential Cpandl\WilliamS | Connect-PSSession
```

Or

```
$s = Get-PSSession -ComputerName Server74, Server38, Server45
-Credential Cpandl\WilliamS | Connect-PSSession
```

Here, you get the sessions that were created on the remote computers and use Connect-PSSession to reconnect the sessions.

> **NOTE** Connect-PSSession has no effect on valid, active sessions. If the servers had sessions that were opened or disconnected but busy, those sessions would not be reconnected.

Once you've reconnected sessions, the sessions can be accessed in the current PowerShell window by ID and name. If you didn't assign the sessions to variables directly, you'll need to do so before you can work with the sessions using Invoke-Command. Enter **Get-PSSession** to get information about the sessions, and then use the (valid) locally assigned ID or the session name to assign sessions to a session variable, such as:

```
$session = get-pssession -id 2, 3, 12
```

Here, you store the session objects for the sessions with the local ID of 2, 3, and 12 in the $session variable. You can then use the $session variable to pass commands to all three remote computers, such as:

```
$session = get-pssession -id 2, 3, 12

invoke-command -session $session { get-eventlog system |
where {$_.entrytype -eq "Error"} }
```

When you are completely finished with a session, you should use Remove-PSSession to remove it. Removing a session stops any commands or scripts that are running, ends the session, and releases the resources the session was using.

Connecting through PowerShell Web Access

PowerShell Web Access allows you to connect to a web gateway application running on IIS, which in turns executes your commands on a specified remote computer. The most commonly used implementation of PowerShell Web Access is with Exchange servers and Exchange Online.

With PowerShell Web Access, you establish connections to a remote computer using the URI address of the related HTTP or HTTPS endpoint. These connections are made over TCP port 80 for HTTP and TCP port 443 for HTTPS.

Before you can establish a connection to an HTTP or HTTPS endpoint and access PowerShell, you need to know:

- The configuration name, which is the naming context you want to use for working with the remote computer. For standard PowerShell, this is **Windows.PowerShell**. For Exchange server and Exchange Online, this is **Microsoft.Exchange**.
- The connection URI, which is the URL to PowerShell Web Access on the remote computer, such as http://server37.imaginedlands.com/PowerShell/.
- The authentication method to use. With Windows workgroups and domains, you typically use Kerberos authentication. With Exchange Online, you typically use Basic authentication.

When your management computer is joined to the domain in which you want to work, you can use either HTTP or HTTPS with Kerberos authentication to establish the PowerShell session. Keep in mind that with Kerberos authentication you must use the server name or the server's fully-qualified domain name and cannot use an IP address, as shown in the following example:

```
$Session = New-PSSession -ConfigurationName Windows.PowerShell
-ConnectionUri http://Server24.imaginedlands.com/PowerShell/
-AllowRedirection -Authentication Kerberos
```

Here, you use the –AllowRedirection parameter to specify that redirection is allowed, which is required if the URI is redirected by the receiving server. You use HTTP with Kerberos authentication to connect to Server24. With Kerberos authentication, your current credentials are used to establish the session. If needed, you can pass in alternate credentials, as shown in this example:

```
$Cred = Get-Credential

$Session = New-PSSession -ConfigurationName Windows.PowerShell
-ConnectionUri http://Server24.imaginedlands.com/PowerShell/
-AllowRedirection -Authentication Kerberos -Credential $Cred
```

Here, when PowerShell executes Get-Credential, you are prompted for a user name and password. This credential is then stored in the $Cred variable. When PowerShell creates the remote session on Server24, the credential is passed in using the –Credential parameter.

If you want to use an authentication mechanism other than Kerberos or your computer isn't connected to the domain in which you want to work, you may need to use HTTPS as the transport (or the destination server must be added to the TrustedHosts configuration settings for WinRM, and HTTP must be enabled in the client configuration). You also must explicitly pass in a credential using the –Credential parameter, as shown in this example:

```
$Cred = Get-Credential

$Session = New-PSSession -ConfigurationName Microsoft.Exchange
-ConnectionUri https://server17.imaginedlands.com/PowerShell/
-AllowRedirection -Authentication Negotiate -Credential $Cred
```

> **REAL WORLD**   Generally to work via HTTPS, the remote computer must have an SSL certificate. Regardless of whether you use Kerberos or another authentication mechanism, this certificate must contain a common name (CN) that matches the identifier you are using. You must install the remote computer's SSL certificate in the certificate store for the management computer you are using (and not the user's certificate store). Finally, you must ensure the remote computer has an HTTPS listener for WSMan. If you don't configure PowerShell in this way, you won't be able to connect using HTTPS.

After you establish a session with a remote server, you can import the server-side session into your client-side session by using the Import-PSSession cmdlet. The basic syntax is:

```
Import-PSSession [-Session] Session [-AllowClobber]
[-CommandType CommandTypes] [-Module Modules] [-Prefix
NounPrefix]
```

With Import-PSSession, you'll usually want to use the –AllowClobber parameter to specify that PowerShell can temporarily overwrite local commands, as shown in the following example:

```
Import-PSSession $Session -AllowClobber
```

Here, you import a session and overwrite local commands. By overwriting local commands, you ensure that any command you run is executed against the remote computer.

When you import a session, PowerShell creates an implicit remoting module and you no longer have to use Invoke-Command to execute commands on the remote computer. In this way, importing a PowerShell session by using Import-PSSession is similar to entering a session by using Enter-PSSession.

Temporarily overwriting commands is referred to as shadowing commands. As long as the remote session is valid, commands remain shadowed and are executed on the remote computer implicitly. If the connection is broken, however, commands won't execute on the remote machine as expected.

> **NOTE**   When commands are shadowed, you can't use session-related commands to manage the session. Why? All commands are executed implicitly on the remote computer, which doesn't recognize the original session. To exit the session, you'll need to close the PowerShell window.

Keep in mind that if you don't use the –AllowClobber parameter, the import process won't temporarily overwrite local commands with those being imported from a remote session. As a result, you'll end up with a mixed environment where locally-defined commands execute against the local computer and imported commands execute against the remote computer. As this typically isn't what you want, you'll want to use –AllowClobber to ensure all commands are executed against the remote computer.

Establishing CIM Sessions

Windows PowerShell 3.0 and later support the Common Information Model (CIM). CIM allows you to use XML to define management information for computer systems, networks, applications and services, and then use these management definitions to exchange information between different types of computers, including computers running non-Windows operating systems.

Currently, CIM modules can only be defined in a special type of XML file called a Cmdlet Definition XML (CDXML) file. Cmdlets and other features in CDXML files are defined using non-managed code assemblies. CIM modules can make use of CIM classes, the CIM .NET Framework, CIM management cmdlets, and WMI providers.

In Windows and Windows Server, support for CIM is implemented in the CimCmdlets module. If you enter **get-command –module cimcmdlets**, you'll find the module includes the following cmdlets:

- Export-BinaryMiLog
- Get-CimAssociatedInstance
- Get-CimClass
- Get-CimInstance
- Get-CimSession
- Import-BinaryMiLog
- Invoke-CimMethod
- New-CimInstance
- New-CimSession
- New-CimSessionOption
- Register-CimIndicationEvent
- Remove-CimInstance
- Remove-CimSession
- Set-CimInstance

CDXML files specify the mapping between Windows PowerShell cmdlets and CIM class operations and methods. CIM cmdlets call a CIM Object Manager (CIMOM) server, such as WMI in Windows, to manage a remote computer.

As long as a remote computer or device supports CIM and has a compliant CIMOM, you can work with the computer or device remotely using Windows PowerShell. This means that not only can you use CimCmdlets to manage Windows 8 or later and Windows Server 2012 or later, you also can use CimCmdlets to manage earlier releases of Windows and non-Windows computers.

You use New-CimSession to create a session with one or more remote computers, as shown in the following example:

```
$s = New-CimSession –ComputerName Server41, Server13, Server39
```

However, if a computer or device does not have the Windows Management Framework, the CIM session can't be established using the standard approach, which relies on Windows Remote Management (WinRM). In this case, you must establish the session using the Distributed Component Object Model (DCOM) protocol. Additionally, as CIM sessions aren't implemented in PowerShell 2.0, you also must use DCOM if you want to work with computers with PowerShell 2.0 installed.

To use DCOM instead of WinRM, you must pass in a CimSessionOption object with the Protocol set when you create the session, as shown in this example:

```
$sopt = New-CimSessionOption –Protocol DCOM

$s = New-CimSession –ComputerName Server41, Server13, Server39
–SessionOption $sopt
```

Here, the first command creates a CimSessionOption object and sets the protocol to DCOM and the second command creates a CIM Session with this option.

Once the remote CIM session is established, you use the CIM-related cmdlets to work with the remote systems and devices. Some cmdlets, such as Get-Module, also have CIM-related parameters that you can use.

In the following example, you use Get-CimInstance to examine the properties of the Win32_Processor object on the remote computers:

```
Get-CimInstance -ClassName Win32_Processor -CimSession $s |fl
```

Here, you specify the CIM session you want to work with using the –CimSession parameter and list the properties of the Win32_Processor object on each computer so you can determine their processor type. You could just as easily examine the properties of the Win32_OperatingSystem, Win32_ComputerSystem or any other CIM object that is available in the session.

Because Windows Management Instrumentation (WMI), which is used to manage Windows resources and components, is a CIMOM server service that implements the CIM standard on Windows, you can use CIM cmdlets to work with MI objects as well. The CIM cmdlets show instances and classes from the default namespace (root/cimv2), unless you specify a different namespace to work with. For example, if you enter **get-cimclass** without specifying another namespace, you'll see a list of all classes in the root/cimv2 namespace.

> **TIP** Working with MI objects is covered extensively in Chapter 8 "Conquering COM, WMI, CMI, .NET, and Objects." When managing remote computers, you may find that working with CIM cmdlets is easier than working with WMI cmdlets. The reason for this is that the CIM cmdlets make it easier to discover and work with Windows resources and components. An added advantage of working with CIM is efficiency. When you establish a persistent session, you work within the context of this session and the computers don't need to repeatedly establish, provision and remove connections.

When you are finished working with CIM, use Remove-CimSession to close the session to free the resources used. Here is an example:

```
Remove-CimSession $s
```

Working Remotely Without WinRM

Some cmdlets have a –ComputerName parameter that lets you work with a remote computer without using Windows PowerShell remoting. This means you can use the cmdlet on any computer that is running Windows PowerShell, even if the computer is not configured for Windows PowerShell remoting. These cmdlets include the following:

- Get-WinEvent, Get-HotFix, Get-Counter
- Get-EventLog, Clear-EventLog, Write-EventLog, Limit-EventLog
- Show-EventLog, New-EventLog, Remove-EventLog
- Get-WmiObject, Get-Process, Get-Service, Set-Service
- Restart-Computer, Stop-Computer, Add-Computer
- Remove-Computer, Rename-Computer

Because these cmdlets don't use remoting, you can run any of these cmdlets on a remote computer in a domain simply by specifying the name of one or more remote computers in the –ComputerName parameter. However, Windows policies and configuration settings must allow remote connections, and you must still have the appropriate credentials.

The following command runs Get-WinEvent on PrintServer35 and FileServer17:

```
get-winevent –computername printserver35, fileserver17
```

When you use the –ComputerName parameter, these cmdlets return objects that include the name of the computer that generated the data. The remote computer name is stored in the MachineName property. Typically, the MachineName property is not displayed by default. The following example shows how you can use the Format-Table cmdlet to add the MachineName property to the output:

```
$procs = {get-process -computername Server56, Server42, Server27
| sort-object -property Name}

&$procs | format-table Name, Handles, WS, CPU, MachineName –auto
```

```
Name                   Handles       WS        CPU MachineName
----                   -------       --        --- -----------
acrotray                    52  3948544          0 Server56
AlertService               139  7532544            Server56
csrss                      594 20463616            Server56
csrss                      655  5283840            Server56
CtHelper                    96  6705152   0.078125 Server56
  . . .
acrotray                    43  3948234          0 Server42
AlertService               136  7532244            Server42
csrss                      528 20463755            Server42
csrss                      644  5283567            Server42
CtHelper                    95  6705576   0.067885 Server42
```

```
acrotray                        55  3967544          0 Server27
AlertService                   141  7566662            Server27
csrss                          590 20434342            Server27
csrss                          654  5242340            Server27
CtHelper                        92  6705231   0.055522 Server27
```

You can get a complete list of all cmdlets with a –ComputerName parameter by typing the following command: **get-help * -parameter ComputerName**. To determine whether the –ComputerName parameter of a particular cmdlet requires Windows PowerShell remoting, display the parameter description by typing **get-help *CmdletName* -parameter ComputerName**, where *CmdletName* is the actual name of the cmdlet, such as

```
get-help Restart-Computer -parameter ComputerName
```

Typically, if the parameter doesn't require remoting, this is stated explicitly. For example, the output often states specifically:

```
This parameter does not rely on Windows PowerShell remoting. You
can use the -ComputerName parameter even if your computer is not
configured to run remote commands.
```

Chapter 5. Using Background Jobs and Scheduled Jobs

When you work with computers, you'll often want to perform routine tasks in the background or on a periodic, scheduled basis. To do this, PowerShell gives you several options, including allowing you to run commands as jobs and allowing you to schedule commands to run via the Task Scheduler service.

Creating Background Jobs

PowerShell supports both local and remote background jobs. A background job is a command that you run asynchronously without interacting with it. When you start a background job, the command prompt returns immediately, and you can continue to work in the session while the job runs, even if it runs for an extended period of time.

Using Background Jobs

PowerShell runs background jobs on the local computer by default. You can run background jobs on remote computers by

- Starting an interactive session with a remote computer and starting a job in the interactive session. This approach allows you to work with the background job the same way as you would on the local computer.
- Running a background job on a remote computer that returns results to the local computer. This approach allows you to collect the results of background jobs and maintain them from your computer.
- Running a background job on a remote computer and maintaining the results on the remote computer. This approach helps ensure the job data is secure.

PowerShell has several commands for working with background jobs. These commands include

- **Get-Job** Gets objects that represent the background jobs started in the current session. Without parameters, Get-Job returns a list of all jobs in the current session. The job object returned does not contain the job results. To get the results, use the Receive-Job cmdlet. You can use the parameters of Get-Job to get background jobs by their command text, names, IDs, or instance IDs. For command text, type the command or the part of the command with wildcards. For IDs, type an integer value that uniquely identifies the job in the current session. For names, type the friendly names previously assigned to the job. An instance ID is a GUID that uniquely identifies a job, even when you have multiple jobs running in PowerShell. To find the names, IDs, or instance IDs of jobs, use Get-Jobs without parameters. You can use the –State parameter to get only jobs in the specified state. Valid values are NotStarted, Running, Completed, Stopped, Failed, and Blocked. Use the –Before or –After parameters to get jobs completed before or after a specified date and time.

- **Receive-Job** Gets the output and errors of the PowerShell background jobs started in the current session. You can get the results of all jobs or identify jobs by their name, ID, instance ID, computer name, location, or session, or by inputting a job object. By default, job results are deleted after you receive them, but you can use the –Keep parameter to save the results so that you can receive them again. To delete the job results, receive them again without the –Keep parameter, close the session, or use the Remove-Job cmdlet to delete the job from the session.

- **Remove-Job** Deletes PowerShell background jobs that were started by using Start-Job or the –AsJob parameter of a cmdlet. Without parameters or parameter values, Remove-Job has no effect. You can delete all jobs or selected jobs based on their command, name, ID, instance ID, or state, or by passing a job object to Remove-Job. Before deleting a running job, you should use Stop-Job to stop the job. If you try to delete a running job, Remove-Job fails. You can use the –Force parameter to delete a running job. If you do not delete a background job, the job remains in the global job cache until you close the session

- **Start-Job** Starts a Windows PowerShell background job on the local computer. To run a background job on a remote computer, use the –AsJob parameter of a cmdlet that supports background jobs, or use the Invoke-Command cmdlet to run a Start-Job command on the remote computer. When you start a Windows PowerShell background job, the job starts, but the results do not appear immediately. Instead, the command returns an object that represents the background job. The job object contains useful information about the job, but it does not contain the results. This approach allows you to continue working while the job runs.

- **Stop-Job**   Stops PowerShell background jobs that are in progress. You can stop all jobs or stop selected jobs based on their name, ID, instance ID, or state, or by passing a job object to Stop-Job. When you stop a background job, PowerShell completes all tasks that are pending in that job queue and then ends the job. No new tasks are added to the queue after you stop the job. Stop-Job does not delete background jobs. To delete a job, use Remove-Job.

- **Wait-Job**   Waits for PowerShell background jobs to complete before it displays the command prompt. You can wait until any specific background jobs are complete or until all background jobs are complete. Use the –Timeout parameter to set a maximum wait time for the job. When the commands in the job are complete, Wait-Job displays the command prompt and returns a job object so that you can pipe it to another command. Use the –Any parameter to display the command prompt when any job completes. By default, Wait-Job waits until all of the specified jobs are complete before displaying the prompt.

Some cmdlets can be run as background jobs automatically using an –AsJob parameter. You can get a complete list of all cmdlets with an –AsJob parameter by typing the following command: **get-help * -parameter AsJob**. These cmdlets include:

- **Invoke-Command**   Runs commands on local and remote computers.
- **Invoke-WmiMethod**   Calls Windows Management Instrumentation (WMI) methods.
- **Test-Connection**   Sends Internet Control Message Protocol (ICMP) echo request packets (*pings*) to one or more computers.
- **Restart-Computer**   Restarts (*reboots*) the operating system on local and remote computers.
- **Stop-Computer**   Stops (shuts down) local and remote computers.

The basic way background jobs work is as follows:

1. You start a background job using Start-Job or the –AsJob parameter of a cmdlet.

2. The job starts, but the results do not appear immediately. Instead, the command returns an object that represents the background job.

3. As necessary, you work with the job object. The job object contains useful information about the job, but it does not contain the results. This approach allows you to continue working while the job runs.

4. To view the results of a job started in the current session, you use Receive-Job. You can identify jobs by their name, ID, instance ID, computer name, location, or session, or by inputting a job object to Receive-Job. After you receive a job, the job results are deleted (unless you use the –Keep parameter).

Starting Jobs in Interactive Sessions

You can start a background job in any interactive session. The procedure for starting a background job is almost the same whether you are working with your local computer or a remote computer. When you work with the local computer, all operations occur on the local computer. When you work with a remote computer, all operations occur on the remote computer.

You can use the Enter-PSSession cmdlet to start an interactive session with a remote computer. Use the –ComputerName parameter to specify the name of the remote computer, such as in the following:

```
enter-pssession -computername filesvr32
```

> **NOTE** To end the interactive session later, type **exit-pssession**.

You start a background job in a local or remote session using the Start-Job cmdlet. You can reference a script block with the –ScriptBlock parameter or a local script using the –FilePath parameter.

The following command runs a background job that gets the events in the System, Application, and Security logs. Because Start-Job returns an object that represents the job, this command saves the job object in the $job variable. Type the command as a single line:

```
$job = start-job -scriptblock {$share = "\\FileServer85\logs";
$logs = "system","application","security";
foreach ($log in $logs) { $filename =
```

```
"$env:computername".ToUpper() + "$log" + "log" +
(get-date -format yyyyMMdd) + ".log";
Get-EventLog $log | set-content $share\$filename; }
}
```

Or use the back apostrophe to continue the line as shown here:

```
$job = start-job -scriptblock {$share = "\\FileServer85\logs"; `
$logs = "system","application","security"; `
foreach ($log in $logs) { `
$filename = "$env:computername".ToUpper() + "$log" + "log" + `
(get-date -format yyyyMMdd) + ".log"; `
Get-EventLog $log | set-content $share\$filename; } `
}
```

Alternatively, you can store the commands as a script on the local computer and then reference the local script using the –FilePath parameter as shown in the examples that follow.

Command line
```
$job = start-job -filepath c:\scripts\eventlogs.ps1
```

Source for Eventlogs.ps1
```
$share = "\\FileServer85\logs"
$logs = "system","application","security"

foreach ($log in $logs) {
  $filename = "$env:computername".ToUpper() + "$log" + "log" + `
(get-date -format yyyyMMdd) + ".log"
  Get-EventLog $log | set-content $share\$filename
}
```

The script must reside on the local computer or in a directory that the local computer can access. When you use FilePath, Windows PowerShell converts the contents of the specified script file to a script block and runs the script block as a background job.

While the job runs, you can continue working and run other commands, including other background jobs. However, you must keep the interactive session open until the job completes. Otherwise, the jobs will be interrupted, and the results will be lost.

> **NOTE** You don't have to store Job objects in variables. However, doing so makes it easier to work with Job objects. But if you do use variables and you run multiple jobs, be sure that you store the returned Job objects in different variables, such as $job1, $job2, and $job3.

You use the Get-Job cmdlet to do the following:

- Find out if a job is complete.
- Display the command passed to the job.
- Get information about jobs so that you can work with them.

You can get all jobs or identify jobs by their name, ID, instance ID, computer name, location, or session, or by inputting a job object. PowerShell gives jobs sequential IDs and names automatically. The first job you run has an ID of 1 and a name of Job1, the second job you run has an ID of 2 and a name of Job2, and so on. You can also name jobs when you start them using the –Name parameter. In the following example, you create a job named Logs:

```
start-job -filepath c:\scripts\eventlogs.ps1 –name Logs
```

You can then get information about this job using Get-Job and the –Name parameter as shown in the following example and sample output:

```
get-job -name Logs
Id   Name   State    HasMoreData    Location    Command
--   ----   -----    -----------    --------    -------
1    Logs   Failed   False          filesvr32   $share =
"\\FileServer...
```

Because this job failed to run, you won't necessarily be able to receive its output or error results. You can, however, take a closer look at the job information. For more detailed information, you need to format the output in a list as shown in this example and sample output:

```
get-job -name logs | format-list
HasMoreData   : False
StatusMessage :
Location      : filesvr32
Command       : $share = "\\FileServer85\logs"; $logs =
"system", "application","security"; foreach ($log in $logs) {
$filename = "$env:computername".ToUpper() + "$log" + "log" +
```

```
(get-date -format yyyyMMdd) + ".log"; Get-EventLog $log | set-
content $share\$filename; }
JobStateInfo  : Failed
Finished      : System.Threading.ManualResetEvent
InstanceId    : 679ed475-4edd-4ba5-ae79-e1e9b3aa590e
Id            : 3
Name          : Logs
ChildJobs     : {Job4}
Output        : {}
Error         : {}
Progress      : {}
Verbose       : {}
Debug         : {}
Warning       : {}
```

If you are running several jobs, type **get-job** to check the status of all jobs as shown in the following example and sample output:

```
get-job
Id Name    State       HasMoreData  Location   Command
-- ----    -----       -----------  --------   -------
1  Job1    Completed   False        localhost  $share =
"\\FileServer...
3  Job3    Running     True         localhost  $logs =
"system","appl...
```

When a job completes, you can use the Receive-Job cmdlet to get the results of the job. However, keep in mind that if a job doesn't produce output or errors to the PowerShell prompt, there won't be any results to receive.

You can receive the results of all jobs by typing **receive-job**, or you can identify jobs by their name, ID, instance ID, computer name, location, or session, or by inputting a job object. The following example receives results by name:

```
receive-job –name Job1, Job3
```

The following example receives results by ID:

```
receive-job –id 1, 3
```

Job results are deleted automatically after you receive them. Use the –Keep parameter to save the results so that you can receive them again. To delete the job results, receive the job results again without the –Keep parameter, close the session, or use the Remove-Job cmdlet to delete the job from the session.

Alternatively, you can write the job results to a file. The following example writes the job results to C:\logs\mylog.txt:

```
receive-job –name Job1 > c:\logs\mylog.txt
```

When working with a remote computer, keep in mind that this command runs on the remote computer. As a result, the file is created on the remote computer. If you are using one log for multiple jobs, be sure to use the append operator as shown in this example:

```
receive-job –name Job1 >> c:\logs\mylog.txt
receive-job –name Job2 >> c:\logs\mylog.txt
receive-job –name Job3 >> c:\logs\mylog.txt
```

While in the current session with the remote computer, you can view the contents of the results file by typing the following command:

```
get-content c:\logs\mylog.txt
```

If you close the session with the remote computer, you can use Invoke-Command to view the file on the remote computer as shown here:

```
$ms = new-pssession -computername fileserver84

invoke-command -session $ms -scriptblock {get-content
c:\logs\mylog.txt}
```

Running Jobs Noninteractively

Rather than working in an interactive session, you can use the Invoke-Command cmdlet with the –AsJob parameter to start background jobs and return results to the local computer. When you use the –AsJob parameter, the job object is created on the local computer, even though the job runs on the remote computer. When the job completes, the results are returned to the local computer.

In the following example, we create a noninteractive PowerShell session with three remote computers and then use Invoke-Command to run a background job that gets the events in the System, Application, and Security logs. This is the same job created earlier, only now the job runs on all the computers listed in the –ComputerName parameter. Type the command as a single line:

```
$s = new-pssession -computername fileserver34, dataserver18
Invoke-command –session $s
-asjob -scriptblock {$share = "\\FileServer85\logs";
$logs = "system","application","security";
foreach ($log in $logs) {
$filename = "$env:computername".ToUpper() + "$log" + "log" +
(get-date -format yyyyMMdd) + ".log";
Get-EventLog $log | set-content $share\$filename; }
}
```

Or use the back apostrophe to continue the line as shown here:

```
$s = new-pssession -computername fileserver34, dataserver18 `
Invoke-command –session $s `
-asjob -scriptblock {$share = "\\FileServer85\logs"; `
$logs = "system","application","security"; `
foreach ($log in $logs) { `
$filename = "$env:computername".ToUpper() + "$log" + "log" + `
(get-date -format yyyyMMdd) + ".log"; `
Get-EventLog $log | set-content $share\$filename; } `
}
```

Alternatively, you can store the commands as a script on the local computer and then reference the local script using the –FilePath parameter as shown in the examples that follow.

Command line
```
$s = new-pssession -computername fileserver34, dataserver18
Invoke-command –session $s -asjob -filepath
c:\scripts\eventlogs.ps1
```

Source for Eventlogs.ps1
```
$share = "\\FileServer85\logs"
$logs = "system","application","security"

foreach ($log in $logs) {
   $filename = "$env:computername".ToUpper() + "$log" + "log" + `
(get-date -format yyyyMMdd) + ".log"
```

```
    Get-EventLog $log | set-content $share\$filename
}
```

The script must reside on the local computer or in a directory that the local computer can access. As before, when you use FilePath, Windows PowerShell converts the contents of the specified script file to a script block and runs the script block as a background job.

Now, you don't necessarily have to run Invoke-Command via a noninteractive session. However, the advantage of doing so is that you can now work with the job objects running in the session. For example, to get information about the jobs on all three computers, you type the following command:

```
get-job
```

To receive job results you type this command:

```
receive-job -keep
```

Or you can type the following if you want to save the results to a file on the local computer:

```
receive-job > c:\logs\mylog.txt
```

A variation on this technique is to use the Invoke-Command cmdlet to run the Start-Job cmdlet. This technique allows you to run background jobs on multiple computers and keep the results on the remote computers. Here's how this works:

1. You use Invoke-Command without the –AsJob parameter to run the Start-Job cmdlet.
2. A job object is created on each remote computer.
3. Commands in the job are run separately on each remote computer.
4. Job results are maintained separately on each remote computer.
5. You work with the job objects and results on each remote computer separately.

Here, you use Invoke-Command to start jobs on three computers and store the Job objects in the $j variable:

```
$s = new-pssession -computername fileserver34, dataserver18

$j = invoke-command -session $s {start-job -filepath
c:\scripts\elogs.ps1}
```

Again, you don't necessarily have to run Invoke-Command via a noninteractive session. However, the advantage of doing so is that you can now work with the job objects running on all three computers via the session. For example, to get information about the jobs on all three computers, you type the following command:

```
invoke-command -session $s -scriptblock {get-job}
```

Or, because you stored the Job objects in the $j variable, you also could enter:

```
$j
```

To receive job results, you type this command:

```
invoke-command -session $s -scriptblock { param($j) receive-job
-job $j -keep} -argumentlist $j
```

Or you can do the following if you want to save the results to a file on each remote computer:

```
invoke-command -session $s -command {param($j) receive-job -job
$j > c:\logs\mylog.txt} -argumentlist $j
```

In both examples, you use Invoke-Command to run a Receive-Job command in each session in $s. Because $j is a local variable, the script block uses the "param" keyword to declare the variable in the command and the ArgumentList parameter to supply the value of $j.

Creating Scheduled Jobs

With Windows PowerShell, you also can create scheduled jobs, which combine the best features of both PowerShell background jobs and Task Scheduler tasks. As scheduled job cmdlets are included in the PSScheduledJob module, you can enter **get-command –module psscheduledjob** to list all the related cmdlets.

You use these commands to create, edit, and modify scheduled jobs, job triggers, and job options.

As scheduled jobs are an enhancement for Windows PowerShell 3.0 and later, the basic commands for working with background jobs have also been extended to work with scheduled jobs. This means you can use Start-Job, Stop-Job, Get-Job, Receive-Job, Remove-Job, and Wait-Job to work with scheduled jobs as well.

Scheduled jobs rely on the Task Scheduler service to monitor the system state and clock. This service must be running and properly configured for job scheduling to work. Like background jobs, scheduled jobs run asynchronously in the background. Creating a schedule jobs requires:

1. Defining one or more job triggers. You create job triggers using New-JobTrigger. You manage Job Trigger objects using Get-JobTrigger, Add-JobTrigger, Enable-JobTrigger, Disable-JobTrigger, Set-JobTrigger, and Remove-JobTrigger.
2. Setting job options as appropriate. You create job options using New-ScheduledJobOption. You manage Job Option objects using Get-ScheduledJobOption and Set-ScheduledJobOption.
3. Registering and running the scheduled job. You register and run scheduled jobs using Register-ScheduledJob. You manage Scheduled Job objects using Get-ScheduledJob, Set-ScheduledJob, Enable-ScheduledJob, Disable-ScheduledJob, and Unregister-ScheduledJob.

Processes related to each of these steps are discussed in the sections that follow. Before getting started, however, keep in mind that triggers and options can be specified directly when you register scheduled jobs or you can create related objects that can be passed to a job when you are registering it.

Defining Job Triggers

You create job triggers using the New-JobTrigger cmdlet. As the cmdlet returns an object, you usually store the object in a variable that is then passed to the scheduled job when you register it. Job triggers specify the circumstances under which a job begins and ends. You can begin a job based on a schedule as well as on computer startup and user logon. As job triggers based on startup and log on are the easiest to define, we'll look at those first.

Running Jobs at Startup or Logon

To create a job trigger based on computer startup, you use the –AtStartup parameter. The basic syntax is:

```
New-JobTrigger -AtStartup [-RandomDelay HH:MM:SS]
```

Where –RandomDelay sets the maximum interval for a random delay. In the following example, you create a trigger that runs at startup with a random delay of up to 30 minutes:

```
$tr = New-JobTrigger -AtStartup -RandomDelay 00:30:00
```

> **NOTE** Setting a random delay for jobs is a best practice whenever many users or computers may run a resource-intensive job at the same time. As all job triggers can use a random delay, I won't include the –RandomDelay parameter in the other syntax examples in this chapter.
>
> **MORE INFO** Time-related values are set using TimeSpan objects or strings that PowerShell can convert automatically to TimeSpan objects. In syntax examples, I typically used the abbreviated syntax HH:MM:SS, which sets the hours, minutes and seconds in a time span. The full syntax, DD.HH:MM:SS, allows you to set day values as well. For example, 1.00:00:00 specifies a time span of 1 day and 2.00:00:00 sets a time span of 2 days.

To create a job trigger based on user logon, you use the –AtLogon parameter. The basic syntax is:

```
New-JobTrigger -AtLogon [-User [Domain\]UserName]
```

Where –User is an optional parameter that specifies the users who trigger the scheduled job. For workgroups and homegroups, users can be identified by their logon name, such as WilliamS. For domains, users should be identified by their logon name in Domain\UserName format, such as ImaginedL\WilliamS. To specify more than one user, enter the user names in a comma-separated list. To apply the trigger to all users, enter * or simply omit the –User parameter. In the following example, you create a trigger that applies only to WilliamS and store the Job Trigger object in the $tr variable:

```
$tr = New-JobTrigger -AtLogon -User ImaginedL\WilliamS
```

To confirm the settings of this job trigger, enter the following command:

```
$tr | fl
```

The resulting output shows the properties of the Job Trigger object stored in the $tr variable. You can make changes to the job trigger using Set-JobTrigger.

Running Jobs Daily or Weekly

In addition to jobs that run at startup or logon, you can create jobs that run daily or weekly. The basic syntax for a job trigger based on a daily run schedule is:

```
New-JobTrigger -Daily [-DaysInterval Int] -At DateTime
```

Where –DaysInterval specifies the number of days between schedules runs and –At specifies date and time to start the job. Keep the following in mind:

- With –DaysInterval, the default value is 1, meaning the scheduled job should run every day. If you specify any other value, the value determines the number of days between schedules runs. For example, a value of 2 specifies that the job should run every other day, a value of 3 specifies the job should run every third day, etc.
- With –At, you can use a DateTime object or any string that can be converted to a DateTime object. Although a string like "2/15/2015 4:50 AM" or "Feb 15, 2015 4:50" sets an exact date and time, you can use a partial value, such as "3:30 PM" or "4/18". When you only specify the time, the command creates a trigger using the current date. When you only specify a date, the command creates a trigger that runs at 12:00:00 AM on the specified date.

In the following example, you create a trigger that runs every other day, starting March 2, 2015 at 3:00:00 AM:

```
$eodt = New-JobTrigger -Daily -DaysInterval 2 -At "March 2, 2015
3:00:00 AM"
```

When you are creating jobs with a weekly run schedule, you specify the number of weeks between run schedules using –WeeksInterval and the days of the week to run using –DaysOfWeek, giving a basic syntax of:

```
New-JobTrigger -Weekly [-WeeksInterval Int] -At DateTime
-DaysOfWeek Day1, Day2, …
```

With –WeeksInterval, the default value is 1, meaning the scheduled job should run every week. If you specify any other value, the value determines the number of weeks between runs. For example, an interval of 2 specifies that the job should run every other week, an interval of 3 specifies the job should run every third week, etc.

With –DaysOfWeek, you enter day names, such as Monday, or the integer values 0 to 6, with 0 representing Sunday. With multiple run days, each day name or value must be separated with a comma, as shown in the following example where the job runs every week on Monday and Thursday:

```
$etwt = New-JobTrigger -Weekly -WeeksInterval 1 -DaysOfWeek
Monday, Thursday -At "June 5, 2015 5:00:00 AM"
```

It's important to point out that if you enclose the day names in quotes, each day name must be specified separately, such as:

```
"Tuesday", "Friday"
```

Creating Jobs that Run Once or Repeatedly

In addition to being able to create scheduled jobs that run daily or weekly, you can create scheduled jobs that run once and also optionally repeat at specific time intervals, such as every hour. The basic syntax is:

```
New-JobTrigger -Once [-RepeatIndefinitely] [-RepetitionDuration
DD.HH:MM:SS] [-RepetitionInterval HH:MM:SS] -At DateTime
```

By default, Run Once jobs do not repeat. If you want a job to repeat, you must use –RepeatIndefinitely to allow a job trigger to repeat without having to set a repetition duration or you must specify an allowed duration for repeating the job. For example, to allow a job to run and repeat for 24 hours, you would set the –RepetitionDuration parameter to 24:00:00. For repeating jobs, you must also specify the repetition interval. For example, if you want a job to repeat every hour, you'd set the –RepetitionInterval to 01:00:00.

In the following example, you create a trigger that runs indefinitely at 3-hour intervals, starting June 1, 2015 at 6:30:00 AM:

```
$rt = New-JobTrigger -Once -RepeatIndefinitely
-RepetitionInterval 00:03:00 -At "June 1, 2015 6:30:00 AM"
```

Rather than running a job indefinitely, you may want a job to run for a specified period of time, such as 24 hours or 7 days. In the following example, you create a job that runs every 2 hours for 5 days:

```
$rt = New-JobTrigger -Once -RepetitionDuration 5.00:00:00
-RepetitionInterval 00:03:00 -At "June 1, 2015 6:30:00 AM"
```

Setting Job Options

You create job options using the New-ScheduledJobOption cmdlet. As the cmdlet returns an object, you usually store the object in a variable that is then passed to the scheduled job when you register it.

Understanding Job Option Parameters

Job options help qualify the conditions under which a job is started or stopped once it is triggered. You can use options to wake the computer to run a job, to specify whether the job runs when a network connection isn't available, and to specify whether a job runs only when AC power is available.

You also can use options to start, stop and restart a job based on the processor idle time. For example, you might want a job to start only if the processor has been idle for at least 5 minutes, stop if the processor is no longer idle, and then restart once the processor is again idle.

You specify job options using the following parameters:

- **–ContinueIfGoingOnBattery** Specifies that a running job should keep running if the computer switches to battery power.
- **–DoNotAllowDemandStart** Specifies that a job cannot be manually started by a user. Thus, the job can only run according to its defined schedule.
- **–HideInTaskScheduler** Creates the job as a hidden task in the Task Scheduler. As users can display hidden tasks in the Task Scheduler, this doesn't prevent users from seeing the scheduled job.
- **–IdleDuration** *HH:MM:SS* Specifies how long a computer must be idle before the job starts. The default is 10 minutes (00:10:00).
- **–IdleTimeout** *HH:MM:SS* Specifies how long a job waits for the computer to be idle. The default value is 1 hour (01:00:00). If the timeout elapses before the computer is idle, the job does not run at that scheduled run time. At the next scheduled run time, the Task Scheduler will again evaluate the computer's idle status and determine whether the job should run.
- **–MultipleInstancePolicy** *PolicyType* Determines how the Task Scheduler handles a request to start a new instance of a scheduled job while another instance of the job is already running. Policy type values you can use are: IgnoreNew, Parallel, Queue, and StopExisting. As the value IgnoreNew is the default, the currently running instance of the job continues execution and a request to start a new instance of that job is ignored.
- **–RequireNetwork** Runs the job only when the computer has a valid and available network connection. If a network is not available, the job does not run at that scheduled run time. At the next scheduled run time, the Task Scheduler will again evaluate the status of network connections and determine whether the job should run.
- **–RestartOnIdleResume** If you use –StopIfGoingOffIdle, you can use this parameter to specify that the computer should restart a scheduled job when the computer is again idle.
- **–RunElevated** Runs the job with elevated, administrator permissions. If you use this option, you should also schedule the job using specific credentials and those credentials must have appropriate administrator permissions.
- **–StartIfIdle** Starts the job if the computer has been idle for the time specified in the IdleDuration, as long as the IdleTimeout has not elapsed.

- **–StartIfOnBattery**   Starts the job if the computer is on battery power.
- **–StopIfGoingOffIdle**   Stops the job if the computer becomes active while the job is running. A computer becomes active when it is being used by a user. By default, a job that is suspended when a computer becomes active resumes when the computer is idle again. If you don't want this to happen, set –RestartOnIdleResume to $False.
- **–WakeToRun**   Wakes the computer from a Hibernate or Sleep state at the scheduled start time so the job can run. If you don't use this parameter, the Task Scheduler will not wake the computer.

Using these options, the basic syntax for New-ScheduledJobOption is:

```
New-ScheduledJobOption [-ContinueIfGoingOnBattery]
[-DoNotAllowDemandStart] [-HideInTaskScheduler]
[-IdleDuration HH:MM:SS] [-IdleTimeout HH:MM:SS]
[-MultipleInstancePolicy PolicyType] [-RequireNetwork]
[-RestartOnIdleResume] [-RunElevated] [-StartIfIdle]
[-StartIfOnBattery] [-StopIfGoingOffIdle] [-WakeToRun]
```

Working with Job Options

By default, jobs created using Register-ScheduledJob:

- Can be started manually by users.
- Are displayed in the Task Scheduler.
- Run with the standard permissions of the user who created the job.
- Start only if a computer is on AC power and stop if the computer switches to battery power.
- Run whether a computer has a network connection or is idle.
- Do not run if a computer is in the Sleep or Hibernate state.
- Only allow one instance of a job to run at a time.

If you want a job to run with different options, you must specify these options when you create the job or pass in a Scheduled Job Option object with the desired options.

- Use –DoNotAllowDemandStart to prevent users from manually starting a job.

- Use –HideInTaskScheduler to create a hidden job rather than a standard job.
- Use –RunElevated to run the job with elevated, administrator permissions rather than the standard permissions of the user who created the job.
- Use –StartIfOnBattery to allow a job to start when the computer is on battery power and –ContinueIfGoingOnBattery to allow a job to continue running if a computer switches from AC power to battery power while the job is running.
- Use –WakeToRun to allow the Task Scheduler to wake the computer to run the job.

Not all of the options are simple switch parameters, however. To control multiple instances of jobs, you must use –MultipleInstancePolicy to specify the policy type to use. Although the default policy, IgnoreNew, simply ignores any request to start another instance of a currently running job, the other policy types give you more control. The other options are:

- **Parallel**   With Parallel, Task Scheduler allows multiple instances of jobs to run at the same time.
- **Queue**   With Queue, Task Scheduler queues additional requests to run a job and then runs each in turn when the current instance finishes running.
- **StopExisting**   With StopExisting, Task Scheduler stops the currently running instance and starts the new instance of the job.

In the following example, you define job options that allow multiple instances of a job to run at the same time and also ensure the job runs regardless of the power state:

```
$opts = New-ScheduledJobOption -MultipleInstancePolicy Parallel
-StartIfOnBattery -ContinueIfGoingOnBattery
```

To confirm these job options, enter the following command:

```
$opts | fl
```

The resulting output shows the properties of the Scheduled Job Option object stored in the $opts variable. You can make changes to the job options using Set-ScheduledJobOption.

If you want a job to run regardless of whether a computer is idle or active, you need only accept the default job options. To start a job only if a computer is idle, you use –StartIfIdle and optionally specify an idle duration and idle timeout. To stop a job if a computer ceases to be idle, add –StopIfGoingOffIdle. To restart a stopped job when a computer resumes an idle state, you must add –RestartOnIdleResume. Rather than using these parameters separately, these parameters are most often used together to ensure scheduled jobs work as expected with idling, as shown in the following example:

```
$joptions = New-ScheduledJobOption -StartIfIdle
-StopIfGoingOffIdle -RestartOnIdleResume
```

Here, you define job options that start a job only if the computer has been idle for 10 minutes and the Task Scheduler hasn't waited more than 1 hour for the computer to enter the idle state. If the computer ceases to be idle, Task Scheduler stops the job, and waits for the computer to resume the idle state before restarting the job. Use the –IdleDuration and –IdleTimeout parameters to override the default idle duration and timeout.

Registering and Running Scheduled Jobs

After you define job triggers and options, you use Register-ScheduledJob to create the job and register it with Task Scheduler. Current jobs configured on a computer are accessible through the Task Scheduler application, which provides a graphical interface for the Task Scheduler service and jobs that have been registered in the Task Scheduler Library.

On Windows desktops, you can access the Task Scheduler application in Computer Management. On Windows servers, select Task Scheduler on the Tools menu in Server Manager to open the Task Scheduler application. As shown in Figure 5-1, jobs registered using PowerShell are displayed in the Task Scheduler Library under Microsoft\Windows\PowerShell\ScheduledJobs.

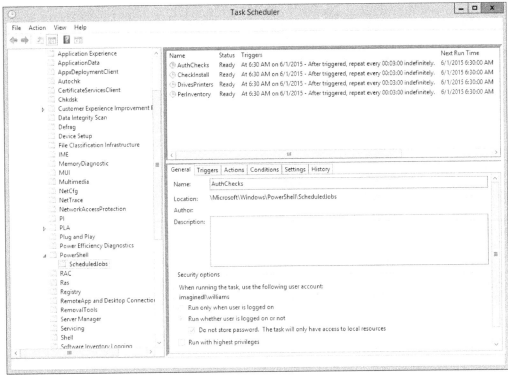

Figure 5-1 Scheduled jobs are registered in Task Scheduler.

You have two options for specifying the commands a scheduled job executes. You can specify the commands to run using a script block and the following basic syntax:

Register-ScheduledJob [-Name] *JobName* [-ScriptBlock] { *ScriptBlock* }
[-Credential *Credential*] [-RunNow] [-ScheduledJobOption *Options*]
[-Trigger *Triggers*]

Or you can specify the full path to a script to run using the following basic syntax:

Register-ScheduledJob [-Name] *JobName* [-FilePath] *FilePath*
[-Credential *Credential*] [-RunNow] [-ScheduledJobOption *Options*]
[-Trigger *Triggers*]

With script blocks, the curly braces { } denote the start and end of the block of commands to run and you use semicolon to specify where one command ends and another begins, such as:

```
$tr = New-JobTrigger -Weekly -WeeksInterval 4 -DaysOfWeek
Tuesday, Thursday -At "June 5, 2015 5:00:00 AM"

$opts = New-ScheduledJobOption -StartIfOnBattery
-ContinueIfGoingOnBattery -RunElevated

Register-ScheduledJob -Name SysChecks -ScriptBlock {
get-process > ./processes.txt; get-eventlog system >
./events.txt} -ScheduledJobOption $opts -Trigger $tr
```

With scripts, you must specify the complete path to the script you want to run. This can be a local path, such as:

```
Register-ScheduledJob -Name SysChecks -FilePath
D:\Scripts\SysChecks.ps1 -ScheduledJobOption
$opts -Trigger $tr
```

Or a UNC path available to the user under which the process runs, such as:

```
Register-ScheduledJob -Name SysChecks -FilePath
\\Server48\Scripts\SysChecks.ps1 -ScheduledJobOption
$opts -Trigger $tr
```

When you are working with remote computers, you can create a session and register the scheduled job using Invoke-Command. As shown in the following example, the techniques used are similar to those discussed previously:

```
$cred = Get-Credential

$ses = New-PSSession -ComputerName (Get-Content .\Computers.txt)
-Credential $cred

invoke-command -session $s { $tr = New-JobTrigger -Daily
-DaysInterval 2 -At "March 31, 2015 5:00:00 AM";
$opt = New-ScheduledJobOption -StopIfGoingOffIdle -StartIfIdle
-RestartOnIdleResume; Register-ScheduledJob -Name SysChecks
-FilePath "\\Server33\Scripts\CheckSys.ps1"
-ScheduledJobOption $opts -Trigger $tr}
```

Here, you establish a PowerShell session with the computers listed in the Computers.txt file, and then you invoke commands on each of those remote computers so that you can create a scheduled job called SysChecks on those computers. Because the jobs are created on remote computers, you must access the remote computers to check the status of the jobs and view any related results. It's important to note that you should define the job triggers and job options using commands invoked on the remote computers. If you don't do this, the objects aren't available for your use on those computers.

An alternative to working with invoked commands would be to create a PowerShell session and then import the session. You could then work directly with the remote computers, as shown in the following example:

```
$cred = Get-Credential

$ses = New-PSSession -ComputerName (Get-Content .\Computers.txt)
-Credential $cred

Import-PSSession -Session $ses -AllowClobber

$tr = New-JobTrigger -Daily -DaysInterval 2 -At "March 31, 2015
5:00:00 AM"

$opt = New-ScheduledJobOption -StopIfGoingOffIdle -StartIfIdle
-RestartOnIdleResume

Register-ScheduledJob -Name SysChecks -FilePath
"\\Server33\Scripts\CheckSys.ps1" -ScheduledJobOption
$opts -Trigger $tr
```

Modifying and Removing Scheduled Jobs

After you create a scheduled job, you'll often need to manage it, which means:

- Using Get-ScheduledJob to view scheduled jobs.
- Using Disable-ScheduledJob to disable a job when it is temporarily not needed.
- Using Enable-ScheduledJob to enable a job that was previously disabled.
- Using Set-ScheduledJob to modify job settings.
- Using Unregister-ScheduledJob to remove scheduled jobs that are no longer needed.

> **NOTE** You can only work with scheduled jobs created by the current user. You can't work with jobs created by other users or any other scheduled tasks available in Task Scheduler.

MORE INFO The only way to work with jobs created in PowerShell by other users is to use the credentials of that user. That said, if you need to remove jobs created by other users and don't have the credentials to do this, you can remove the jobs in the Task Scheduler application, provided you have administrator permissions. In Task Scheduler, navigate the Task Scheduler Library to Microsoft\Windows\PowerShell\ScheduledJobs. Select a job that you want to delete and then press the Delete key. When prompted to confirm the action, select Yes.

Tasks Scheduler also allows you to delete tasks using the Actions pane. In the Actions pane, make sure you don't select Delete Folder (which is listed under ScheduledJobs and likely the first delete option). Instead, choose the Delete option under Selected Item.

Get-ScheduledJob returns information about jobs scheduled on a computer. If you enter the command without options, information about all the jobs you scheduled via PowerShell are listed. If you add the –Name or –Id parameter, you can get information about a specific job by name or ID number.

As Get-ScheduledJob doesn't have a –ComputerName parameter, you can only view information about jobs on computers to which you are connected. Thus, if you are working in a remote session, Get-ScheduledJob returns information about the computers you've connected to in the remote session. Otherwise, Get-ScheduledJob returns information only about jobs on the local computer.

Enable-ScheduledJob, Disable-ScheduledJob and Unregister-ScheduledJob work in much the same way as Get-ScheduledJob. Add the –Name or –Id parameter to specify the job you want to work with by name or ID number. In this example, you enable the HTasks scheduled job which was previously registered and disabled by the current user:

```
Enable-ScheduledJob HTasks
```

If you don't specify a job by name or ID number, you may accidentally modify all jobs created by the current user. Consider the following example:

```
Get-ScheduledJob | Enable-ScheduledJob
```

Here, you enable all scheduled jobs previously registered and disabled by the current user. Keep in mind that if you are working in a remote session, these commands modify jobs defined on the computers you've connected to in the remote session. Otherwise, these commands modify jobs on the local computer.

Chapter 6. Navigating Core Windows PowerShell Structures

The core structures of any programming language determine what you can do with the available options and how you can use the programming language. The programming language at the heart of Windows PowerShell is C#, and the core structures of PowerShell include

- Expressions and operators
- Variables, values, and data types
- Strings, arrays, and collections

Whenever you work with Windows PowerShell, you use these core structures. You'll want to read this chapter closely to learn the core mechanics and determine exactly how you can put PowerShell to work. Because we discuss these core mechanics extensively in this chapter, we won't rehash these discussions when we put the core mechanics to work in upcoming chapters.

Working with Expressions and Operators

In Windows PowerShell, an expression is a calculation that evaluates an equation and returns a result. PowerShell supports many types of expressions, including arithmetic expressions (which return numerical values), assignment expressions (which assign or set a value), and comparison expressions (which compare values).

An *operator* is the element of an expression that tells PowerShell how to perform the calculation. You use operators as part of expressions to perform mathematical operations, make assignments, and compare values. The three common operator types are arithmetic operators, assignment operators, and comparison operators. Windows PowerShell also supports an extended type of operator used with regular expressions, logical operators, and type operators.

Arithmetic, Grouping, and Assignment Operators

Windows PowerShell supports a standard set of arithmetic operators. These operators are summarized in Table 6-1.

TABLE 6-1 Arithmetic Operators in Windows PowerShell

OPERATOR	OPERATION & USAGE
+	Addition. For numbers, returns their sum. For strings, returns a joined string. For arrays, returns a joined array. Example: 3 + 4.
/	Division. For numbers, returns their quotient. Not applicable to strings or arrays. Example: 5 / 2.
%	Modulus. For numbers, returns the remainder of their division. Not applicable to strings or arrays. Example: 5 % 2.
*	Multiplication. For numbers, returns their product. For strings, appends the string to itself the number of times you specify. For arrays, appends the array to itself the number of times you specify. Example: 6 * 3.
–	Subtraction, negation. For numbers, returns their difference. Not applicable to strings or arrays. Example: 3 – 2.

Table 6-2 lists the assignment operators available in PowerShell. Assignment operators assign one or more values to a variable and can perform numeric operations on the values before the assignment. PowerShell supports two special assignment operators that you might not be familiar with: the increment operator (++) and the decrement operator (--). These operators provide a quick way to add or subtract 1 from the value of a variable, property, or array element.

TABLE 6-2 Windows PowerShell Assignment Operators

OPERATOR	OPERATION & USAGE
=	Assign value. Example: $a = 7. Meaning: $a = 7.
+=	Add or append to current value. Example: $g += $h. Meaning: $g = $g + $h.
–=	Subtract from current value. Example: $g –= $h. Meaning: $g = $g – $h.
*=	Multiply current value. Example: $g *= $h. Meaning: $g = $g * $h.

OPERATOR	OPERATION & USAGE
/=	Divide current value. Example: $g /= $h. Meaning: $g = $g / $h.
%=	Modulus current value. Example: $g %= $h. Meaning: $g = $g % $h.
++	Increment by 1. Example: $g++ or ++$g. Meaning: $g = $g + 1.
--	Decrement by 1. Example: $g-- or --$g. Meaning: $g = $g − 1.

As you can see in Tables 6-1 and 6-2, there are few surprises when it comes to PowerShell's arithmetic and assignment operators. Still, there are a few things worth mentioning. In PowerShell, you determine remainders using the Modulus function. In this example, $Remainder is set to 0 (zero):

```
$Remainder = 12 % 4
```

However, $Remainder is set to 1 with the following expression:

```
$Remainder = 10 % 3
```

You can negate a value using the − operator. In the following example, $Answer is set to −15:

```
$Answer = -5 * 3
```

Command expansion and execution operators bring together sets of elements. The grouping operators are described in the following list and examples:

- **&** Used to invoke a script block or the name of a command or function.

```
$a = {Get-Process -id 0}
&$a
Handles  NPM(K)  PM(K)   WS(K) VM(M)  CPU(s)   Id ProcessName
-------  ------  -----   ----- -----  ------   -- -----------
      0       0      0      24     0            0 Idle
```

- **( )** Used to group expression operators. It returns the result of the expression.

```
$a = (5 + 4) * 2; $a
18
```

- **$( )**   Used to group collections of statements. The grouped commands are executed, and then results are returned.

```
$($p= "win*"; get-process $p)
Handles  NPM(K)  PM(K)  WS(K) VM(M)  CPU(s)  Id ProcessName
-------  ------  -----  ----- -----  ------  -- -----------
    106       4   1448   4092    46          636 wininit
    145       4   2360   6536    56          780 winlogon
```

- **@( )**   Used to group collections of statements, execute them, and insert the results into an array.

```
@(get-date;$env:computername;$env:logonserver)
Friday, February 12, 2014 9:01:49 AM
CORSERVER34
\\CORDC92
```

> **NOTE**   An array is simply a data structure for storing a series of values. You'll learn more about arrays in the "Working with Arrays and Collections" section.

If you mix operators, PowerShell performs calculations using the same precedence order you learned in school. For example, multiplication and division in equations are carried out before subtraction and addition, which means

```
5 + 4 * 2 outputs 13
```

and

```
10 / 10 + 6 outputs 7
```

Table 6-3 shows the precedence order for arithmetic operators. As the table shows, the grouping is always evaluated first, and then PowerShell determines whether any values have been incremented or decremented. Next, PowerShell sets positive and negative values as such. Then PowerShell performs multiplication and division before performing any modulus operations. Finally, PowerShell performs addition and subtraction and then assigns the results as appropriate.

TABLE 6-3 Operator Precedence in Windows PowerShell

ORDER	OPERATION
1	Grouping ( ) { }
2	Increment ++, Decrement --
3	Unary + -
4	Multiplication *, Division /
5	Remainders %
6	Addition +, Subtraction −
7	Assignment =

One of the interesting things about Windows PowerShell is that it supports the data storage concepts of

- Kilobytes (KB)
- Megabytes (MB)
- Gigabytes (GB)
- Terabytes (TB)
- Petabytes (PB)

Knowing this, you can perform some simple calculations at the prompt. For example, if you are backing up a drive that uses 1 TB of storage to Blu-Ray DVD, you might want to find out the maximum number of dual-layer Blu-Ray DVDs you'll need, and you can do this simply by entering

```
1TB / 50GB
```

The answer is

```
20.48
```

In the following example, you list all files in the C:\Data directory that are larger than 100 KB:

```
get-item c:\data\* | where-object {$_.length -gt 100kb}
```

Comparison Operators

When you perform comparisons, you check for certain conditions, such as whether A is greater than B or whether A is equal to C. You primarily use comparison operators with conditional statements, such as If and If Else.

Table 6-4 lists the comparison operators available in PowerShell. Most of these operators are straightforward. By default, PowerShell uses non–case-sensitive comparisons. However, you can perform case-sensitive and non–case-sensitive comparisons, respectively, by adding the letter C or I to the operator, such as –ceq or –ieq.

Table 6-4 Windows PowerShell Comparison Operators

OPERATOR	OPERATION & USAGE
–eq	Equal $g –eq $h Is g equal to h? Boolean
	Include string $g –eq $h Does g include h? Boolean
–ne	Not equal $g –ne $h Is g not equal to h?

OPERATOR	OPERATION & USAGE
	Boolean
	Different string
	$g –ne $h
	Does g include a different value than h?
	Boolean
–lt	Less than
	$g –lt $h
	Is g less than h?
	Boolean
–gt	Greater than
	$g –gt $h
	Is g greater than h?
	Boolean
–le	Less than or equal
	$g –le $h
	Is g less than or equal to h?
	Boolean
–ge	Greater than or equal
	$g –ge $h
	Is g greater than or equal to h?
	Boolean

OPERATOR	OPERATION & USAGE
–contains	Contains $g –contains $h Does g include h? Boolean
–notcontains	Does not contain $g –notcontains $h Does g not include h? Boolean
–like	Like $g –like $h Does g include a value like h? Boolean
–notlike	Not like $g –notlike $h Does g not include a value like h? Boolean
–match	Match $g –match $h Does g include any matches for the expression defined in h? Boolean
–notmatch	Not match $g –notmatch $h

OPERATOR	OPERATION & USAGE
	Does g not include matches for the expression defined in h?
	Boolean
–replace	Replace
	$g –replace $h, $i
	If g has occurrences of h, replace them with i.
	String

Note that you can use these operators to compare numbers as well as strings and that there is no set precedence order for comparisons. Comparisons are always performed from left to right.

Most of the comparison operators return a Boolean value that indicates whether a match was found in the compared values. In this example and sample output, we evaluate whether $a equals $b, and the output is False because the values are different:

```
$a = 5; $b = 6
$a -eq $b
```

```
False
```

In this example and sample output, we evaluate whether $a does not equal $b, and the output is True because the values are different:

```
$a = 5; $b = 6
$a -ne $b
```

```
True
```

In this example and sample output, we evaluate whether $a is less than $b, and the output is True:

```
$a = 5; $b = 6
$a -lt $b
```

```
True
```

When you are working with arrays and collections, the –eq, –ne, –lt, –gt, –le, and –ge operators return all values that match the given expression. For example, the –eq operator checks to see if an array of values contains any identical values. If it does, the output shows all the identical values as shown in this example and sample output:

```
$a = "iexplorer", "iexplorer", "powershell"; $b = "iexplorer"
$a -eq $b

iexplorer
iexplorer
```

Similarly, when you are working with arrays and collections, the –ne operator checks to see if an array of values contains values other than a particular value. If it does, the output shows the different values as shown in this example and sample output:

```
$a = "svchost", "iexplorer", "powershell"; $b = "iexplorer"
$a -ne $b

svchost
powershell
```

You use the –contains and –notcontains operators with strings, arrays, and collections. These operators are used to determine whether there is or is not an identical match for a value. In the following example, you check to see whether $a has a resulting match for winlogon:

```
$a = "svchost", "iexplorer", "powershell"
$a -contains "winlogon"

False
```

The –like, –notlike, –match, and –notmatch operators are used for pattern matching. With –like and –notlike, you can use wildcard characters to determine whether a value is like or not like another value. In the following example, you check to see whether $a has a resulting match for *host:

```
$a = "svchost"
$a -like "*host"
```

```
True
```

In examples in other chapters, I've used the *match all* wildcard (*) to match part of a string. PowerShell supports several other wildcards as well, including ? and [ ]. Table 6-5 summarizes these wildcards and their uses.

TABLE 6-5 Wildcard Characters in Windows PowerShell

WILDCARD CHARACTER	DESCRIPTION & USAGE
*	Matches zero or more characters help *-alias export-alias, import-alias, get-alias, new-alias, set-alias
?	Matches exactly one character in the specified position help ??port-alias export-alias, import-alias
[ ]	Matches one character in a specified range of characters help [a-z]e[t-w]-alias get-alias, new-alias, set-alias
[ ]	Matches one character in a specified subset of characters help [efg]et-alias get-alias

When you are working with arrays and collections, the –like and –notlike operators return all values that match the given expression. The following example returns two values that are like 4:

```
1,1,2,3,4,5,5,6,3,4 -like 4
```

4
4

The following example returns five values that are not like 4:

```
2,3,4,5,5,6,4 -notlike 4
```

```
2
3
5
5
6
```

With –match and –notmatch, you use regular expressions to determine whether a value does or does not contain a match for an expression. You can think of regular expressions as an extended set of wildcard characters. In the following example, you check to see whether $a contains the letter s, t, or u:

```
$a = "svchost"
$a -match "[stu]"
```

```
True
```

Table 6-6 shows the characters you can use with regular expressions. Each of the usage examples in the table evaluates to true. When you use .NET Framework regular expressions, you also can add .NET Framework quantifiers to more strictly control what is considered a match.

TABLE 6-6 Characters Used with Regular Expressions

CHARACTER	DESCRIPTION & USAGE
[chars]	Matches exact characters anywhere in the original value. "powershell" –match "er"
.	Matches any single character. "svchost" –match "s.....t"

CHARACTER	DESCRIPTION & USAGE
[value]	Matches at least one of the characters in the brackets. "get" –match "g[aeiou]t"
[range]	Matches at least one of the characters within the range. Use a hyphen (-) to specify a block of contiguous characters. "out" –match "[o-r]ut"
[^]	Matches any character except those in brackets. "bell" –match "[^tuv]ell"
^	Matches the beginning characters. "powershell" –match "^po"
$	Matches the end characters. "powershell" –match "ell$"
*	Matches any pattern in a string. "powershell" –match "p*"
?	Matches a single character in a string. "powershell" –match "powershel?"
+	Matches repeated instances of the preceding characters. "zbzbzb" –match "zb+"
\	Matches the character that follows as a literal character. For example, when \ precedes a double quotation mark, PowerShell interprets the double quotation mark as a character, not as a string delimiter. "Shell$" –match "Shell\$"

CHARACTER	DESCRIPTION & USAGE	
.NET REGEX		
\p{name}	Matches any character in the named character class specified by {name}. Supported names are Unicode groups and block ranges—for example, Ll, Nd, Z, IsGreek, and IsBoxDrawing. "abcd" –match "\p{Ll}+"	
\P{name}	Matches text not included in groups and block ranges specified in {name}. 1234 –match "\P{Ll}+"	
\w	Matches any word character. Equivalent to the Unicode character categories [\p{Ll} \p{Lu}\p{Lt}\p{Lo}\p{Nd}\p{Pc}]. If ECMAScript-compliant behavior is specified with the ECMAScript option, \w is equivalent to [a-zA-Z_0-9]. "abcd defg" –match "\w+"	
\W	Matches any nonword character. Equivalent to the Unicode categories [^\p{Ll}\p{Lu}\p{Lt} \p{Lo}\p{Nd}\p{Pc}]. "abcd defg" –match "\W+"	
\s	Matches any white-space character. Equivalent to the Unicode character categories [\f\n\r\t\v\x85\p{Z}]. "abcd defg" –match "\s+"	
\S	Matches any non–white-space character. Equivalent to the Unicode character categories [^\f\n\r\t\v\x85\p{Z}]. "abcd defg" –match "\S+"	
\d	Matches any decimal digit. Equivalent to \p{Nd} for Unicode and [0–9] for non-Unicode behavior. 12345 –match "\d+"	

CHARACTER	DESCRIPTION & USAGE
\D	Matches any nondigit. Equivalent to \P{Nd} for Unicode and [^0-9] for non-Unicode behavior. "abcd" –match "\D+"
.NET FRAMEWORK QUANTIFER	
*	Matches zero or more occurrences of a pattern specified in a .NET Framework regex. "abc" –match "\w*"
?	Matches zero or one occurrences of a pattern specified in a .NET Framework regex. "abc" –match "\w?"
{n}	Matches exactly *n* occurrences of a pattern specified in a .NET Framework regex. "abc" –match "\w{2}"
{n,}	Matches at least *n* occurrences of a pattern specified in a .NET Framework regex. "abc" –match "\w{2,}"
{n,m}	Matches at least *n* occurrences of a pattern specified in a .NET Framework regex, but no more than *m*. "abc" –match "\w{2,3}"

In addition to using the –match and –notmatch operators with regular expressions, you can explicitly declare regular expressions and then check values against the regular expression. The following example declares a regular expression that matches strings with the letters a to z or A to Z:

```
[regex]$regex="^([a-zA-Z]*)$"
```

When you work with regular expressions, you use the ^ to represent the beginning of a string and $ to represent the end of a string. You then use parentheses to define a group of characters to match. The value [a-zA-Z]* specifies that we want to match zero or more occurrences of the letters a to z or A to Z.

Now that we've defined a regular expression, we can use the IsMatch() method of the expression to verify that a value matches or does not match the expression as shown in the following example:

```
$a = "Tuesday"

[regex]$regex="^([a-zA-Z]*)$"

$regex.ismatch($a)

True
```

However, if we use a string with numbers, spaces, punctuation, or other special characters, the IsMatch test fails as shown in the following example:

```
$days ="Monday Tuesday"

[regex]$regex="^([a-zA-Z]*)$"

$regex.ismatch($days)

False
```

> **TIP** PowerShell also provides operators for splitting, joining, and formatting strings. These operators are discussed in the "Working with Strings" section later in this chapter.

Another comparison operator you can use is –replace. You use this operator to replace all occurrences of a value in a specified element. In the following example, you replace all occurrences of "host" in $a with "console":

```
$a = "svchost", "iexplorer", "loghost"

$a -replace "host", "console"

svcconsole
```

```
iexplorer
logconsole
```

Other Operators

Windows PowerShell includes several other types of operators, including logical and type operators. Table 6-7 provides an overview of these additional operators.

TABLE 6-7 Logical and Type Operators in Windows PowerShell

OP	OPERATION & USAGE
–and	Logical AND True only when both statements are True. (5 –eq 5) –and (3 –eq 6) False
–or	Logical OR True only when either statement or both statements are True. (5 –eq 5) –or (3 –eq 6) True
–xor	Logical XOR True only when one of the statements is True and one is False. (5 –eq 5) –xor (3 –eq 6) True
–not, !	Logical NOT Negates the statement that follows it. True only when the statement is False. False only when the statement is True. –not (5 –eq 5) False ! (5 –eq 5) False
–is	Object equality Returns True only when the input is an instance of a specified .NET Framework type.

OP	OPERATION & USAGE
	(get-date) –is [datetime] True
–isnot	Object inequality Returns True only when the input is not an instance of a specified .NET Framework type. (get-date) –isnot [datetime] False
–as	Object conversion Converts the input to the specified .NET Framework type. "3/31/17" –as [datetime] Wednesday, March 31, 2017 12:00:00 AM
,	Array constructor Creates an array from the comma-separated values. $a = 1,2,4,6,4,2
..	Range operator Establishes a range of values. $a = 2..24
–band	Binary AND Performs a binary AND. –
–bor	Binary OR Performs a binary OR. –

OP	OPERATION & USAGE
–bnot	Binary NOT Performs a binary complement. –
–bxor	Binary XOR Performs a binary exclusive OR. –

One operator you should learn about is the special operator Is. You use Is to compare objects according to their .NET Framework type. If the objects are of the same type, the result of the comparison is True. If the objects are not of the same type, the result of the comparison is False.

Table 6-8 shows the expanded precedence order for all available operators. This precedence order takes into account all the possible combinations of operators and defines an order of evaluation.

TABLE 6-8 Extended Operator Precedence in Windows PowerShell

ORDER	OPERATION
1	Grouping ( ) { }
2	Command expansion @ $
3	Not !
4	Wildcard expansion [ ]
5	Dot sourcing .
6	Invoke &

ORDER	OPERATION
7	Increment ++, Decrement --
8	Unary + −
9	Multiplication *, Division /
10	Remainders %
11	Addition +, Subtraction −
12	Comparison operators
13	−and, −or
14	Pipelining |
15	Redirection > > >
16	Assignment =

Working with Variables and Values

Variables are placeholders for values. A value can be a string, a number, or an object. You can access this information later simply by referencing the variable name. With variables that store objects (from the output of commands), you can pass the stored information down the pipeline to other commands as if it were the output of the original command.

Your scripts and command text can use any of the available variables. By default, variables you create exist only in the current session and are lost when you exit or close the session. To maintain your variables, you must store them in a profile. For detailed information on profiles, see Chapter 3, "Managing Your PowerShell Environment."

In scripts, if configuration information doesn't need to be hard-coded, you should consider using variables to represent the information because this makes scripts easier to update and maintain. Additionally, you should try to define your variables in one place at the beginning of a script to make it easier to find and maintain variables.

PowerShell supports four classes of variables: automatic, preference, environment, and user-created variables. Unlike the command line, where variable values are stored as text strings, PowerShell stores values as either text strings or objects. Technically, a string is a type of object as well, and you'll learn more about strings in "Working with Strings" later in this chapter.

Variable Essentials

The following cmdlets are available for working with variables:

- **Get-Variable**   Lists all or specified variables set in the current session by name and value.

  ```
  Get-Variable [[-Name] VarNames] [AddtlParams]

  AddtlParams=
  [-Scope String] [-Exclude Strings] [-Include Strings]
  [-ValueOnly]
  ```

- **New-Variable**   Creates a new variable.

  ```
  New-Variable [[-Value] Object] [-Name] VarName [AddtlParams]

  AddtlParams=
  [-Description String] [-Force] [-Option None | ReadOnly |
  Constant | Private | AllScope] [-PassThru] [-Scope String]
  [-Visibility Public | Private]
  ```

- **Set-Variable**   Creates a new variable or changes the definition of an existing variable.

  ```
  Set-Variable [[-Value] Object] [-Name] VarNames [AddtlParams]

  AddtlParams=
  [-Description String] [-Exclude Strings] [-Force] [-Include
  Strings] [-Option None | ReadOnly | Constant | Private |
  ```

```
AllScope] [-PassThru] [-Scope String] [-Visibility Public |
Private]
```

- **Remove-Variable** Removes a variable and its value. Use the –Force parameter to remove a read-only variable.

```
Remove-Variable [-Name] VarNames [AddtlParams]

AddtlParams=
[-Scope String] [-Force] [-Exclude Strings] [-Include
Strings]
```

- **Clear-Variable** Deletes the value of a variable. The value of the variable is then set to NULL.

```
Clear-Variable [-Force] [-PassThru] [-Scope String] [-Exclude
Strings] [-Include Strings] [-Name] VarNames
```

Regardless of the class of variable you are working with, you reference variables by preceding the variable name with a dollar sign ($). This is true whether you are defining a new variable or trying to work with a value stored in an existing variable. The dollar sign helps distinguish variables from aliases, functions, cmdlets, and other elements you use with PowerShell. Table 6-9 provides an overview of the options for defining variables.

TABLE 6-9 Windows PowerShell Variable Syntaxes

SYNTAX	DESCRIPTION
$myVar = "Value"	Defines a variable with a standard name, which is prefixed by $ and can contain the alphanumeric characters (a to z, A to Z, and 0–9) and the underscore (_). Variable names are not case sensitive.
${my.var!!!!} = "Value"	Defines a variable with a nonstandard name, which is prefixed by $, is enclosed in curly braces, and can contain any character. If curly braces are part of the name, you must prevent substitution using the back apostrophe (`).
[type] $myVar = "Value"	Defines a strongly typed variable that ensures the variable can contain only data of the specified type. PowerShell throws an error if it cannot coerce the data into the declared type.

SYNTAX	DESCRIPTION
$SCOPE:$myVar = "Value"	Declares a variable with a specific scope. Scopes set the logical boundaries for variables. For more information, see "Managing Variable Scopes" later in the chapter.
New-Item Variable:\myVar –Value Value	Creates a new variable using the variable provider. For more on providers, see the "Using Providers" section in Chapter 3.
Get-Item Variable:\myVar Get-Variable myVar	Gets a variable using the variable provider or the Get-Variable cmdlet.
${path\filename.ext}	Defines a variable using the Get-Content and Set-Content syntax. If the path\filename.ext value points to a valid path, you can get and set the content of the item by reading and writing to the variable.

To define a variable, you must assign the variable a name and a value using the equals operator (=). Standard variable names are not case sensitive and can contain any combination of alphanumeric characters (a to z, A to Z, and 0–9) and the underscore (_) character. Following these rules, these are all valid and separate variables:

```
$myString = "String 1"
$myVar = "String 2"
$myObjects = "String 3"
$s = "String 4"
```

To access the value stored in a variable, you simply reference the variable name. For example, to display the contents of the $myString variable defined earlier, you type **$myString** at the PowerShell prompt, and you get the following output:

```
String 1
```

You can list available variables by typing **get-variable** at the PowerShell prompt. The output includes variables you've defined as well as current automatic and preference variables. Because environment variables are accessed through the environment provider, you must reference $env: and then the name of the variable you want to work with. For example, to display the value of the %UserName% variable, you must enter **$env:username**.

Variables can have nonstandard names that include special characters, such as dashes, periods, colons, and parentheses, but you must enclose nonstandard variable names in curly braces. Enclosing the variable name in curly braces forces PowerShell to interpret the variable name literally. Following these rules, these are all valid and separate variables:

```
${my.var} = "String 1"
${my-var} = "String 2"
${my:var} = "String 3"
${my(var)} = "String 4"
```

To refer to a variable name that includes braces, you must enclose the variable name in braces and use the back apostrophe character (`) to force PowerShell to interpret the brace characters literally when used as part of the variable name. For example, you can create a variable named "my{var}string" with a value of "String 5" by typing

```
${my`{var`}string} = "String 5"
```

In previous examples, we assigned string values to variables, but you can just as easily assign numeric, array, and object values. Numeric values are values entered as numbers rather than strings. Arrays are data structures for storing collections of like-typed data items. The values stored in an array can be delimited with a comma or initialized using the range operator (..). A collection of objects can be obtained by assigning the output of a cmdlet to a variable. Consider the following examples:

```
$myFirstNumber = 10
$mySecondNumber = 500
$myFirstArray = 0,1,2,3,4,8,13,21
$mySecondArray = 1..9
$myString = "Hello!"
$myObjectCollection1 = get-service
$myObjectCollection2 = get-process -name svchost
```

Here, you create variables to store integer values, arrays of values, strings, and collections of objects. You can then work with the values stored in the variable just as you would the original values. For example, you can count the number of service objects stored in $myObjectCollection1 by typing the following:

```
$myObjectCollection1.Count
```

You even can sort the service objects by status and display the sorted output by typing the following command:

```
$myObjectCollection1 | sort-object -property status
```

You aren't limited to values of these data types. You can assign any .NET Framework data type as a value, including the common data types listed in Table 6-10.

TABLE 6-10 Data Type Aliases

DATA TYPE ALIAS	DATA TYPE
[adsi]	An Active Directory Services Interface (ADSI) object
[array]	An array of values
[bool]	A Boolean value (True/False)
[byte]	An 8-bit unsigned integer in the range 0 to 255
[char]	A Unicode 16-bit character
[datetime]	A datetime value
[decimal]	A 128-bit decimal value
[double]	A double-precision, 64-bit floating-point number

DATA TYPE ALIAS	DATA TYPE
[float]	A single-precision, 32-bit floating-point number
[hashtable]	An associative array defined in a hashtable object
[int]	A 32-bit signed integer
[long]	A 64-bit signed integer
[psobject]	A common object type that can encapsulate any base object
[regex]	A regular expression
[scriptblock]	A series of commands
[single]	A single-precision, 32-bit floating-point number
[string]	A fixed-length string value with Unicode characters
[wmi]	A Windows Management Instrumentation (WMI) object
[xml]	An XML object

Variables also can be used to store the results of evaluated expressions. Consider the following example and result:

```
$theFirstResult = 10 + 10 + 10

$theSecondResult = $(if($theFirstResult -gt 25) {$true} else
{$false})

write-host "$theFirstResult is greater than 25? `t
$theSecondResult"
```

```
30 is greater than 25?        True
```

Here, Windows PowerShell evaluates the first expression and stores the result in the first variable. Next PowerShell evaluates the second expression and stores the result in the second variable. The expression determines whether the first variable is greater than 25. If it is, PowerShell sets the second variable to True. Otherwise, PowerShell sets the second variable to False. Finally, PowerShell displays output to the console containing the results.

In these examples, the first variable is defined as the Integer data type, and the second is defined as the Boolean data type. Generally, if you use whole numbers (such as 3 or 5) with a variable, PowerShell creates the variable as an Integer. Variables with values that use decimal points, such as 6.87 or 3.2, are generally assigned as Doubles—that is, double-precision, floating-point values. Variables with values entered with a mixture of alphabetical and numeric characters, such as Hello or S35, are created as Strings.

In PowerShell, you use Boolean values quite frequently. Whenever PowerShell evaluates variables as part of a Boolean expression, such as in an If statement, PowerShell maps the result to a Boolean representation. A Boolean value is always either True or False, and it can be represented literally using the values $true for True or $false for False.

Table 6-11 shows examples of items and results and how they are represented as Booleans by PowerShell. Note that a reference to any object is represented as True whereas a reference to $null is represented as False.

TABLE 6-11 Results Represented as Boolean Values

ITEM OR RESULT	BOOLEAN REPRESENTATION
$true	True
$false	False
$null	False

ITEM OR RESULT	BOOLEAN REPRESENTATION
Object reference	True
Nonzero number	True
Zero	False
Nonempty string	True
Empty string	False
Nonempty array	True
Empty array	False
Empty associative array	True
Nonempty associative array	True

Assigning and Converting Data Types

You can directly assign values without declaring the data type because PowerShell has the built-in capability to automatically determine the data type. If you ever have a question about a variable's data type, you can display the data type using the following syntax:

```
VariableName.GetType()
```

where *VariableName* is the actual name of the variable as shown in the following example and sample output:

```
$myFirstNumber.GetType()
```

```
IsPublic IsSerial Name                    BaseType
-------- -------- ----                    --------
True     True     Int32                   System.ValueType
```

Note that the base type is listed as System.ValueType, and the name is listed as Int32. Based on this output, you know the base type for the variable is a valid type in the System namespace and that the specific value type is Int32, meaning a 32-bit integer value.

Although the easiest way to declare a variable type is to use an alias, you also can declare variable types using the following:

- Fully qualified class names, such as [System.Array], [System.String], or [System.Diagnostics.Service]
- Class names under the System namespace, such as [Array], [String], or [Diagnostics.Service]

Be careful though: PowerShell throws an error if it cannot coerce the data into the specified data type. This is why you'll typically want to allow PowerShell to determine the data type for you. That way, you don't have to worry about PowerShell throwing errors if data cannot be coerced into a specified data type. However, after the data type is set, PowerShell tries to coerce any subsequent values you add to a variable to be of this type and throws an error if data types are mismatched. Consider the following example:

```
$myNumber = 52

$myNumber += "William"
```

Here, you create a variable and assign an integer value of 52. Next, you try to add a string value to the existing value using the increment operator (+=). This causes PowerShell to throw the following type mismatch error:

```
Cannot convert value "William" to type "System.Int32". Error:
"Input string was not in a correct format."
At line:1 char:1
+ $myNumber += "William"
+ ~~~~~~~~~~~~~~~~~~~~~~~
    + CategoryInfo          : InvalidArgument: (:) [],
RuntimeException
    + FullyQualifiedErrorId : InvalidCastFromStringToInteger
```

This error occurs because PowerShell cannot automatically convert the string value to a numeric value. However, in other cases, PowerShell silently converts value types for you. Consider the following example:

```
$myNumber = "William"
$myNumber += 52
```

Here, you create a variable and assign a string value. Next, you try to add the numeric value 52 to the existing string value using the increment operator (+=). This causes PowerShell to silently convert a numeric value to a string, and the result is that the value of $myNumber is then set to "William52".

When you create variables, you can specify the value type using any of the data type aliases listed previously in Table 6-10. These data type aliases are used in the same way whenever you declare a data type in PowerShell.

In the following example, you declare the data type as a 32-bit integer, specify the variable name as $myNumber, and assign a value of 10:

```
[int]$myNumber = 10
```

This creates a strongly typed variable and ensures that the variable can contain only the data of the type you declare. PowerShell throws an error if it cannot coerce the data to this type when you assign it. For more information about data types, see the "Object Types" section in Chapter 8.

To explicitly assign a number as a long integer or decimal, you can use the suffixes L and D, respectively. Here are examples:

```
$myLongInt = 52432424L
$myDecimal = 2.2425D
```

Windows PowerShell also supports scientific notation. For example,

```
$mathPi = 3141592653e-9
```

sets the value for $mathPi as 3.141592653.

> **TIP**   In Windows PowerShell, you can reference the mathematical constants Pi and E via the static properties of the [System.Math] class.

> [System.Math]::Pi equals 3.14159265358979. [System.Math]::E equals 2.71828182845905.

You can enter hexadecimal numbers using the 0x prefix, and PowerShell stores the hexadecimal number as an integer. If you enter the following statement

```
$ErrorCode = 0xAEB4
```

PowerShell converts the hexadecimal value AEB4 and then stores that value as 44724.

PowerShell does not natively support other number bases. However, you can use the [Convert] class in the .NET Framework to perform many types of data conversions. The [Convert] class supports the static conversion methods shown in Table 6-12.

TABLE 6-12 Commonly Used Static Methods of the [Convert] Class

STATIC METHOD	DESCRIPTION
ToBase64CharArray()	Converts the value to a base64 character array
ToBase64String()	Converts the value to a base64 string
ToBoolean()	Converts the value to a Boolean
ToByte()	Converts the value to an 8-bit unsigned integer
ToChar()	Converts the value to a Unicode 16-bit char
ToDateTime()	Converts the value to a datetime value
ToDecimal()	Converts the value to a decimal value
ToDouble()	Converts the value to a double-precision, 64-bit floating-point number

STATIC METHOD	DESCRIPTION
ToInt16()	Converts the value to a 16-bit integer
ToInt32()	Converts the value to a 32-bit integer
ToInt64()	Converts the value to a 64-bit integer
ToSByte()	Converts the value to an 8-bit signed integer
ToSingle()	Converts the value to a single-precision, 32-bit floating-point number
ToString()	Converts the value to a string
ToUInt16()	Converts the value to an unsigned 16-bit integer
ToUInt32()	Converts the value to an unsigned 32-bit integer
ToUInt64()	Converts the value to an unsigned 64-bit integer

You can use the [Convert] class methods to convert to and from binary, octal, decimal, and hexadecimal values. The following example converts the binary value to a 32-bit integer:

```
$myBinary = [Convert]::ToInt32("1011111011110001", 2)
```

The result is 48881. The following example converts an octal value to a 32-bit integer:

```
$myOctal = [Convert]::ToInt32("7452", 8)
```

The result is 3882. The following example converts a hexadecimal value to a 32-bit integer:

```
$myHex = [Convert]::ToInt32("FEA07E", 16)
```

The result is 16687230. You can just as easily convert an integer value to binary, octal, or hexadecimal. The following example takes the value 16687230 and converts it to a string containing a hexadecimal value:

```
$myString = [Convert]::ToString(16687230, 16)
```

The result is "FEA07E".

Although PowerShell can convert between some variable types, you might sometimes want to force PowerShell to use a variable value as a string rather than another data type. To do this, you can use the ToString() method to convert a variable value to a string. This works with Boolean, Byte, Char, and Datetime objects, as well as any of the numeric data types. It does not work with most other data types.

To convert a value to a string, just pass the value to the ToString() method as shown in this example and sample output:

```
$myNumber = 505
$myString = $myNumber.ToString()
$myString.GetType()
IsPublic IsSerial Name                 BaseType
-------- -------- ----                 --------
True     True     String               System.Object
```

In the [System.Datetime] and [System.Math] classes, you find other useful static methods and properties. Table 6-13 lists the class members you'll use most often.

TABLE 6-13 Commonly Used Static Members of [DateTime] and [Math] Classes

CLASS/MEMBERS	DESCRIPTION & SYNTAX	
[Datetime]		
Compare()	Compares two date objects. Returns 0 if they are equal and –1 otherwise. [Datetime]::Compare(d1,d2)	

CLASS/MEMBERS	DESCRIPTION & SYNTAX	
DaysInMonth()	Returns the number of days in a given year and month. [Datetime]::DaysInMonth(year, month)	
Equals	Determines if two date objects are equal. Returns True if they are equal. [Datetime]::Equals(d1,d2)	
IsLeapYear	Returns True if the specified year is a leap year. [Datetime]::IsLeapYear(year)	
Now	Returns the current date and time. [Datetime]::Now	
Today	Returns the current date as of 12:00 A.M. [Datetime]::Today	
[MATH]		
Abs()	Returns the absolute value. [Math]::Abs(value1)	
Acos()	Returns the arccosine of the value. [Math]::Acos(value1)	
Asin()	Returns the arcsine of the value. [Math]::Asin(value1)	
Atan()	Returns the arctangent of the value. [Math]::Atan(value1)	

CLASS/MEMBERS	DESCRIPTION & SYNTAX
Atan2()	Returns the inverse arccosine of the value. [Math]::Atan2(value1)
BigMul()	Returns the multiple as a 64-bit integer. [Math]::BigMul(val1,val2)
Ceiling()	Returns the mathematical ceiling of the value. [Math]::Ceiling(val1)
Cos()	Returns the cosine of the value. [Math]::Cos(val1)
Cosh()	Returns the inverse cosine of the value. [Math]::Cosh(val1)
DivRem()	Returns the dividend remainder for value1 / value2. [Math]::DivRem(val1,val2)
Equals()	Evaluates whether object1 equals object2. [Math]::Equals(obj1,obj2)
Exp()	Returns the exponent. [Math]::Exp(value1)
Floor()	Returns the mathematical floor of the value. [Math]::Floor(val1)
Log()	Returns the Log of the value. [Math]::Log(value1)

CLASS/MEMBERS	DESCRIPTION & SYNTAX
Log10()	Returns the Log10 of the value. [Math]::Log10(value1)
Max()	Returns the larger of two values. [Math]::Max(val1,val2)
Min()	Returns the smaller of two values. [Math]::Min(val1,val2)
Pow()	Returns the value to the power of the exponent. [Math]::Pow(val1,val2)
Round()	Returns the rounded value. [Math]::Round(val1)
Sign()	Returns a signed 16-bit integer value. [Math]::Sign(val1)
Sin()	Returns the sine of the value. [Math]::Sin(value1)
Sinh()	Returns the inverse sine of the value. [Math]::Sinh(value1)
Sqrt()	Returns the square root of the value. [Math]::Sqrt(value1)
Tan()	Returns the tangent of the value. [Math]::Tan(value1)

CLASS/MEMBERS	DESCRIPTION & SYNTAX
Tanh()	Returns the inverse tangent of the value. [Math]::Tanh(value1)
Truncate()	Truncates the decimal value. [Math]::Truncate(value1)
E	Returns the mathematical constant E. [Math]::E
Pi	Returns the mathematical constant Pi. [Math]::Pi

Table 6-14 provides an overview of the instance methods and properties of the String object. You'll use the String object often when working with values in PowerShell.

TABLE 6-14 Commonly Used Instance Methods and Properties of String Objects

INSTANCE MEMBER	DESCRIPTION & USAGE
Length	Returns the character length of the string. $s.Length
Contains()	Returns True if string2 is contained within string1. $s.Contains("string2")
EndsWith()	Returns True if string1 ends with string2. $s.EndsWith("string2")
Insert()	Inserts string2 into string1 at the specified character position.

INSTANCE MEMBER	DESCRIPTION & USAGE
	$s.Insert(0,"string2") $s.Insert($s.Length,"string2")
Remove()	Removes characters from string1 based on a starting position and length. If no length is provided, all characters after the starting position are removed. $s.Remove(5,3) $s.Remove(5)
Replace()	Replaces occurrences of substr1 in the string with the substr2 value. $s.Replace("this","that")
StartsWith()	Returns True if string1 starts with string2. $s.StartsWith("string2")
SubString()	Gets a substring from string1 based on a starting position and length. If no length is provided, all characters after the starting position are returned. $s.Substring(3,5) $s.Substring(3)
ToLower()	Converts the string to lowercase letters. $s.ToLower()
ToString()	Converts an object to a string. $s.ToString()
ToUpper()	Converts the string to uppercase letters. $s.ToUpper()

Managing Variable Scopes

The scope of a variable determines its logical boundaries. You can set variable scope as global, local, script, or private. The scopes exist in a logical hierarchy in which scope information is accessible downward in this order:

global > script/local > private

Following this, you can see that the local and script scopes can read information from the global scope, but the global scope cannot read a local or script scope. Further, private scopes can read information from higher-level scopes, but other scopes cannot read the contents of a private scope.

> **REAL WORLD** Scope applies to aliases, functions, and PowerShell drives as well as to variables. You can think of the global scope as the parent or root scope and script/local scripts as child scopes of the global scope. Child scopes can always read information from parent scopes. Technically speaking, variables, aliases, and functions in a parent scope are not part of the child scope. A child scope does not inherit the variables, aliases, or functions from the parent scope. However, a child scope can view the variables, aliases, or functions from the parent scope, and it can change these items in the parent scope by explicitly specifying the parent scope.
>
> The default scope for a script is a script scope that exists only for that script. The default scope for a function is a local scope that exists only for that function, even if the function is defined in a script.
>
> Regardless of whether you are working with variables, aliases, functions, or PowerShell drives, scopes work the same. An item you include in a scope is visible in the scope in which it was created and any child scopes, unless you explicitly make it private. An item in a particular scope can be changed only in that scope, unless you explicitly specify a different scope. If you create an item in a child scope and that item already exists in another scope, the original item is not accessible in the child scope, but it is not overridden or changed in the original (parent) scope.

You can create a new scope by running a script or function, by defining a script block, by creating a local or remote session, or by starting a new instance of

PowerShell. When you create a new scope through a script, function, script block, or nesting of instances, the scope is a child scope of the original (parent) scope. However, when you create a new session, the session is not a child scope of the original scope. The session starts with its own global scope, and that global scope is independent from the original scope.

You can explicitly or implicitly set the scope of a variable. You explicitly set scope by adding the Global, Local, Script, or Private keyword prefix to the variable name. The following example creates a global variable:

```
$Global:myVar = 55
```

You implicitly set scope whenever you define a variable at the prompt, in a script, or in a function. A variable with an implicit scope resides in the scope in which it is defined.

The default scope is the current scope and is determined as follows:

- Global when defined interactively at the PowerShell prompt
- Script when defined outside functions or script blocks in a script
- Local within functions, script blocks, or anywhere else

The global scope applies to an entire PowerShell instance. Because data defined in the global scope is inherited by all child scopes, this means any commands, functions, or scripts that you run can make use of variables defined in the global scope.

Global scopes are not shared across instances of PowerShell. With regard to the PowerShell console, this means the variables you define in one console are not available in another console (unless you define them in that console session). With regard to the PowerShell application, this means variables you define in one tab are not available in another tab (unless you define them in that tab session).

Local scopes are created automatically each time a function, script, or filter runs. A local scope can read information from the global scope, but it can make changes to global information only by explicitly declaring the scope. After a function, script, or filter has finished running, the information in the related local scope is discarded.

To learn more about scopes, consider the following example and sample output:

```
function numservices {$serv = get-service}
numservices
write-host "The number of services is: `t" $serv.count

The number of services is: 0
```

Here, $serv is created as a variable inside the numservices function. As a result, when you run the function, a local variable instance is created. When you then try to access the $s variable in the global scope, the variable has no value. In contrast, if you explicitly declare the variable as global, you can access the variable in the global scope as shown in the following example and sample output:

```
function numservices {$Global:serv = get-service}
numservices
write-host "The number of services is: `t" $serv.count

The number of services is:          164
```

Script scopes are created whenever a script runs. Only commands in a script run in the script scope; to these commands, the script scope is the local scope. As functions in a script run in their own local scope, any variables set in a script function are not accessible to the script itself. To remedy this, you can set the scope of variables defined in a script function explicitly as shown in this example:

```
function numservices {$Script:serv1 = get-service}
numservices
write-host "The number of services is: `t" $serv1.count
```

Normally, when a function or script finishes running, the related scope and all related information is discarded. However, you can use dot sourcing to tell PowerShell to load a function's or script's scope into the calling parent's scope rather than creating a new local scope for the function or script. To do this, simply prefix the function or script name with a period (.) when running the function or script, as shown in this example:

```
. c:\scripts\runtasks.ps1
```

The final scope type you can use is the private scope. You must create privately scoped items explicitly. Because any information in a private scope is not available to any other scopes, including child scopes, a privately scoped variable is available only in the scope in which it is created. The following example and sample output shows this:

```
function numservices {$Private:serv = get-service

write-host "The number of services is: `t" $serv.count

 &{write-host "Again, the number of services is: `t"
$serv.count}

}
numservices


The number of services is:      164
Again, the number of services is:
```

Here, you create a function with a private variable and then define a script block within the function. Within the function, you have access to the private variable, and this is why you can write the number of services when you call the function. Because the script block automatically runs in its own local scope, you cannot access the private variable in the script block. This is why you cannot write the number of services from within the script block when you call the function.

Automatic, Preference, and Environment Variables

In addition to user-created variables, PowerShell supports automatic, preference, and environment variables. Automatic variables are fixed and used to store state information. Preference variables are changeable and used to store working values for PowerShell configuration settings. Environment variables store the working environment for the current user and the operating system.

Table 6-15 lists the common automatic variables in PowerShell. You'll use many of these variables when you are working with PowerShell, especially $_, $Args, $Error, $Input, and $MyInvocation.

TABLE 6-15 Common Automatic Variables in Windows PowerShell

AUTOMATIC VARIABLE	DESCRIPTION
$$	Stores the last token in the last line received by the PowerShell session.
$?	Stores the execution status of the last operation as TRUE if the last operation succeeded or as FALSE if it failed.
$^	Stores the first token in the last line received by the session.
$_	Stores the current object in the pipeline object set. Use this variable in commands that perform an action on every object or on selected objects in a pipeline.
$Args	Stores an array of the undeclared parameters, parameter values, or both that are passed to a function, script, or script block.
$ConsoleFileName	Stores the path of the console file (.psc1) that was most recently used in the session.
$Error	Stores an array of error objects that represent the most recent errors. $Error[0] references the most recent error in the array.
$ExecutionContext	Stores an EngineIntrinsics object that represents the execution context of the Windows PowerShell host.
$False	Stores FALSE. It can be used instead of the string "false".
$ForEach	Stores the enumerator of a ForEach-Object loop.
$Home	Stores the full path of the user's home directory.

AUTOMATIC VARIABLE	DESCRIPTION
$Host	Stores an object that represents the current host application.
$Input	Stores the input that is passed to a function or script block. The $Input variable is case sensitive. When the Process block is completed, the value of $Input is NULL. If the function does not have a Process block, the value of $Input is available to the End block, and it stores all the input to the function.
$LastExitCode	Stores the exit code of the last Windows-based program that was run.
$Matches	Stores a hash table of any string values that were matched when you use the –Match operator.
$MyInvocation	Stores an object with information about the current command, including the run path and file name for scripts.
$NestedPromptLevel	Stores the current prompt level. A value of 0 (zero) indicates the original prompt level. The value is incremented when you enter a nested level and decremented when you exit nested levels.
$NULL	Stores a NULL or empty value. It can be used instead of the string "NULL".
$PID	Stores the process identifier (PID) of the process that is hosting the current Windows PowerShell session.
$Profile	Stores the full path of the Windows PowerShell profile for the current user and the current host application.
$PSBoundParameters	Stores a hash table of the active parameters and their current values.
$PsCulture	Stores the name of the culture setting currently in use in the operating system.

AUTOMATIC VARIABLE	DESCRIPTION
$PSDebugContext	Stores information about the debugging environment (if applicable). Otherwise, it stores a NULL value.
$PsHome	Stores the full path of the installation directory for Windows PowerShell.
$PsUICulture	Stores the name of the user interface (UI) culture that is currently in use in the operating system.
$PsVersionTable	Stores a read-only hash table with the following items: PSVersion (the Windows PowerShell version number), BuildVersion (the build number of the current version), CLRVersion (the version of the common language runtime), and PSCompatibleVersions (versions of Windows PowerShell that are compatible with the current version).
$Pwd	Stores a path object representing the full path of the current working directory.
$ShellID	Stores the identifier of the current shell.
$This	Defines a script property or script method within a script block. Refers to the object that is being extended.
$True	Stores TRUE. It can be used instead of the string "true".

You use $_ with the Where-Object cmdlet to perform an action on every object or on selected objects in a pipeline. The basic syntax is

```
where-object {$_.PropertyName -ComparisonOp "Value"}
```

where *PropertyName* is the name of the property to examine, *–ComparisonOp* specifies the type of comparison to perform, and *Value* sets the value to compare—for example:

```
get-process | where-object {$_.Name -match "svchost"}
```

Here, you use $_ to examine the Name property of each object passed in the pipeline. If the Name property is set to "svchost", you pass the related object along the pipeline.

You can extend this example using a regular expression, such as:

```
get-process | where-object {$_.Name -match "^s.*"}
```

Here, you examine the Name property of each object passed in the pipeline. If the Name property begins with the letter S, you pass the related object along the pipeline. You can just as easily use any other comparison operator listed previously in Table 6-4, such as –eq, –ne, –gt, –lt,–contains, –notcontains, –like, or –notlike.

Another useful automatic variable is $Error. You use $Error to list all error objects for the current session and $Error[0] to access the most recent error object. Simply type **$Error** or **$Error[0]**. Because errors are represented in objects, you can format the properties of error objects as you would any other output, such as

```
$error[0] | format-list -property * -force
```

Error objects have the following properties:

- **CategoryInfo**   Indicates the category under which an error is classified, such as InvalidArgument or PSArgumentException
- **Exception**   Provides detailed information about the error that occurred
- **FullyQualifiedErrorId**   Identifies the exact error that occurred, such as Argument
- **InvocationInfo**   Provides detailed information about the command that caused an error
- **PipelineIterationInfo**   Provides detailed information about the pipeline iteration
- **PSMessageDetails**   Provides PowerShell message details, if applicable
- **TargetObject**   Indicates the object being operated on

You can access any of these properties via a specified error object. To list detailed information about the command that caused the last error, you can use the InvocationInfo property as shown in the following example and sample output:

```
$currError = $error[0]
$currError

$currError.InvocationInfo
MyCommand          : Sort-Object
BoundParameters    : {}
UnboundArguments   : {}
ScriptLineNumber   : 1
OffsetInLine       : 25
ScriptName         :
Line               : $p | sort-object -status
PositionMessage    :
                     At line:1 char:25
                     + $p | sort-object -status <<<<
InvocationName     : sort-object
PipelineLength     : 0
PipelinePosition   : 0
ExpectingInput     : False
CommandOrigin      : Internal
```

You can clear all the errors in the current sessions by entering the following command:

```
$error.clear()
```

Another handy automatic variable is $Args. You can access command-line arguments using the array stored in this variable—for example:

```
$argCount = $args.Count
$firstArg = $args[0]
$secondArg = $args[1]
$lastArg = $args[$args.Count -1]
```

Here, you determine the number of arguments passed in the command line using $args.Count. You get the first argument using $args[0], the second argument using $args[1], and the last argument using $args[$args.Count -1].

Data being passed to a function or script block via the pipeline is stored in the $Input variable. This variable is a .NET Framework enumerator. With enumerators, you can access the input stream but not an arbitrary element as you can with an array. After you process the input stream, you must call the Reset() method on the $Input enumerator before you can process the elements again. One way to access the input stream is in a For Each loop, such as

```
foreach($element in $input) { "The input was: `t $element" }
```

Or you can store the input element in an array, such as

```
$iArray = @($input)
```

You can access information about the context under which you are running a script using $MyInvocation. In a script, you can access detailed information about the current command through $MyInvocation.MyCommand. To access the path and file name of the script, use $MyInvocation.MyCommand.Path. Use $MyInvocation.MyCommand.Name to identify the name of a function. Use $MyInvocation.ScriptName to display the name of the script.

Table 6-16 provides a summary of the common preference variables. As you use these variables to customize how PowerShell works, you should familiarize yourself with them. Some of these variables were discussed previously in the "Writing to Output Streams" section in Chapter 2, "Getting the Most from Windows PowerShell."

TABLE 6-16 Common Preference Variables in Windows PowerShell

PREFERENCE VARIABLE	DESCRIPTION & DEFAULT VALUE
$ConfirmPreference	Controls whether cmdlet actions request confirmation from the user before they are performed. Acceptable values are **High** (actions with a high risk are confirmed), **Medium** (actions with a medium or high risk are confirmed), **Low** (actions with a low, medium, or high risk are confirmed), or **None** (no actions are confirmed; use the –Confirm parameter to request confirmation). High
$DebugPreference	Controls how PowerShell responds to debugging messages. SilentlyContinue

PREFERENCE VARIABLE	DESCRIPTION & DEFAULT VALUE
$ErrorAction Preference	Controls how PowerShell responds to an error that does not stop the cmdlet processing. Continue
$ErrorView	Controls the display format of error messages in PowerShell. Acceptable values are **NormalView** (the detailed normal view) or **CategoryView** (a streamlined view). NormalView
$FormatEnumerationLimit	Controls how many enumerated items are included in a grouped display. Acceptable values are **Integers**. 4
$LogCommand HealthEvent	Controls whether errors and exceptions in command initialization and processing are written to the PowerShell event log. Acceptable values are **$true** (logged) or **$false** (not logged). $false
$LogCommand LifecycleEvent	Controls whether PowerShell logs the starting and stopping of commands and command pipelines and security exceptions in command discovery. Acceptable values are **$true** (logged) or **$false** (not logged). $false
$LogEngine HealthEvent	Controls whether PowerShell logs errors and failures of sessions. Acceptable values are **$true** (logged) or **$false** (not logged). $true
$LogEngine LifecycleEvent	Controls whether PowerShell logs the opening and closing of sessions. Acceptable values are **$true** (logged) or **$false** (not logged). $true

PREFERENCE VARIABLE	DESCRIPTION & DEFAULT VALUE
$LogProvider HealthEvent	Controls whether PowerShell logs provider errors, such as read and write errors, lookup errors, and invocation errors. Acceptable values are **$true** (logged) or **$false** (not logged). Default value: $true.
$LogProvider LifecycleEvent	Controls whether PowerShell logs adding and removing of PowerShell providers. Acceptable values are **$true** (logged) or **$false** (not logged). Default value: $true.
$MaximumAlias Count	Specifies how many aliases are permitted in a PowerShell session. Valid values are **1024–32768**. Count aliases using (get-alias).count. Default value: 4096.
$MaximumDrive Count	Specifies how many PowerShell drives are permitted in a session. This includes file system drives and data stores that are exposed by providers and appear as drives. Valid values are **1024–32768**. Count drives using (get-psdrive).count. Default value: 4096.
$MaximumError Count	Specifies how many errors are saved in the error history for the session. Valid values are **256–32768**. Objects that represent each retained error are stored in the $Error automatic variable. Count errors using $Error.count. Default value: 256.
$MaximumFunction Count	Specifies how many functions are permitted in a given session. Valid values are **1024–32768**. Count functions using (get-childitem function:).count. Default value: 4096.
$MaximumHistory Count	Specifies how many commands are saved in the command history for the current session. Valid values are **1–32768**. Count commands saved using (get-history).count. Default value: 4096.
$MaximumVariable Count	Specifies how many variables are permitted in a given session, including automatic variables, preference variables, and user-created variables. Valid values are **1024–32768**. Count variables using (get-variable).count. Default value: 4096.

PREFERENCE VARIABLE	DESCRIPTION & DEFAULT VALUE
$OFS	Sets the Output Field Separator. This determines the character that separates the elements of an array when the array is converted to a string. Valid values are **Any string**, such as "+" instead of " ". Default value: " ".
$OutputEncoding	Sets the character encoding method used by PowerShell when it sends text to other applications. Valid values are **ASCIIEncoding**, **SBCSCodePageEncoding**, **UTF7Encoding**, **UTF8Encoding**, **UTF32Encoding**, and **UnicodeEncoding**. Default value: ASCIIEncoding.
$ProgressPreference	Specifies how PowerShell responds to progress updates generated by Write-Progress. Valid values are **Stop** (displays an error and stops executing), **Inquire** (prompts for permission to continue), **Continue** (displays the progress bar and continues), and **SilentlyContinue** (executes the command but does not display the progress bar). Default value: Continue.
$PSDefault ParameterValues	Allows you to specify default values for the parameters of any cmdlet. Enter **help about_Parameters_Default_Values** for more details.
$PSEmailServer	Specifies the default email server for messages.
$PSModuleAuto LoadingPreference	Controls whether PowerShell modules are imported automatically. By default, modules are imported automatically. If you specify a value of None, modules always must be imported manually using Import-Module. Default value: All.
$PSSessionApplication Name	Specifies the default application that is used when you identify a remote computer by an HTTP endpoint. Internet Information Services (IIS) forwards requests to WSMAN by default. Default value: WSMAN.

PREFERENCE VARIABLE	DESCRIPTION & DEFAULT VALUE
$PSSession ConfigurationName	Specifies the default session configuration for remote sessions. The value must be a name that appears in the WinRM custom remote session table and that is associated with the executable file that runs the session and a URI for the session resource. Default value: Microsoft.PowerShell.
$PSSessionOption	Sets option preferences for remote sessions that override the system default values.
$VerbosePreference	Controls how PowerShell responds to verbose messages. Default value: SilentlyContinue.
$WarningPreference	Controls how PowerShell responds to warning messages. Default value: Continue.
$WhatIfPreference	Specifies whether the –WhatIf parameter is automatically enabled for every command that supports it. When –WhatIf is enabled, the cmdlet reports the expected effect of the command, but it does not execute the command. Valid values are **0** (disabled) and **1** (enabled). Default value: $false.

You can view the value of automatic and preference variables simply by typing their name at the PowerShell prompt. For example, to see the current value of the $pshome variable, type **$pshome** at the PowerShell prompt. Although you cannot change the value of automatic variables, you can change the value of preference variables. To do so, you use the basic assignment syntax as with user-created variables. For example, if you want to set $WarningPreference to SilentlyContinue, you can do this by typing the following command:

```
$warningpreference = "silentlycontinue"
```

With environment variables, you must work within the context of the environment provider. One way to do this is to reference the $env: provider drive and then reference the name of the variable, such as

```
$env:logonserver
```

You also can get or set the location with respect to the env: provider drive. For example, if you set the location to the env: provider drive as shown in this example

```
set-location env:
```

the PowerShell prompt changes to

```
PS Env:\>
```

You can then work with any or all environment variables. To list all environment variables you type the following command:

```
get-childitem
```

To list a particular environment variable, you use Get-ChildItem and type the variable name or part of the variable name with wildcards, such as

```
get-childitem userdomain
get-childitem user*
```

When you are finished working with the environment provider, you can return to the file system drive you were using by typing **set-location** and the drive designator, such as

```
set-location c:
```

Another way to work with the environment provider is to use the Get-Item cmdlet to examine its path values. If you do this, you don't need to switch to the environment provider drive. For example, regardless of which provider drive you are working with, you can type the following command to list all environment variables:

```
get-item -path env:*
```

You also can get an environment variable by name:

```
get-item -path env:username
```

Or you can get it by using a wildcard:

```
get-item -path env:user*
```

You can change environment variables using the Set-Item cmdlet. The basic syntax is

```
set-item -path env:VariableName -value NewValue
```

where *VariableName* is the name of the environment variable you want to change, and *NewValue* sets the desired value, such as

```
set-item -path env:homedrive -value D:
```

You also can change the value of an environment variable using simple assignment, such as

```
$env:homedrive = D:
```

When you change environment variables using either technique, the change is made only for the current session. To permanently change environment variables, you can use the Setx command-line utility.

Working with Strings

Although we've used strings in some previous examples, we haven't really talked about what exactly a string is and isn't. A string is a series of alphanumeric or non-alphanumeric characters. PowerShell has several parsing rules for strings, and these rules modify the way values are handled. You need a good understanding of how strings are parsed to be successful with PowerShell, whether you enter commands at the PowerShell prompt or use PowerShell scripts.

Single-Quoted and Double-Quoted Strings

You use quotation marks to denote the beginning and ending of literal string expressions. You can enclose strings in single quotation marks (' ') or double quotation marks (" "). However, PowerShell parses values within single-quoted strings and double-quoted strings differently.

When you enclose a string in single-quotation marks, the string is passed to the command exactly as you type it. No substitution is performed. Consider the following example and output:

```
$varA = 200
Write-Host 'The value of $varA is $varA.'
```

The output of this command is

```
The value $varA is $varA.
```

Similarly, expressions in single-quoted strings are not evaluated. They are interpreted as literals—for example:

```
'The value of $(2+3) is 5.'
```

The output of this command is

```
The value of $(2+3) is 5.
```

When you enclose a string in double quotation marks, variable names that are preceded by a dollar sign ($) are replaced with the variable's value before the string is passed to the command for processing. Consider the following example:

```
$varA = 200
Write-Host "The value of $varA is $varA."
```

The output of this command is

```
The value 200 is 200.
```

To prevent the substitution of a variable value in a double-quoted string, use the back apostrophe character (`), which serves as the escape character as well as the line-continuation character. Consider following example:

```
$varA = 200
Write-Host "The value of `$varA is $varA."
```

Here, the back apostrophe character that precedes the first variable reference prevents Windows PowerShell from replacing the variable name with its value. This means the output is

```
The value $varA is 200.
```

Additionally, in a double-quoted string, expressions are evaluated, and the result is inserted in the string. Consider the following example:

```
"The value of $(100+100) is 200."
```

The output of this command is

```
The value of 200 is 200.
```

You can make double quotation marks appear in a string by enclosing the entire string in single quotation marks or by using double quotation marks, such as

```
'He said, "Hello, Bob"'
```

or

```
"He said, ""Hello, Bob"""
```

You can include a single quotation mark in a single-quoted string as well. Simply use a second single quote, such as

```
'He won''t go to the store.'
```

Finally, you can use the back apostrophe (`) character to force PowerShell to interpret a single quotation mark or a double quotation mark literally, such as

```
"You use a double quotation mark (`") with expandable strings."
```

Escape Codes and Wildcards

In several previous examples, we used the back apostrophe (`) as an escape character to force PowerShell to interpret a single quotation mark, a double quotation mark, or a variable literally. When an escape character precedes a single or double quotation mark, Windows PowerShell interprets the single or double quotation mark as a literal character, not as a string delimiter. When an escape character precedes a variable, it prevents a value from being substituted for the variable.

Within a string, the escape character also can indicate a special character. PowerShell recognizes the special characters listed in Table 6-17. To see how you can use a tab character in a string, review the following example and sample output:

```
$s = "Please specify the computer name `t []"
$c = read-host $s
write-host "You entered: `t $c"


Please specify the computer name          []: corpserver45

You entered:          corpserver45
```

Here, you create a string with a tab character. You then use the Read-Host cmdlet to display the string while waiting for input from the user. You store the input from the user in a variable for later user, and then you use the Write-Host cmdlet to display a string with a tab character and the value the user entered.

TABLE 6-17 Escape Codes in Windows PowerShell

ESCAPE CODE	MEANING
`'	Single quotation mark
`"	Double quotation mark
`0	Null character
`a	Alert (sends a bell or beep signal to the computer speaker)
`b	Backspace
`f	Form feed (used with printer output)
`n	New line
`r	Carriage return

ESCAPE CODE	MEANING
`t	Horizontal tab (eight spaces)
`v	Vertical tab (used with printer output)

Often when you are working with strings, you might need to match part of a string to get a desired result. To do this, you use the wildcards listed previously in Table 6-5. When you work with character ranges and subsets, keep in mind the characters can be in these ranges:

- [a to z] or [A to Z] for alphabetic characters
- [0-9] for numeric characters

Generally, PowerShell matches characters whether they are uppercase or lowercase. Because of this, in most instances, these ranges are interpreted the same whether you use uppercase or lowercase letters—for example:

- [a-c] and [A-C] are the same.
- [abc] and [ABC] are the same.

However, when you get into regular expressions, there are times when PowerShell performs case-sensitive matches. As you've seen in past examples, wildcards are useful when you want to perform pattern matching within strings, especially when you are passing string values to cmdlet parameters. Although some cmdlet parameters support wildcards being passed in values, not all do, and you'll want to confirm whether a parameter supports wildcards using the –Full help details. For example, if you type **get-help get-alias –full**, you see the full help details for the Get-Alias cmdlet as shown partially in this example:

```
NAME
    Get-Alias

SYNOPSIS
    Gets the aliases for the current session.

SYNTAX
    Get-Alias [-Exclude <string[]>] [-Name <string[]>]
[-Scope <string>] [<CommonParameters>]
```

```
   Get-Alias [-Definition <String[]>] [-Exclude <String[]>]
[-Scope <String>] [<CommonParameter>]

DETAILED DESCRIPTION
    The Get-Alias cmdlet gets the aliases (alternate names for
commands and executable files) in the current session.

PARAMETERS
    -Definition <string[]>
        Gets the aliases for the specified item. Enter the name
of a cmdlet, function, script, file, or executable file.

        Required?                      false
        Position?                      named
        Default value
        Accept pipeline input?         false
        Accept wildcard characters?    true
```

Here, you know the –Definition parameter accepts wildcards being passed in values because Accept WildCard Characters is set to True. If the parameter does not accept wildcards, Accept WildCard Characters is set to False.

Multiline Strings

When you want a string to have multiple lines, precede and follow the string value with @. This type of string is referred to as a *here-string*, and the same rules for single quotes and double quotes apply. Consider the following example and sample output:

```
$myString = @"
=========================
$env:computername
=========================
"@
write-host $myString

=========================
EngPC85
=========================
```

Data strings are another type of multiline string. PowerShell supports data strings primarily for script internationalization because data strings make it easier to separate data and code by isolating strings that might be translated into other languages. There's no reason, however, that you can't use data strings for other purposes, and they are much more versatile than other types of strings. Primarily, this is because data strings are referenced with a variable name and can include programming logic.

The basic syntax for a data string is

```
DATA StringName {
    StringText
}
```

where *StringName* sets the name for the data string as a variable, and *StringText* can include the following: one or more single-quoted strings, double-quoted strings, here-strings, or any combination thereof. Note that the DATA keyword is not case sensitive, meaning you can use DATA, data, or even Data to denote the beginning of the data string.

The following example declares a data string named MyValues:

```
DATA MyValues {
  "This is a data string."
  "You can use data strings in many different ways."
}
```

You use or reference the MyValues string by its name. To display the data string's contents at the prompt, type the following command:

```
Write-Host $MyValues
```

You can also type

```
$MyValues
```

The extended syntax for data strings is

```
DATA StringName [-supportedCommand CmdletNames] {
PermittedContent
}
```

Here, *CmdletName* provides a comma-separated list of cmdlets that you use in the data string, and *PermittedContent* includes any of the following elements:

- Strings and string literals
- Any PowerShell operators, except –match
- If, Else, and ElseIf statements
- Certain automatic variables, including $PsCulture, $PsUICulture, $True, $False, and $Null
- Statements separated by semicolons, comments, and pipelines

Adding cmdlets and programming elements to data strings makes them work much like functions, and in many cases you'll find it easier to simply use a function than to treat a data string like a function. For more information on functions, see the "Creating and Using Functions" section in Chapter 6, "Mastering Aliases and Functions."

Strings that contain prohibited elements, such as variables or subexpressions, must be enclosed in single-quoted strings or here-strings so that the variables are not expanded and subexpressions are not executable. The only cmdlet you don't have to declare as supported is ConvertFrom-StringData. The ConvertFrom-StringData cmdlet converts strings that contain one or more "name=value" pairs into associative arrays. Because each "name=value" pair must be on a separate line, you typically use here-strings as the input format. However, PowerShell allows you to use single-quoted or double-quoted strings or here-strings.

The following example shows how the ConvertFrom-StringData cmdlet can be used with data strings:

```
DATA DisplayNotes {
  ConvertFrom-StringData -stringdata @'
  Note1 = This appears to be the wrong syntax.
  Note2 = There is a value missing.
  Note3 = Cannot connect at this time.
  '@
}
```

In this example, you create a data string called DisplayNotes and use ConvertFrom-StringData to create a related associative array with three separate strings: Note1, Note2, and Note3. You are then able to reference the strings using dot notation. To display the first string, you use $DisplayNotes.Note1; for the second string, you use $DisplayNotes.Note2; and for the third string, you use $DisplayNotes.Note3. To display all the notes, you simply type **$DisplayNotes**.

With a here-string, you can use a similar technique to create an array of strings—for example:

```
$string = @'
  Note1 = This appears to be the wrong syntax.
  Note2 = There is a value missing.
  Note3 = Cannot connect at this time.
  '@

$strArray = $string | convertfrom-stringdata
```

The here-string defined in this example contains the same strings as the previous example. You then use a pipeline operator (|) to send the value of the here-string to ConvertFrom-StringData. The command saves the result in the $strArray variable, and you can use the same techniques discussed previously to access the strings.

String Operators

As you learned in "Comparison Operators" earlier in the chapter, you can use many operators with strings and arrays. These include –eq, –ne, –lt, –gt, –le, –ge, –like, –notlike, –match, –notmatch, –contains, –notcontains, and –replace.

You also can use the following special operators with strings:

- = Assigns a string value to a variable
- + Concatenates strings by adding them together
- * Repeats a string some number of times
- **–Join** Joins strings by adding them together with or without delimiters
- **–Split** Splits a string on spaces or a specified delimiter
- **–f** Formats a string using the extended formatting syntax

The most common string operations you'll want to perform are assignment and concatenation. As you've seen in previous examples, you assign values to strings using the equal sign, such as

```
$myString = "This is a String."
```

Concatenation is the technical term for adding strings together. The normal operator for string concatenation is the + operator. Using the + operator, you can add strings together as follows:

```
$streetAdd = "123 Main St."
$cityState = "Anywhere, NY"
$zipCode = "12345"
$custAddress = $streetAdd + " " + $cityState + " " + $zipCode
$custAddress
```

```
123 Main St. Anywhere, NY 12345
```

Sometimes you might also want to add a string stored in a variable to output you are displaying. You can do this simply by referencing the variable containing the string as part of the double-quoted output string as shown here:

```
$company = "XYZ Company"
Write-Host "The company is: $company"
```

```
The company is: XYZ Company
```

Concatenation of arrays works much like concatenation of strings. Using the + operator, you can add arrays together as shown in this example:

```
$array1 = "PC85", "PC25", "PC92"
$array2 = "SERVER41", "SERVER32", "SERVER87"
$joinedArray = $array1 + $array2
$joinedArray
```

```
PC85
PC25
PC92
SERVER41
SERVER32
SERVER87
```

Multiplication of strings and arrays can be handy when you want to repeat the character in a string or the values in an array a specified number of times. For example, if you have a string with the + character stored in it, you might want to make an 80-character string of + characters act as a dividing line in output. You can do this as shown in the following example and sample output:

```
$separator = "+"
$sepLine = $separator * 60
$sepLine
```

```
++++++++++++++++++++++++++++++++++++++++++++++++++++++++++++
```

You use the –Join and –Split operators to join and split strings, respectively. The basic syntaxes for joining strings are

```
-Join (String1, String2, String3 …)
```

```
String1, String2, String3 … -Join "Delimiter"
```

The first syntax simply joins a collection of strings together. The second syntax joins a collection of strings while specifying a delimiter to use between them. To see how you can join strings without delimiters, consider the following example and sample output:

```
$a =  -join ("abc", "def", "ghi")
$a
```

```
abcdefghi
```

To see how you can join strings with delimiters, consider the following example and sample output:

```
$a = "abc", "def", "ghi" –join ":"
$a
```

```
abc:def:ghi
```

The basic syntaxes for splitting strings are

```
-Split String
```

```
String -Split "Delimiter" [,MaxSubStrings]
```

With the first syntax, you can split a string using the spaces between words as delimiters. To see how, consider the following example and sample output:

```
$a = "abc def ghi"
-Split $a

abc
def
ghi
```

You also can split strings based on a delimiter as shown in this example:

```
$a = "jkl:mno:pqr"
$a -Split ":"

jkl
mno
pqr
```

You use the –f operator to format a string using the extended formatting syntax. With this syntax, you specify exactly how you want to format a series of numeric, alphabetic, or alphanumeric values.

The basic structure is to specify the desired formatting on the left of the –f operator and the values to format in a comma-separated list on the right, as shown in this example:

```
'FormatingInstructions' -f "Value1", "Value2", "Value3", …
```

In the formatting instructions, {0} represents the first value, {1} the second value, and so on. Knowing this, you can use the formatting instructions to modify the order of values, convert values to different formats, or both. In the following example and sample output, you reverse the order of the values in the output:

```
'{2} {1} {0}' -f "Monday", "Tuesday", "Wednesday"

Wednesday Tuesday Monday
```

You are not limited to forward or reverse order. You control the output order and can specify any desired order, such as

```
'{2} {0} {1}' -f "Cloudy", "Sunny", "Rainy"
```

```
Rainy Cloudy Sunny
```

The number of formatting instructions must exactly match the number of values to format. Otherwise, values will be omitted, which is fine if this is your intention. In the following example, you omit the second value:

```
'{0} {2}' -f "Server15", "Server16", "Server17"
```

```
Server15 Server17
```

To each individual formatting instruction, you can add one of the conversion indicators listed in Table 6-18. The usage example provided for each format specifier is followed by the output.

TABLE 6-18 Conversion Indicators for Formatting

FORMAT SPECIFIER	DESCRIPTION & USAGE
:c or :C	Converts a numeric format to currency format (based on the computer's locale). '{0:c}' –f 145.50 $145.50
:e or :E	Converts to scientific (exponential) notation. Add a numeric value to specify precision (the number of digits past the decimal point). '{0:e4}' –f [Math]::Pi 3.1416e+000
:f or :F	Converts to fixed-point notation. Add a numeric value to specify precision (the number of digits past the decimal point). '{0:f4}' –f [Math]::Pi 3.1426
:g or :G	Converts to the most compact notation, either fixed-point or scientific notation. Add a numeric value to specify the number of significant digits. '{0:g3}' –f [Math]::Pi

FORMAT SPECIFIER	DESCRIPTION & USAGE
	3.14
:n or :N	Converts to a number with culture-specific separators between number groups. Add a numeric value to specify precision (the number of digits past the decimal point). '{0:n2}' –f 1GB 1,073,741,824.00
:p or :P	Converts a numeric value to a percentage. Add a numeric value to specify precision (the number of digits past the decimal point). '{0:p2}' –f .112 11.20 %
:r or :R	Converts a number with precision to guarantee the original value is returned if parsing is reversed. '{0:r}' –f (1GB/2.0) 536870912 Note: (536870912 * 2) = 1,073,741,824
:x or :X	Converts the numeric value to hexadecimal format. '{0:x}' –f 12345678 bc614e
{N:hh:mm:ss}	Converts a datetime object to a two-digit hour, minute, and second format. You can omit any portion to get a subset. '{0:hh:mm}' –f (get-date) 02:35

FORMAT SPECIFIER	DESCRIPTION & USAGE
{N:ddd}	Converts a datetime object to a day of the week. It can be combined with the previous format listed. '{0:ddd} {0:hh:mm}' –f (get-date) Mon 12:57

Working with Arrays and Collections

In Windows PowerShell, the terms *array* and *collection* are interchangeable. Arrays are data structures for storing a series of values. Using arrays, you can group related sets of data together, and PowerShell doesn't care whether the data you group is like-typed or not. For example, although you can group sets of numbers, strings, or objects in separate arrays, you also can combine values of different types in the same array.

The most common type of array you'll use is a one-dimensional array. A one-dimensional array is like a column of tabular data, a two-dimensional array is like a spreadsheet with rows and columns, and a three-dimensional (3-D) array is like a 3-D grid.

Elements in an array are indexed and can be accessed by referencing their index position. With a one-dimensional array, you access elements in the array by specifying a single index value. You also can create arrays with multiple dimensions if you want to. With multidimensional arrays, you access elements in the array by specifying multiple index values.

> **NOTE** Windows PowerShell also supports associative arrays, which are name-value pairs stored in arrays. For more information, see the "Multiline Strings" section earlier in this chapter.

Creating and Using One-Dimensional Arrays

Windows PowerShell has several operators for working with arrays. The one you'll use most is the comma. You use the comma to separate elements in a one-dimensional array. The basic syntax for this type of array is

```
$VarName = Element1, Element2, Element3, …
```

where *VarName* is the variable in which the array will be stored, *Element1* is the first item in the array, *Element2* is the second, and so on.

The following example creates an array of numbers:

```
$myArray = 2, 4, 6, 8, 10, 12, 14
```

You can just as easily create an array of strings, such as

```
$myStringArray = "This", "That", "Why", "When", "How", "Where"
```

You access the elements in the array by passing the index position to the [ ] operator. PowerShell numbers the array elements starting from zero. This means the first element has an index position of 0, the second has an index position of 1, and so on. The basic syntax is

```
$VarName[Index]
```

where *VarName* is the variable in which the array is stored, and *Index* is the index position you want to work with. Knowing this, you can return the first element in the $myStringArray as shown here:

```
$myStringArray[0]
```

```
This
```

You can work with the index in several ways. You can use an index value of –1 to reference the last element of the array, –2 to reference the second to last, and so on. This example returns the last element in the array:

```
$myStringArray[-1]
```

```
Where
```

You also can access ranges of elements in an array using the range operator (..). The following example returns elements 1, 2, and 3:

```
$myStringArray[0..2]
```

```
This
That
Why
```

By mixing these techniques, you can work with arrays in different ways. For example, the following statement returns the last, first, and second elements in the array:

```
$myStringArray[-1..1]
```

```
Where
This
That
```

This example goes through the array backward from the last to the second-to-last to the third-to-last:

```
$myStringArray[-1..-3]
```

```
Where
How
When
```

However, to return both a series of elements and a range of elements, you must separate the series and the range using the + operator. The following example returns element 1, element 2, and elements 4 to 6:

```
$myStringArray[0,1+3..5]
```

```
This
That
When
How
Where
```

Using the Length property, you can determine the number of elements in an array. For example, typing **$myArray.Length** returns a value of 7. You can use the Length property when accessing elements in the array as well. The following example returns elements 5 to 6:

```
$myStringArray[4..($myArray.Length-1)]
```

```
How
Where
```

Using the Cast Array Structure

Another way to create an array is to use the array cast structure. The basic syntax is

```
$VarName = @(Element1, Element2, Element3, …)
```

where *VarName* is the variable in which the array will be stored, *Element1* is the first item in the array, *Element2* is the second, and so on.

The following example creates an array of numbers:

```
$myArray = @(3, 6, 9, 12, 15, 18, 21)
```

The advantage of the cast array syntax is that if you use semicolons instead of commas to separate values, PowerShell treats each value as command text. This means PowerShell executes the value as if you typed it at the prompt and then stores the result. Consider the following example:

```
$myArray = @(14; "This"; get-process)
```

As shown in the following example and sample output, the first element is created as an integer:

```
$myArray[0].gettype()
```

```
IsPublic IsSerial Name                        BaseType
-------- -------- ----                        --------
True     True     Int32                       System.ValueType
```

The second element is created as a string:

```
$myArray[1].gettype()
```

```
IsPublic IsSerial Name                    BaseType
-------- -------- ----                    --------
True     True     String                  System.Object
```

And the third element is created as a collection of Process objects:

```
$myArray[2].gettype()
```

```
IsPublic IsSerial Name          BaseType
-------- -------- ----          --------
True     False    Process       System.ComponentModel.Component
```

Assigning and Removing Values

After you create an array, you can change the array's values through a simple assignment. For example, if you define the following array,

```
$myArray = @(3, 6, 9, 12, 15, 18, 21)
```

you can change the value of the second element in $myArray using the following assignment:

```
$myArray[1] = 27
```

You also can use the SetValue() method to change a value in an array. The syntax is

```
$VarName.SetValue(NewValue, IndexPos)
```

where *VarName* is the variable in which the array was stored, *NewValue* is the new value you want to assign, and *IndexPos* is the index position of the value to change. Following this, you can change the value of the first element in $myArray using the following assignment:

```
$myArray.SetValue(52,0)
```

To add elements to an existing array, you can use the += operator to assign a new value. For example, to append an element to $myArray with a value of 75, you type the following command:

```
$myArray += 75
```

PowerShell won't let you easily delete elements in an array, but you can create a new array that contains only a subset of elements from an existing array. For example, to create the $myNewArray array with all elements in $myArray, except for the value at index position 3, you type

```
$myNewArray = $myArray[0..2+4..($myArray.length - 1)]
```

You can combine multiple arrays into a single array using the plus operator (+). The following example creates three arrays and then combines them into one array:

```
$array1 = 1,2,3,4
$array2 = 5,6,7,8
$array3 = 9,10,11,12
$cArray = $array1 + $array2 + $array3
```

Because large arrays can use up memory, you might want to delete an array when you are finished working with it. To delete an array, use the Remove-Item cmdlet to delete the variable that contains the array. The following command deletes $myArray:

```
remove-item variable:myArray
```

Using Strict Types in Arrays

Sometimes when you are working with arrays, you might want to ensure an array can store only strings, numbers, or objects of a particular type. The way to do this is to declare the array's type when you create the array.

You can declare an array of any type, but the declared type uses the [] operator as shown here:

- **[int32[]]$myArray**   Creates an array of integers
- **[bool[]]$myArray**   Creates an array of Booleans
- **[object[]]$myArray**   Creates an array of objects
- **[string[]]$myArray**   Creates an array of strings

For example, if you want to create an array of integers and assign integer values, you can use the following declaration:

```
[int32[]]$myArray = 5,10,15,20,25,30,35
```

Because the array is strictly typed, you can use only the declared value type with it. For example, if you try to change a value to a string, you get an error as shown in the following example and sample output:

```
$myArray[0]= "Kansas"
```

```
Cannot convert value "Kansas" to type "System.Int32". Error:
"Input string was not in a correct format."
At line:1 char:1
+ $myArray[0]= "Kansas"
+ ~~~~~~~~~~~~~~~~~~~~~~
    + CategoryInfo          : InvalidArgument: (:) [],
RuntimeException
    + FullyQualifiedErrorId : InvalidCastFromStringToInteger
```

Using Multidimensional Arrays

Multidimensional arrays are arrays that support multiple index positions. With a two-dimensional array, you create a table with rows and columns. Because you access any row using the first index and any column using the second index, these can be thought of as x-coordinates and y-coordinates as well.

Consider the following example.

INDEX	COLUMNS 0, 1, 2
ROW 0	Red, Green, Blue
ROW 1	Washington, Ohio, Florida
ROW 2	Ocean, Lake, Stream
ROW 3	Sky, Clouds, Rain

Here, you have a table with rows and columns that you want to store in an array. The convention is to reference the row index and then the column index. The value in row 0, column 0 is Red. The value in row 0, column 1 is Green, and so on.

Although you can create one-dimensional arrays with simple constructors, PowerShell handles arrays of two or more dimensions as objects. Because of this, you must first create the array and then populate the array. The syntax for creating a two-dimensional array is

```
$VarName = new-object 'object[,]' numRows,numColumns
```

where *VarName* is the variable in which the array will be stored, *object[,]* specifies you are creating a two-dimensional array, *numRows* sets the number of rows, and *numColumns* sets the number of columns.

The following example creates an array with 4 rows and 3 columns:

```
$myArray = new-object 'object[,]' 4,3
```

After you create the array, you can populate each value according to its row and column index position as shown in this example:

```
$myArray[0,0] = "Red"
$myArray[0,1] = "Green"
$myArray[0,2] = "Blue"
$myArray[1,0] = "Washington"
$myArray[1,1] = "Ohio"
$myArray[1,2] = "Florida"
$myArray[2,0] = "Ocean"
$myArray[2,1] = "Lake"
$myArray[2,2] = "Stream"
$myArray[3,0] = "Sky"
$myArray[3,1] = "Clouds"
$myArray[3,2] = "Rain"
```

After you populate the array, you can return a value at a row/column position, such as

```
$myArray[0,1]
```

```
Green
```

Creating an array of three or more dimensions works in much the same way. The difference is that you must accommodate dimension. The syntax for creating a three-dimensional array is

```
$VarName = new-object 'object[,,]' numX,numY,numZ
```

where *VarName* is the variable in which the array will be stored, *object[,,]* specifies you are creating a three-dimensional array, and *numX*, *numY*, and *numZ* set the X, Y, and Z grid coordinates.

The following example creates an array with 5 rows, 5 columns, and 3 levels:

```
$a = new-object 'object[,,]' 5,5,3
```

This array is like 3 tables, each of 5 rows and 5 columns, stacked on top of each other. Knowing this, you can set the value for the 0, 0, 0 coordinate as

```
$a[0,0,0] = "Texas"
```

At the time of this writing, PowerShell supports up to 17 dimensions, and you can create an array of 17 dimensions, using 16 commas for the object[] constructor and then entering 17 coordinate values, as in the following example:

```
$myHugeArray = new-object 'object[,,,,,,,,,,,,,,,,]'
5,5,5,5,3,3,3,3,3,3,3,3,3,3,3,4,4
```

If you create such a large array, be sure to remove it when you are finished, to free up memory.

Chapter 7. Mastering Aliases and Functions

Beyond the core structures discussed in the previous chapter, you'll find a number of other essential elements you'll use whenever you work with Windows PowerShell. These include

- Aliases
- Functions
- Objects

You'll learn how to use aliases and functions in this chapter and about objects in the next chapter. Whenever you work with Windows PowerShell, you'll use these essential elements to help you do more with less and to help you use PowerShell to perform any conceivable administrative task. Because the discussion in this chapter ties in closely with the discussion in previous chapters, you should read those chapters before continuing.

Creating and Using Aliases

PowerShell aliases provide alternate names for commands, functions, scripts, files, executables, and other command elements. PowerShell has many default aliases that map to commands, and you can create your own aliases as well.

Aliases are designed to save you keystrokes, and each command can have multiple aliases. For example, ls is also an alias of Get-ChildItem. In UNIX environments, ls is used to list the contents of a directory and, in fact, the output of Get-ChildItem is more similar to UNIX ls than to Windows dir.

Using the Built-In Aliases

Table 7-1 shows some of the default aliases. Although there are many other default aliases, you'll use these aliases most frequently.

TABLE 7-1 Commonly Used Aliases

ALIAS	ASSOCIATED CMDLET
clear, cls	Clear-Host
Diff	Compare-Object
cp, copy	Copy-Item
Epal	Export-Alias
Epcsv	Export-Csv
Foreach	ForEach-Object
Fl	Format-List
Ft	Format-Table
Fw	Format-Wide
Gal	Get-Alias
ls, dir	Get-ChildItem
Gcm	Get-Command
cat, type	Get-Content
h, history	Get-History
gl, pwd	Get-Location
gps, ps	Get-Process

ALIAS	ASSOCIATED CMDLET
Gsv	Get-Service
Gv	Get-Variable
Group	Group-Object
Ipal	Import-Alias
Ipcsv	Import-Csv
R	Invoke-History
Ni	New-Item
Mount	New-MshDrive
Nv	New-Variable
rd, rm, rmdir, del, erase	Remove-Item
Rv	Remove-Variable
Sal	Set-Alias
sl, cd, chdir	Set-Location
sv, set	Set-Variable
Sort	Sort-Object
Sasv	Start-Service

ALIAS	ASSOCIATED CMDLET
Sleep	Start-Sleep
spps, kill	Stop-Process
Spsv	Stop-Service
write, echo	Write-Output

Table 7-2 lists commands that exist internally within the Windows command shell (cmd.exe) and do not have separate executable files. Each internal command is followed by a brief description. Because cmdlets behave differently from these commands, you must know exactly what you are executing. For this reason, I also provide a notation when a default alias precludes use of the command. You can run commands internal to the Windows command shell at the PowerShell prompt or in a PowerShell script. To do so, invoke the command shell with appropriate parameters followed by the name of the internal command to execute. Typically, you'll want to use the /c parameter, which tells the command shell to carry out the specified command and then terminate. For example, if you want to use the internal dir command, you can type the following at the PowerShell prompt:

```
cmd /c dir
```

TABLE 7-2 Internal Commands for the Windows Command Shell

NAME	DESCRIPTION
assoc	Displays or modifies the current file extension associations.
break	Sets breaks for debugging.
call	Calls a procedure or another script from within a script.

NAME	DESCRIPTION
cd (chdir)	Displays the current directory name, or changes the location of the current directory. Overridden by: Set-Location.
cls	Clears the command window and erases the screen buffer. Overridden by: Clear-Host.
color	Sets the text and background colors of the command-shell window.
copy	Copies files from one location to another, or concatenates files. Overridden by: Copy-Item.
date	Displays or sets the system date.
del (erase)	Deletes the specified file, files, or directory. Overridden by: Remove-Item.
dir	Displays a list of subdirectories and files in the current or specified directory. Overridden by: Get-ChildItem.
dpath	Allows programs to open data files in specified directories as if they were in the current directory.
echo	Displays text strings to PowerShell; sets command echoing state (on | off). Overridden by: Write-Output.
endlocal	Ends localization of variables.
exit	Exits the command shell.
for	Runs a specified command for each file in a set of files.
ftype	Displays current file types, or modifies file types used in file extension associations.
goto	Directs the command interpreter to a labeled line in a batch script.

NAME	DESCRIPTION
if	Performs conditional execution of commands.
md (mkdir)	Creates a subdirectory in the current or specified directory. *md invokes mkdir (via cmd.exe)
mklink	Creates either a symbolic link or a hard link, for either a file or a directory.
move	Moves a file or files from the current or designated source directory to a designated target directory. It can also be used to rename a directory. Overridden by: Move-Item.
path	Displays or sets the command path the operating system uses when searching for executables and scripts.
pause	Suspends processing of a batch file, and waits for keyboard input.
popd	Makes the directory saved by PUSHD the current directory. Overridden by: Pop-Location.
prompt	Sets the text for the command prompt.
pushd	Saves the current directory location and then optionally changes to the specified directory. Overridden by: Push-Location.
rd (rmdir)	Removes a directory or a directory and its subdirectories. Overridden by: Remove-Item.
rem	Sets a remark in batch scripts or Config.sys.
ren (rename)	Renames a file or files. Overridden by: Rename-Item (for ren only).
set	Displays current environment variables, or sets temporary variables for the current command shell. Overridden by: Set-Variable.

NAME	DESCRIPTION
setlocal	Marks the start of variable localization in batch scripts.
shift	Shifts the position of replaceable parameters in batch scripts.
start	Starts a separate window to run a specified program or command. Overridden by: Start-Process.
time	Displays or sets the system time.
title	Sets the title for the command-shell window.
type	Displays the contents of a text file. Overridden by: Get-Content.
verify	Causes the operating system to verify files after writing files to disk.
vol	Displays the disk's volume label and serial number.

Creating Aliases

The following cmdlets are available for working with aliases:

- **Get-Alias** Lists all or specified aliases set in the current session by name and definition.

  ```
  Get-Alias [[-Name | -Definition] Strings] [AddtlParams]

  AddtlParams=
  [-Exclude Strings] [-Scope String]
  ```

- **New-Alias** Creates a new alias.

  ```
  New-Alias [-Description String] [-Name] String [-Value]
  String
  [AddtlParams]

  AddtlParams=
  ```

```
[-Force] [-PassThru] [-Scope String] [-Option None | ReadOnly
| Constant | Private | AllScope]
```

- **Set-Alias**   Creates a new alias, or changes the definition of an existing alias.

```
Set-Alias [-Description String] [-Name] String [-Value]
String
[AddtlParams]

AddtlParams=
[-Force] [-PassThru] [-Scope String] [-Option None | ReadOnly
| Constant | Private | AllScope]
```

- **Export-Alias**   Exports all the aliases that are currently in use in the PowerShell console to an alias file. This includes the built-in aliases as well as aliases you've created.

```
Export-Alias [-Append] [-As Csv | Script] [-Path] String
[AddtlParams]

AddtlParams=
[-Description String] [-Force] [-NoClobber] [-PassThru]
[-Scope String] [[-Name] Strings]
```

- **Import-Alias**   Imports an alias file into a PowerShell console. The aliases can then be used in that PowerShell session. You must reload the aliases each time you open a PowerShell console.

```
Import-Alias [-Path] String [AddtlParams]

AddtlParams=
[-PassThru] [-Force] [-Scope String]
```

As mentioned previously, you can use the Get-Alias cmdlet to list all of the available aliases. To get particular aliases, use the –Name parameter of the Get-Alias cmdlet. For example, to get aliases that begin with "a", use the following command:

```
get-alias -name a*
```

To get aliases according to their values, use the –Definition parameter. For example, to get aliases for the Remove-Item cmdlet, type the following command:

```
get-alias -definition Remove-Item
```

You can create aliases using either the New-Alias cmdlet or the Set-Alias cmdlet. The primary difference between them is that New-Alias creates an alias only if a like-named alias does not yet exist, while Set-Alias overwrites an existing alias with the new association you provide. The basic syntax is

```
set-alias –name AliasName –value CommandName
```

where *AliasName* is the alias you want to use or modify, and *CommandName* is the cmdlet you want to associate with the alias. The following example creates a "cm" alias for Computer Management:

```
set-alias -name cm -value c:\windows\system32\compmgmt.msc
```

Because the –Name and –Value parameters are position sensitive, you pass the related values in order without having to specify the parameter name, as shown in this example:

```
set-alias cm c:\windows\system32\compmgmt.msc
```

> **MORE INFO**   Sometimes, you might want to use the –Option parameter to set optional properties of an alias. Valid values are None, ReadOnly, Constant, Private, and AllScope. The default, None, sets no options. When you use ReadOnly, this specifies that the alias cannot be changed unless you use the –Force parameter. Constant specifies that the alias cannot be changed, even by using the –Force parameter. Private specifies that the alias is available only within the scope specified by the –Scope parameter. AllScope specifies that the alias is available in all scopes.

You can use the alias with any applicable parameters just as you would the full command name. If you always want to use certain startup parameters, external utilities, or applications, you can define those as well as part of the alias. To do this, enclose the value in double quotation marks as shown in this example:

```
set-alias cm "c:\windows\system32\compmgmt.msc
/computer=engpc57"
```

However, you cannot define startup parameters for cmdlets in this way. For example, you can create an alias of *gs* for Get-Service, but you cannot create an alias with the following definition: get-service –name winrm. The workaround is to create a function that includes the command as discussed in the "Creating and Using Functions" section later in this chapter.

Importing and Exporting Aliases

Normally, you save the aliases you want to use by typing the related commands into a profile file. If you create a number of aliases in a PowerShell session and want to save those aliases, you also can use the Export-Alias cmdlet to do so. This cmdlet exports all the aliases that are currently in use in the PowerShell console to an alias file. You can export aliases as a list of comma-separated values or a list of Set-Alias commands in a PowerShell script.

The basic syntax for Export-Alias is

```
export-alias –path AliasFileName
```

where *AliasFileName* is the full file path to the alias file you want to create, such as

```
export-alias –path myaliases.csv
```

The default output format is a list of comma-separated values. You can use the –As parameter to set the output format as a script containing Set-Alias commands as shown in this example:

```
export-alias –as script –path myaliases.ps1
```

Other parameters you can use include

- –Append, to write the output to the end of an existing file rather than overwrite the file as per the default setting
- –Force, to force overwriting an existing alias file if the read-only attribute is set
- –Noclobber, to prevent automatic overwriting of an existing alias file

The Import-Alias cmdlet imports an alias file into the PowerShell console. The basic syntax for Import-Alias is

```
import-alias –path AliasFileName
```

where *AliasFileName* is the full file path to the alias file you want to import, such as

```
import-alias –path c:\powershell\myaliases.csv
```

Use the –Force parameter to import aliases that are already defined and set as read-only.

Creating and Using Functions

Windows PowerShell functions are named sets of commands that can accept input from the pipeline. When you call a function by its name, the related commands run just as if you had typed them at the command line. Normally, you save functions that you want to use frequently by typing the related commands into a profile file. You also can add functions to scripts.

Creating Functions

To create a function, type the word **function** followed by a name for the function. Type your command text, and enclose it in braces ({ }). For example, the following command creates the getwinrm function. This function represents the "get-service -name winrm" command:

```
function getwinrm {get-service -name winrm}
```

The braces ({ }) create a code block that the function uses. You can now type **getwinrm** instead of the command. And you can even create aliases for the getwinrm function. For example, you can create a *gr* alias for the getwinrm function using the following command:

```
new-alias gr getwinrm
```

Because functions use code blocks, you can create functions with multiple commands. Functions also can use piping, redirection, and other coding techniques. For example, you can use piping to format the output of Get-Service as shown in this example:

```
function getwinrm {get-service -name winrm | format-list}
```

Functions are very powerful because you can define parameters for them and use the parameter names to pass in values. The basic syntax for using parameters with functions is

```
function FunctionName {
  param ($Parameter1Name, $Parameter2Name, ...)
  Commands }
```

where *FunctionName* sets the name of the function, *$Parameter1Name* sets the name of the first parameter, *$Parameter2Name* sets the name of the second parameter, and so on. Consider the following example:

```
function ss {param ($status) get-service | where { $_.status -eq
$status} }
```

This line of code defines an *ss* function with a parameter called *status*. The *ss* function examines all the configured services on the computer and uses the Where-Object cmdlet to return a formatted list of services with the status you specify. To return a list of all services with a status of Stopped, you type

```
ss -status stopped
```

To return a list of all services with a status of Running, you type

```
ss -status running
```

Because the name of the parameter is optional, you also can simply specify the value to check, such as

```
ss stopped
```

or

```
ss running
```

Keep in mind that functions run within the context of their own local scope. The items created in a function, such as variables, exist only in the function scope. Additionally, if a function is part of a script, the function is available only to statements within that script. This means a function in a script is not available at the command prompt by default. When you define a function in the global scope, you can use the function in scripts, in functions, and at the command line.

To set the scope for a function, simply prefix the name of the function with the desired scope. This example sets the scope of the function to *global*:

```
function global:getwinrm {get-service -name winrm}
```

Using Extended Functions

Now that you know the basics, let's look at the extended syntax for functions:

```
function $FunctionName {
  param ($Parameter1Name, $Parameter2Name, ...)
  Begin {
    <one-time, pre-processing commands>
  }
  Process{
    <commands to execute on each object>
  }
  End{
    <one-time, post-processing commands>
  }
}
```

In the extended syntax, you can add Begin, Process, and End code blocks to make a function behave exactly like a cmdlet. The Begin block is optional and used to specify one-time preprocessing commands. Statements in the Begin block are executed before any objects in the pipeline are evaluated by the function. This means no pipeline objects are available.

The Process block is required if you want to process input. In the basic syntax, the Process block is implied. However, when you use the other optional blocks and want to process input, you must explicitly declare the Process block. Statements in the Process block are executed once for each object in the pipeline.

The End block is optional and used to specify one-time postprocessing commands. Statements in the End block are executed after all objects in the pipeline are evaluated by the function. As with the Begin block, this means no pipeline objects are available.

The following example uses Begin, Process, and End code blocks:

```
function scheck {
param ($status)
 Begin {
   Write-Warning "############### Services on $env:computername"
  }
 Process {
  get-service | where { $_.status -eq $status}
  }
 End {
   Write-Warning "############################################"
  }
}
```

If you define this function at the prompt or use it in a script, you can return a list of all services with a status of Stopped by typing

```
scheck stopped
```

To return a list of all services with a status of Running, you type

```
scheck -status running
```

Using Filter Functions

Filters are a type of function that run on each object in the pipeline. You can think of a filter as a function with all its statements in a Process block.

The basic syntax for a filter is

```
filter FilterName {
   param ($Parameter1Name, $Parameter2Name, ...)
   Commands }
```

where *FilterName* sets the name of the filter, *$Parameter1Name* sets the name of the first parameter, *$Parameter2Name* sets the name of the second parameter, and so on.

The power of a filter is that it processes a single pipeline object at a time. This makes a filter ideal for working with large amounts of data and returning an appropriate subset of the pipeline data. As with functions, you can specify a scope for a filter. Simply prefix the name of the function with the desired scope.

When you work with filters, you'll often use the $_ automatic variable to operate on the current object in the pipeline as shown in this example:

```
filter Name { $_.Name }
```

Here, you define a filter that outputs the name property of any object sent to the filter. For example, if you pipeline the output of Get-PSDrive to the function as shown here:

```
get-psdrive | name
```

the filter returns the name of each PSDrive that is available. Because a filter is essentially a function with only a Process block, the following function works the same as the previously defined filter:

```
function Name {
    Process { $_.Name }
}
```

Digging Deeper into Functions

You can extend the function concepts we've discussed previously in many ways. For example, you can set a default value for a parameter by assigning an initial value as shown in this example:

```
function ss {param ($status = "stopped") get-service |
where { $_.status -eq $status} }
```

Now the –Status parameter is set to Stopped by default. You can override the default by specifying a different value.

When you create functions, you can specify the parameter value type using any of the data type aliases listed previously in Table 6-10. These data type aliases are used in the same way whenever you declare a data type in PowerShell.

In the following example, you create a function to dynamically set the PowerShell window size:

```
function set-windowsize {

param([int]$width=$host.ui.rawui.windowsize.width,
[int]$height=$host.ui.rawui.windowsize.height)

$size=New-Object
System.Management.Automation.Host.Size($width,$height);

$host.ui.rawui.WindowSize=$size

}
```

The function defines two parameters: $width and $height. Both parameters are defined as having 32-bit integer values. Because of this, PowerShell expects the parameters to be in this format when you call the function. If you pass values in another format, PowerShell attempts to convert the values you provide to the correct format. If PowerShell cannot do this, an error is returned stating that the value cannot be converted to the specified type and that the input string was not in the correct format.

The Get-Command cmdlet lists all currently defined cmdlets and functions. If you want to see only the available functions, you can filter the output using the Where-Object cmdlet as shown in the following example:

```
get-command | where {$_.commandtype -eq "function"}
```

Here, you look for command objects where CommandType is set as Function. This lists all the functions that currently are defined. Add **| format-list** to see the extended definition of each function, such as

```
get-command | where {$_.commandtype -eq "function"} |
format-list
```

The technique of calling a function and passing parameter values directly works great when you want to do either of the following:

- Define a function at the prompt and then run the function from the prompt.

- Define a function in a script and then run the function in the script.

However, this technique won't work if you want to pass parameter values to a function in a script from the prompt. The reason for this is that values passed to a script are read as arguments. For example, if you save a library of functions in a script and then want to run the functions from the prompt, you have to design the function to understand script-passed arguments or modify the script to work with arguments. One solution is shown in this example script:

Contents of CheckIt.ps1

```
function scheck {param ($status)
 Begin {
  Write-Warning "############### Services on $env:computername"
 }
 Process {
  get-service | where { $_.status -eq $status}
 }
 End {
  Write-Warning "###############################################"
 }
}
if ($args[0] = "scheck") {scheck $args[1]}
```

Note that the last line of the script determines whether the Scheck function is called. If you call the script with the first argument as *scheck* and the second argument as the status to check, the Scheck function is called and you get a list of services with that status. An alternative solution is to simply set the Status parameter to the value of the first argument passed to the script, as shown in the example that follows. You can then call the script with the first argument as the status to check. Note that the last line of the script invokes the function.

Contents of CheckIt2.ps1

```
function scheck {param ($status = $args[0])
 Begin {
  Write-Warning "############### Services on $env:computername"
 }
 Process {
  get-service | where { $_.status -eq $status}
 }
 End {
  Write-Warning "###############################################"
 }
```

```
}
scheck
```

Examining Function Definitions

If desired, you can work with functions via the *function:* provider drive. For example, if you set the location to the function: provider drive as shown in this example

```
set-location function:
```

the PowerShell prompt changes to

```
PS Function:\>
```

You can then work with any function or all functions. To list all functions by name and definition, you type

```
get-childitem
```

To list a particular function by name and definition, you use Get-ChildItem and type the function name or part of the function name with wildcards, such as

```
get-childitem get-filehash
get-childitem *filehash
```

When you are finished working with the function: provider drive, you can return to the file system drive you were using by typing **set-location** and the drive designator, such as

```
set-location c:
```

Another way to work with the function: provider drive is to use the Get-Item cmdlet to examine its definitions. If you do this, you don't need to switch to the function: provider drive. For example, regardless of which provider drive you are working with, you can type the following command to list all functions:

```
get-item -path function:*
```

You also can get a function by name:

```
get-item -path function:prompt
```

Or you can get it by wildcard:

```
get-item -path function:pr*
```

Using the Built-In Functions

Table 7-3 shows commonly used default functions. As you can see, most of the default functions are created to allow you to access drives and file paths, and the definition for these matches the definition set in the actual function. For other functions, the definition shows the essential command text at the heart of the function when possible.

TABLE 7-3 Commonly Used Default Functions

FUNCTION NAME	DEFINITION & PURPOSE
A:, B:, C:, D:, E:, F:, G:, H:, I:, J:, K:, L:, M:, N:, O:, P:, Q:, R:, S:, T:, U:, V:, W:, X:, Y:, Z:	Set-Location *DriveLetter*, where *DriveLetter* is the letter of the drive you want to access.
	Allows you to change to a particular drive letter. Thus, rather than having to type **Set-Location C:**, you can simply type **C:**.
CD..	Set-Location ..
	Allows you to go back one directory level. Thus, rather than having to type **Set-Location ..**, you can simply type **CD..**.
CD\	Set-Location \
	Allows you to go to the root directory of the current drive. Thus, rather than having to type **Set-Location **, you can simply type **CD**.
Clear-Host	$space = New-Object System.Management. Automation.Host. BufferCell
	$space.Character = ' '
	Clears the history buffer in the PowerShell console. Thus, rather than having to invoke the host run space and clear the buffer, you can simply type **Clear-Host**.

FUNCTION NAME	DEFINITION & PURPOSE
Help	Get-help | More Gets the help text for a cmdlet and pages it one screen at a time. Thus, rather than having to type **get-help *CmdletName* | More**, you can simply type **Help *CmdletName***.
Mkdir	New-Item –path *Path* –name *Name* –type directory Creates a directory with a specified name along a specified path. Thus, rather than having to use New-Item to create a directory in a named path, you can simply type **mkdir *DirName***.
More	| More Pages file contents or output one screen at a time. Thus, rather than having to type ***CommandText* | More**, you can simply type **More *CommandText***.
Prompt	$(if (test-path variable:/ PSDebugContext) { '[DBG]: ' } else { '' }) + 'PS ' + $(Get-Location) + $(if ($nestedpromptlevel –ge 1) { '>>' }) + '> ' Displays the PowerShell prompt. By default, the prompt displays PS, a space, and then the current directory. The prompt changes to >> when you do not terminate a line properly and PowerShell is looking for more input to complete the command entry.
TabExpansion2	* Enables tab expansion of command and parameter names. When you are typing part of a name value, press Tab to expand.

Practice using these functions because they provide handy shortcuts for many common tasks, especially the Prompt and TabExpansion functions. By default, the prompt displays PS, a space, and then the current directory. Also, the prompt changes to >> when you do not terminate a line properly and PowerShell is looking for more input to complete the command entry. When you are in debugging mode, the prompt changes to [DBG]:.

You can create your own Prompt function. If you do, your Prompt function simply overwrites and takes the place of the default prompt function. For example, if you want to the prompt to display the date instead of the current location, you can define the Prompt function as

```
function prompt {"$(get-date)> "}
```

Or to display the computer name, define the prompt as

```
function prompt {"PS [$env:computername]> "}
```

To maintain the original behavior of the prompt, copy the original definition and then modify it to meet your needs. The original prompt is created using the following function entered as a single line of code:

```
function prompt {
$(if (test-path variable:/PSDebugContext) { '[DBG]: ' }
else { '' }) + 'PS ' + $(Get-Location)
+ $(if ($nestedpromptlevel -ge 1) { '>>' }) + '> '
}
```

Typically, you'll want to replace the bold text with the desired value. For example, to display the date, you enter the following definition as a single line:

```
function prompt {
$(if (test-path variable:/PSDebugContext) { '[DBG]: ' }
else { '' }) + "$(get-date)> "
+ $(if ($nestedpromptlevel -ge 1) { '>>' }) + '> '
}
```

To display the computer name, you enter the following definition as a single line:

```
function prompt {
$(if (test-path variable:/PSDebugContext) { '[DBG]: ' }
else { '' }) + "PS [$env:computername]> "
+ $(if ($nestedpromptlevel -ge 1) { '>>' }) + '> '
}
```

While the Prompt function is a nice extra, the TabExpansion function is one you won't be able to live without once you start using it. The TabExpansion function allows you to complete cmdlet names, parameter names, and even parameter values using the Tab key. Here's how it works:

- When you are typing a cmdlet name, type the first few letters of the name and then press the Tab key to cycle through matching cmdlet names in alphabetical order. For example, if you know the cmdlet you want to use begins with Get-, you can type Get- and then press Tab to cycle through the matching cmdlets. Here, Get-Acl is listed first, followed by Get-Alias, Get-AuthenticateSignature, and so on. Similarly, if you know the cmdlet verb is Get and the cmdlet noun begins with C, you can type Get-C and then press Tab to cycle through possible values. A little-known secret is that you can press Shift+Tab to go through the values backwards, such as when you know the value you are looking for is later in the alphabet.
- After you type a cmdlet name, you can use tab expansion to select parameter names as well. If you don't know what parameter to use, type a hyphen (-) and then press Tab to cycle through all available parameter names. If you know a parameter begins with a certain letter, type a hyphen (-) followed by the letters you know and then press Tab. Again, you can press Shift+Tab to go through the values backward.

Chapter 8. Conquering COM, WMI, CMI, .NET, and Objects

Every action you take in Windows PowerShell occurs within the context of objects. Objects are the fundamental unit in object-oriented programming. Programming languages that follow object-oriented concepts describe the interaction among objects, and PowerShell uses objects in exactly the same way.

Object Essentials

In Windows PowerShell, objects do the real work. As data moves from one command to the next, it moves as it does within objects. Essentially, this means that objects are simply collections of data that represent items in defined namespaces.

Understanding Objects

All objects have a type, state, and behavior. The type provides details about what the object represents. For example, an object that represents a system process is a Process object. The state of an object pertains to data elements and their associated values. Everything the object knows about these elements and values describes the state of the object. Data elements associated with objects are stored in properties.

The behavior of an object depends on the actions the object can perform on the item that the object represents. In object-oriented terminology, this construct is called a *method*. A method belongs to the object class it is a member of, and you use a method when you need to perform a specific action on an object. For example, the Process object includes a method for stopping the process. You can use this method to halt execution of the process that the object represents.

Putting this together, you can see that the state of an object depends on the things the object knows, and the behavior of the object depends on the actions the object can perform. Objects encapsulate properties and related methods into a single identifiable unit. Therefore, objects are easy to reuse, update, and maintain.

Object classes encapsulate objects. A single class can be used to instantiate multiple objects. This means that you can have many active objects or instances of a class. By encapsulating objects within a class structure, you can group sets of objects by type. For example, when you type **get-process** at the PowerShell prompt, PowerShell returns a collection of objects representing all processing that are running on the computer. Although all the objects are returned together in a single collection, each object is separate, retaining its own states and behaviors.

PowerShell supports several dozen object types. When you combine commands in a pipeline, the commands pass information to each other as objects. When the first command runs, it sends one or more objects of a particular class along the pipeline to the second command. The second command receives the collection of objects from the first command, processes the objects, and then either displays output or passes new or modified objects to the next command in the pipeline. This continues until all commands in the pipeline run and the final command's output is displayed.

You can examine the properties and methods of any object by sending the output through the Get-Member cmdlet. For example, system processes and services are represented by the Process and Service objects, respectively. To determine the properties and methods of a Process object, you type **get-process | get-member**. To determine the properties and methods of a Service object, you type **get-service | get-member**. In both instances, the pipe character (|) sends the output of the first cmdlet to the Get-Member cmdlet, and Get-Member shows you the formal type of the object class and a complete listing of its members, as shown in the following example and sample output:

```
get-service | get-member
   TypeName: System.ServiceProcess.ServiceController
```

Name	MemberType	Definition
Name	AliasProperty	Name = ServiceName
Disposed	Event	System.EventHandler
Disposed		
Close	Method	System.Void Close()
. . .		
CanPauseAndContinue	Property	System.Boolean

```
CanPauseAndCo
. . .
Status                          Property  System.ServiceProcess.Service
```

> **TIP** By default, the Get-Member cmdlet does not show you the static methods and static properties of object classes. To get the static members of an object class, type get-member –static. For example, to get the static members of the ServiceProcess object, you'd enter get-service | get-member –static.

In the output, note that each facet of the Service object is listed by member type. You can make better sense of the list of available information when you filter for elements you want to see by adding the –MemberType parameter. The allowed values of –MemberType include

- AliasProperty, CodeProperty, NoteProperty, ParameterizedProperty, Property, PropertySet, ScriptProperty, CodeMethod, MemberSet, Method, and ScriptMethod, for examining elements of a particular type
- Properties, for examining all property-related elements
- Methods, for examining all method-related elements
- All, for examining all properties and methods (the default)

When you examine an object using Get-Member, note the alias properties. Aliases to properties work the same as other aliases. They're friendly names that you can use as shortcuts when you are working with an object. Whereas Service objects have only one alias property (Name), most well-known objects have several alias properties. For example, Process objects have the alias properties shown in the following example and sample output:

```
get-process | get-member
   TypeName: System.Diagnostics.Process

Name                    MemberType     Definition
----                    ----------     ----------
Handles                 AliasProperty  Handles = Handlecount
Name                    AliasProperty  Name = ProcessName
NPM                     AliasProperty  NPM =
NonpagedSystemMemory
PM                      AliasProperty  PM = PagedMemorySize
VM                      AliasProperty  VM = VirtualMemorySize
WS                      AliasProperty  WS = WorkingSet
```

And these aliases are displayed when you list running processes, as shown in the following example and sample output:

```
get-process
```

Handles	NPM(K)	PM(K)	WS(K)	VM(M)	CPU(s)	Id	ProcessName
52	3	1296	3844	51	3.24	3004	acrotray
139	4	2560	7344	75	6.11	1292	AlertService
573	14	14680	11028	120	7.41	2764	aolsoftware
97	4	2872	4476	53	8.02	1512	AppleMobil

When you type **get-process | get-member** and see that Process objects have dozens of other properties not listed, you might wonder what happened to these other properties and why they aren't listed. This occurs because PowerShell shows only streamlined views of well-known objects as part of the standard output. Typically, this output includes only the most important properties of an object.

PowerShell determines how to display an object of a particular type by using information stored in XML files that have names ending in .format.ps1xml. The formatting definitions for many well-known objects are in the types.ps1xml file. This file is stored in the $pshome directory.

The properties you don't see are still part of the object, and you have full access to them. For example, type **get-process winlogon | format-list –property ***, and you get complete details on every property of the Winlogon process by name and value.

Object Methods and Properties

Some methods and properties relate only to actual instances of an object, and this is why they are called *instance methods* and *instance properties*. The term *instance* is simply another word for *object*.

Often you will want to reference the methods and properties of objects through a variable in which the object is stored. To see how this works, consider the following example:

```
$myString = "THIS IS A TEST!"
```

Here, you store a character string in a variable named $myString. In PowerShell, the string is represented as a String object. String objects have a Length property that stores the length of the string. Therefore, you can determine the length of the string created previously by typing the following command:

```
$myString.Length
```

In this example, the length of the string is 15 characters, so the output is 15.

Although String objects have only one property, they have a number of methods, including ToUpper() and ToLower(). You use the ToUpper() method to display all the characters in the string in uppercase letters. You use the ToLower() method to display all the characters in the string in lowercase letters. For example, to change the previously created string to "this is a test!", you type the following command:

```
$myString.ToLower()
```

From these examples, you can see that you access a property of an object by placing a dot between the variable name that represents the object and the property name as shown here:

```
$ObjectName.PropertyName
$ObjectName.PropertyName = Value
```

And you can see that you access a method of an object by placing a dot between the variable name that represents the object and the method name, such as

```
$ObjectName.MethodName()
```

Because methods perform actions on objects, you often need to pass parameter values in the method call. The syntax for passing parameters in a method call is

```
$ObjectName.MethodName(parameter1, parameter2, …)
```

So far the techniques we've discussed for working with methods and properties are for actual instances of an object. However, you won't always be working with a tangible instance of an object. Sometimes, you'll want to work directly with the static methods and static properties that apply to a particular .NET Framework class type as a whole.

The .NET Framework includes a wide range of class types. Generally, .NET Framework class names are always enclosed in brackets. Examples of class type names include [System.Datetime], for working with dates and times, and [System.Diagnostics.Process], for working with system processes. However, PowerShell automatically prepends *System.* to type names, so you can also use [Datetime] for working with dates and times and [Diagnostics.Process] for working with system processes.

Static methods and static properties of a .NET Framework class are always available when you are working with an object class. However, if you try to display them with the Get-Member cmdlet, you won't see them unless you use the –Static parameter as well, such as

```
[System.Datetime] | get-member -Static
```

You access a static property of a .NET Framework class by placing two colon characters (::) between the bracketed class name and the property name as shown here:

```
[ClassName]::PropertyName
[ClassName]::PropertyName = Value
```

In this example, you use a static property of the [System.Datetime] class to display the current date and time:

```
[System.Datetime]::Now
```

```
Monday, February 15, 2017 11:05:22 PM
```

You access a static method of a .NET Framework class by placing two colon characters (::) between the bracketed class name and the method name, such as

```
[ClassName]::MethodName()
```

The syntax for passing parameters in a call to a static method is

```
[ClassName]::MethodName(parameter1, parameter2, …)
```

In this example, you use a static method of the [System.Diagnostics.Process] class to display information about a process:

```
[System.Diagnostics.Process]::GetProcessById(0)

Handles  NPM(K)   PM(K)     WS(K) VM(M)    CPU(s)     Id ProcessName
-------  ------   -----     ----- -----    ------     -- -----------
      0       0       0        24     0     64.22      0 Idle
```

Object Types

By default, all object types that are used by PowerShell are defined in .ps1xml files in the $pshome directory. The default formatting and type files include the following:

- **Certificate.Format.ps1xml** Provides formatting guidelines for certificate objects and X.509 certificates
- **Diagnostics.Format.ps1xml** Provides formatting guidelines for objects created when you are working with performance counters and diagnostics in PowerShell
- **DotNetTypes.Format.ps1xml** Provides formatting guidelines for .NET Framework objects not covered in other formatting files, including CultureInfo, FileVersionInfo, and EventLogEntry objects
- **FileSystem.Format.ps1xml** Provides formatting guidelines for file system objects
- **GetEvent.Types.ps1xml** Provides formatting guidelines for event log configuration, event log records, and performance counters
- **Help.Format.ps1xml** Provides formatting guidelines for the views PowerShell uses to display help file content
- **PowerShellCore.Format.ps1xml** Provides formatting guidelines for objects that are created by the PowerShell core cmdlets
- **PowerShellTrace.Format.ps1xml** Provides formatting guidelines for PSTraceSource objects generated when you are performing traces in PowerShell
- **Registry.Format.ps1xml** Provides formatting guidelines for Registry objects

- **Types.ps1xml**   Provides formatting guidelines for System objects
- **WSMan.Format.ps1xml**   Provides formatting guidelines for objects created when you are working with WS Management configurations in PowerShell

PowerShell accomplishes automatic typing by using a common object that has the capability to state its type dynamically, add members dynamically, and interact with other objects through a consistent abstraction layer. This object is the PSObject. The PSObject can encapsulate any base object, whether it is a system object, a WMI object, a Component Object Model (COM) object, or an Active Directory Service Interfaces (ADSI) object.

By acting as a wrapper for an existing base object, the PSObject can be used to access adapted views of a base object or to extend a base object. Although an adapted view of a base object exposes only members that are directly accessible, you can access alternate views of a base object, and those alternate views can provide access to the extended members of a base object. Available views for base objects include the following:

- **PSBase**   Used to access the original properties of the object without extension or adaptation
- **PSAdapted**   Used to access an adapted view of the object
- **PSExtended**   Used to access the extended properties and methods of the object that were added in the Types.ps1xml files or by using the Add-Member cmdlet
- **PSObject**   Used to access the adapter that converts the base object to a PSObject
- **PSTypeNames**   Used to access a list of types that describe the object

By default, PowerShell returns information only from the PSObject, PSExtended, and PSTypeNames views. However, you can use dot notation to access alternate views. In the following example, you obtain a Win32_Process object representing the winlogon.exe process:

```
$pr = Get-WmiObject Win32_Process | where-object {
$_.ProcessName -eq "winlogon.exe" }
```

If you then type **$pr** at the PowerShell prompt, you see all the information for this process from the PSObject, PSExtended, and PSTypeNames views. You can access the PSBase view to expose the members of the base object as shown in this example:

```
$pr.PSBase
```

Because there might be times when you want to extend an object yourself, you can do this using a custom Types.ps1xml file or by using the Add-Member cmdlet. The three most common extensions you'll want to use are

- **ScriptProperty**   Allows you to add properties to types, including those that are based on a calculation
- **AliasProperty**   Allows you to define an alias for a property
- **ScriptMethod**   Allows you to define an action to take on an object

In custom Types.ps1xml files, you can define these extensions using XML elements, and there are many examples available in the $pshome directory. These extensions also can be added dynamically at the prompt or in your scripts. For example, a ScriptProperty is a type of object member that uses a block of code to process or extract information related to an object. The basic syntax is

```
$ObjectName | add-member -membertype scriptproperty
-name Name -value {CodeBlock}
```

Because the –Name and –Value parameters are position sensitive, you don't have to specify them explicitly. Knowing this, consider the following example and sample output:

```
$proc = get-process powershell;
$proc | add-member -Type scriptproperty "UpTime" {return ((date)
- ($this.starttime))};
$proc | select Name, @{name='Uptime'; Expression={"{0:n0}" -f
$_.UpTime.TotalMinutes}};


Name                                                Uptime
----                                                ------
powershell                                             242
```

Here, you obtain a process object for any Powershell.exe processes running on the computer. You then use the Add-Member cmdlet to extend the standard process object by adding a ScriptProperty. The script block defined in the ScriptProperty is used to calculate the time that a process has been running. Then you get the process object and format its output to include the process name and new Uptime property. Using a regular expression, you convert the output value of the Uptime property to a value in minutes. The result is as shown.

What you don't see happening here is that the first time you assign a value to $proc, you are adding a collection of process objects. You then generate a second collection of process objects because you use the Add-Member cmdlet to wrap the original Process objects in a new PSObject instance that includes the new property you've defined.

While a ScriptProperty extends an object, an AliasProperty simply makes it easier to work with an object. To see how, let's access the C: drive using the Get-PSDrive cmdlet and then create a new PSDriveInfo object so that we can access information about the C: drive. Here's an example:

```
$myDrive = get-psdrive C
$myDriveInfo = New-Object System.IO.DriveInfo $myDrive
```

Now that you have an object you can work with, you can display information about the C: drive simply by typing **$myDriveInfo**. The output you see provides information about the drive, its status, its size, and its free space, and it will be similar to the following:

```
Name                 : C:\
DriveType            : Fixed
DriveFormat          : NTFS
IsReady              : True
AvailableFreeSpace   : 302748798976
TotalFreeSpace       : 302748798976
TotalSize            : 490580373504
RootDirectory        : C:\
VolumeLabel          : OS
```

Although the default format is a list, you can also view the information in table format, such as when you are working with multiple drives. When you type

$myDriveInfo | format-table –property *, the output you get isn't pretty (unless you have a very wide console window). To clean up the output, you might want to create aliases for properties, such as AvailableFreeSpace, TotalFreeSpace, and RootDirectory. You can do this using the Add-Member cmdlet as well. The basic syntax is

```
$ObjectName | add-member -membertype aliasproperty -name
AliasName -value PropertyName
```

where *ObjectName* is the name of the object you are working with, *AliasName* is the new alias for the property, and *PropertyName* is the original name of the property, such as

```
$myDriveInfo | add-member -membertype aliasproperty
-name Free -value AvailableFreeSpace
```

```
$myDriveInfo | add-member -membertype aliasproperty
-name Format -value DriveFormat
```

You can access an alias property as you would any other property. For example, to display the value of the AvailableFreeSpace property, you can type either

```
$myDriveInfo.AvailableFreeSpace
```

or

```
$myDriveInfo.Free
```

You can use alias properties in formatted output as well. An example is shown in the following command and sample output:

```
$myDriveInfo | format-table –property Name, Free, Format
```

Name	Free	Format
C:\	302748483584	NTFS

You use ScriptMethod extensions to define additional methods for an object. The basic syntax is

```
$ObjectName | add-member -membertype scriptmethod -name Name
 -value {CodeBlock}
```

Because the –Name and –Value parameters are position sensitive, you don't have to specify them explicitly. Knowing this, consider the following example:

```
$myDrive = get-psdrive C

$myDrive | add-member -membertype scriptmethod -name Remove
 -value { $force = [bool] $args[0];
 if ($force) {$this | Remove-PSDrive }
 else {$this | Remove-PSDrive -Confirm}
}
```

Here you define a Remote method for a PSDrive object. If you call the method without passing any argument values, PowerShell prompts you to confirm that you want to remove the drive from the current session. If you call the method and pass $true or 0 (zero) as the first argument, PowerShell removes the drive from the current session without requiring confirmation.

Digging Deeper into Objects

To dig a bit deeper into objects, let's look at the $host object. As discussed in the "Configuring Windows PowerShell Console Properties" section in Chapter 1, "Windows PowerShell Essentials," you can use the PowerShell console's Properties dialog box to specify the options, fonts, layouts, and colors to use. The $host object also gives you access to the underlying user interface, which can be either the PowerShell console or the PowerShell application.

To view the current settings of the $host object, type the following command:

```
$host.ui.rawui | format-list -property *
```

The output you see will be similar to the following:

```
ForegroundColor        : DarkYellow
BackgroundColor        : DarkMagenta
CursorPosition         : 0,1050
WindowPosition         : 0,1001
CursorSize             : 25
BufferSize             : 120,3000
WindowSize             : 120,50
```

```
MaxWindowSize         : 120,95
MaxPhysicalWindowSize : 240,95
KeyAvailable          : False
WindowTitle           : Windows PowerShell
```

In the output, you see a number of properties, including the following:

- ForegroundColor, which sets the color of the prompt and text
- BackgroundColor, which sets the background color of the window
- WindowTitle, which sets the name of the PowerShell window

To work with the PowerShell window, you must obtain a reference to the $host object. The easiest way to do this is to store the $host object in a variable, such as

```
$myHostWin = $host.ui.rawui
```

After you have a reference to an object, you can work with the object through the available properties and methods. You can set the foreground or background color to any of the following default color values:

- Black, DarkBlue, DarkGreen, DarkCyan
- DarkRed, DarkMagenta, DarkYellow, Gray
- DarkGray, Blue, Green, Cyan
- Red, Magenta, Yellow, White

To do so, reference the host window object with the property name and the desired value, such as

```
$myHostWin.ForegroundColor = "White"
```

or

```
$myHostWin.BackgroundColor = "DarkGray"
```

Similarly, you can use the WindowTitle property to specify the title for the window. Here's an example:

```
$myHostWin.WindowTitle = "PowerShell on $env.computername"
```

Here, you set the window title to a value based on the computer name. Thus, if you are logged on to TechPC32, the window title is set to

```
PowerShell on TechPC32
```

Take a look back at the output values for the properties of the $host object. Several of properties have values separated by commas. This tells you the value is an array of subproperties. To view the subproperties of a property, you can examine that property separately and format the output as a list. For example, to examine the subproperties of CursorPosition, you can type the following command:

```
$host.ui.rawui.CursorPosition | format-list -property *
```

The output will look similar to the following:

```
X : 0
Y : 2999
```

This tells you the CursorPosition property has two subproperties: X and Y. You reference subproperties of properties by extending the dot notation as shown in these examples:

```
$host.ui.rawui.CursorPosition.X
```

or

```
$host.ui.rawui.CursorPosition.Y
```

If you continue examining subproperties of properties, you'll find both CursorPosition and WindowPosition have X and Y subproperties. You'll also find that BufferSize, WindowSize, MaxWindowSize, and MaxPhysicalWindowSize have Width and Height properties.

After you know what the subproperties are, you can examine their values in the same way you examine the values of standard properties. However, in this case the subproperties cannot be set directly; you must create an instance of the $host object using the New-Object cmdlet and then modify the properties of the object instance.

This means you must first get a reference to the $host object as shown here:

```
$myHost = $host.ui.rawui
```

Then you create a new object instance and set the desired subproperties on the new instance as shown here:

```
$myHostWindowSize = New-Object
System.Management.Automation.Host.Size(150,100)
```

In this example, you dynamically set the host window size. The first value passed is the desired width. The second value passed is the desired height.

Working with COM and .NET Framework Objects

The Component Object Model (COM) and the .NET Framework are two object models you'll work with frequently in PowerShell. Although many applications provide scripting and administrative objects through COM, .NET Framework and even PowerShell cmdlets are becoming increasingly prevalent.

Creating and Using COM Objects

You can create instances of COM objects using the New-Object cmdlet. The basic syntax is

```
New-Object [-Set AssocArray] [-Strict] [-ComObject] String
```

When creating the object, set the –ComObject parameter to the object's programmatic identifier (ProgID). Most well-known COM objects can be used within PowerShell, including those for Windows Script Host (WSH). The following example creates a shortcut on your desktop:

```
$spath = "$Home\Desktop\PowerShellHome.lnk"
$WshShell = New-Object -ComObject WScript.Shell
$scut = $WshShell.CreateShortcut($spath)
$scut.TargetPath = $PSHome
$scut.Save()
```

This shortcut is called *PowerShellHome*, and it links to the $PSHome directory.

> **TIP** After you've attached to a COM object, you can use tab expansion to view available options. For example, if $a is your object, type **$a.** and then press Tab or Shift+Tab to browse available methods and properties.

Beyond WSH, there are many other COM objects you can use. Table 8-1 lists some of these by their ProgID.

TABLE 8-1 Common COM Objects for Use with Windows PowerShell

PROGID	DESCRIPTION
Access.Application	Accesses Microsoft Office Access
CEnroll.Cenroll	Accesses certificate enrollment services
Excel.Application	Accesses Microsoft Office Excel
Excel.Sheet	Accesses worksheets in Excel
HNetCfg.FwMgr	Accesses Windows Firewall
InternetExplorer.Application	Accesses Internet Explorer
MAPI.Session	Accesses Messaging Application Programming Interface (MAPI) sessions
Microsoft.Update.AutoUpdate	Accesses the autoupdate schedule for Microsoft Update
Microsoft.Update.Installer	Allows you to install updates from Microsoft Update
Microsoft.Update.Searches	Allows you to search for updates from Microsoft Update
Microsoft.Update.Session	Accesses the update history for Microsoft Update
Microsoft.Update.SystemInfo	Accesses system information for Microsoft Update

PROGID	DESCRIPTION
Outlook.Application	Accesses Microsoft Office Outlook
OutlookExpress.MessageList	Allows for automation of e-mail in Microsoft Office Outlook Express
PowerPoint.Application	Accesses Microsoft Office PowerPoint
Publisher.Application	Accesses Microsoft Office Publisher
SAPI.SpVoice	Accesses the Microsoft Speech application programming interface (API)
Scripting.FileSystemObject	Accesses the computer's file system
SharePoint.OpenDocuments	Accesses Microsoft SharePoint Services
Shell.Application	Accesses the File Explorer shell
Shell.LocalMachine	Accesses information about the Windows shell on the local computer
SQLDMO.SQLServer	Accesses the management features of Microsoft SQL Server
WMPlayer.OCX	Accesses Windows Media Player
Word.Application	Accesses Microsoft Office Word
Word.Document	Accesses documents in Word

To show you how easy it is to work with COM objects, I'll work through a series of basic examples with File Explorer, Internet Explorer, and Excel. The following example creates an instance of the File Explorer shell and then uses its

Windows() method to display the location name of all open instances of File Explorer and Internet Explorer:

```
$shell = new-object -comobject shell.application
$shell.windows() | select-object locationname
```

Data
This PC
Network

By piping the output to Select-Object LocationName, you display the value of the LocationName property for each shell object. File Explorer windows are listed by name or folder, such as Computer or Network. Internet Explorer windows are listed by Web page title. With Internet Explorer 11 and later, you get a listing for each page opened in a tabbed window as well. You get details about both File Explorer and Internet Explorer because both applications use the File Explorer shell.

If you want to know all the properties available for each shell object, pipe the output to Select-Object without specifying properties to display, as shown in this example and sample output:

```
$shell = new-object -comobject shell.application
$shell.windows() | select-object
Application         : System.__ComObject
Parent              : System.__ComObject
Container           :
Document            : mshtml.HTMLDocumentClass
TopLevelContainer   : True
Type                : HTML Document
Left                : 959
Top                 : 1
Width               : 961
Height              : 1169
LocationName        : Windows Nation: Home of Tech Author
William Stanek
LocationURL         : http://www.williamstanek.com/
Busy                : False
Name                : Windows Internet Explorer
HWND                : 854818
FullName            : C:\Program Files\Internet
Explorer\iexplore.exe
Path                : C:\Program Files\Internet Explorer\
```

```
Visible             : True
StatusBar           : True
StatusText          : Done
ToolBar             : 1
MenuBar             : True
FullScreen          : False
ReadyState          : 4
Offline             : False
Silent              : False
RegisterAsBrowser   : False
RegisterAsDropTarget : True
TheaterMode         : False
AddressBar          : True
Resizable           : True
```

> **REAL WORLD**   Some COM objects have a .NET Framework wrapper that connects them to the .NET Framework. Because the behavior of the wrapper might be different from the behavior of the normal COM object, New-Object has a –Strict parameter to warn you about wrappers. When you use this flag, PowerShell displays a warning message to tell you that you are not working with a standard COM object. The COM object is still created, however.

The following example opens Internet Explorer to *www.williamstanek.com*:

```
$iexp = new-object -comobject "InternetExplorer.Application"
$iexp.navigate("www.williamstanek.com")
$iexp.visible = $true
```

Here, you create a new COM object for Internet Explorer. The new object has the same properties as those for the shell window listed previously. You use the Navigate() method to set the location to browse and the Visible property to display the window. To see a list of all methods and properties you can work with, enter the example and then type **$iexp | get-member**. You can call any method listed as shown in the example. You can modify properties that you can get and set.

The following example accesses the Microsoft Speech API and talks to you:

```
$v = new-object -comobject "SAPI.SPVoice"
$v.speak("Well, hello there. How are you?")
```

Here, you create a new COM object for the Speech API. You use the Speak()
method to say something. To see a list of all methods and properties you can
work with, enter the example and then enter $v | get-member. You can call any
method listed as shown in the example. You can modify any property that you
can get and set.

The following example works with Microsoft Excel:

```
$a = New-Object -comobject "Excel.Application"
$a.Visible = $True
$wb = $a.workbooks.add()
$ws = $wb.worksheets.item(1)


$ws.cells.item(1,1) = "Computer Name"
$ws.cells.item(1,2) = "Location"
$ws.cells.item(1,3) = "OS Type"
$ws.cells.item(2,1) = "TechPC84"
$ws.cells.item(2,2) = "5th Floor"
$ws.cells.item(2,3) = "Windows 8.1"


$a.activeworkbook.saveas("c:\data\myws.xls")
```

Here, you create a new COM object for Excel and then you display the Excel
window by setting the Visible property. When you instantiate the Excel object,
you have a number of methods and properties available for working with the
Excel application and a number of related subobjects that represent workbooks,
worksheets, and individual table cells. To view the default values for properties
of the Excel object, enter the example and then enter **$a**. To view the methods
and properties available for working with the top-level Excel application object,
enter **$a | get-member**.

After you create the Excel object, you add a workbook to the application
window by using the Add() method of the Workbooks object. This creates a
Workbook object, which also has methods and properties as well as a related
Worksheets object array. To view the default values for properties of the
Workbook object, enter **$wb**. To view the methods and properties available for
working with the Workbook object, type **$wb | get-member**.

Next, you specify that you want to work with the first worksheet in the
workbook you just created. You do this by using the Item() method of the

Worksheets object array. This creates a Worksheet object, which also has methods and properties as well as a related Cells object array. To view the default values for properties of the Worksheet object, enter **$ws**. To view the methods and properties available for working with the Worksheet object, enter **$ws | get-member**.

Once you've created a worksheet, you can add data to the worksheet. You do this by using the Item() method of the Cells object array. When you call the Item() method, you specify the column and row position of the cell you want to write to and then specify the value you want. To view the default values for properties of the Cells object, enter **$ws.cells**. To view the methods and properties available for working with the Cells object, enter **$ws.cells | get-member**.

Individual table cells are represented by Cell objects. To view the default values for properties of the cell in column 1 row 1, enter **$ws.cells.item(1,1)**. To view the methods and properties available for working with the Cell object in column 1 row 1, enter **$ws.cells.item(1,1) | get-member**.

Working with .NET Framework Classes and Objects

The .NET Framework is so tightly integrated with PowerShell that it is difficult to talk about PowerShell and not talk about .NET as well. We've used .NET classes and .NET objects in this and other chapters.

One way to instantiate and use a .NET Framework object is to make a direct invocation to a static class. To do this, you enclose the class name in square brackets, insert two colon characters, and then add a method or property call. This is the same technique we previously used to work with instances of [System.Datetime], [System.Math], and other classes.

The following example creates an instance of the [System.Environment] class and gets the current directory:

```
[system.environment]::CurrentDirectory

C:\data\scripts\myscripts
```

> **TIP** You can use tab expansion to view static members of a .NET Framework class. Type the class name in brackets, type **::** and then press Tab or Shift+Tab to browse available methods and properties.

You also can create a reference to an instance of a .NET Framework object using the New-Object cmdlet. The basic syntax is

```
New-Object [-Set AssocArray] [-TypePath Strings]
[[-ArgumentList] Objects] [-TypeName] String
```

The following example creates a reference object for the Application log through the System.Diagnostic.Eventlog object:

```
$log = new-object -type system.diagnostics.eventlog
-argumentlist application
```

```
Max(K) Retain OverflowAction         Entries Name
------ ------ --------------         ------- ----
20,480      0 OverwriteAsNeeded       45,061 application
```

> **TIP** After you've attached to a .NET Framework class instance, you can use tab expansion to view instance members. For example, if you store the object in $log, you type **$log,** type a dot (**.**), and then press Tab or Shift+Tab to browse available methods and properties.

Although we've looked at many .NET Framework classes in this chapter, there are many more available. Table 8-2 lists some of these by their class name.

TABLE 8-2 Common .NET Framework Objects for Use with Windows PowerShell

CLASS	DESCRIPTION
Microsoft.Win32.Registry	Provides Registry objects for working with root keys
Microsoft.Win32.RegistryKey	Represents keys in the registry
System.AppDomain	Represents the environment where applications execute
System.Array	Provides interaction with arrays

CLASS	DESCRIPTION
System.Console	Represents the standard input, output, and error streams for the console
System.Convert	Provides static methods and a property for converting data types
System.Datetime	Represents a datetime value
System.Diagnostics.Debug	Provides methods and properties for debugging
System.Diagnostics.EventLog	Provides interaction with Windows event logs
System.Diagnostics.Process	Provides interaction with Windows processes
System.Drawing.Bitmap	Represents pixel data for images
System.Drawing.Image	Provides methods and properties for working with images
System.Environment	Provides information about the working environment and platform
System.Guid	Represents a globally unique identifier (GUID)
System.IO.Stream	Represents IO streams
System.Management. Automation.PowerShell	Represents a PowerShell object to which you can add notes, properties, and so on
System.Math	Provides static methods and properties for performing mathematical functions
System.Net.Dns	Provides interaction with Domain Name System (DNS)

CLASS	DESCRIPTION
System.Net.NetworkCredential	Provides credentials for network authentication
System.Net.WebClient	Provides interaction with the Web client
System.Random	Represents a random number generator
System.Reflection.Assembly	Represents .NET Framework assemblies so that you can load and work with them
System.Security.Principal.WellKnownSidType	Represents security identifiers (SIDs)
System.Security.Principal.WindowsBuiltInRole	Specifies built-in roles
System.Security.Principal.WindowsIdentity	Represents a Windows user
System.Security.Principal.WindowsPrincipal	Allows checking of a user's group membership
System.Security.SecureString	Represents secure text that is encrypted for privacy
System.String	Provides interaction with strings
System.Text.RegularExpressions.Regex	Represents immutable regular expressions
System.Threading.Thread	Provides interaction with threads
System.Type	Represents type declarations
System.Uri	Represents uniform resource identifiers (URIs)

CLASS	DESCRIPTION
System.Windows.Forms. FlowLayoutPanel	Represents a layout panel
System.Windows.Forms.Form	Represents a window or dialog box in an application

Some .NET Framework objects require that related .NET Framework assemblies be loaded before you can use them. Assemblies are simply sets of files, which can include dynamic-link libraries (DLLs), EXE files, and other resources that the .NET Framework object needs to work properly. You'll know that a .NET Framework object requires an assembly because PowerShell will throw an error if the assembly is not loaded, such as

```
Unable to find type [system.drawing.image]: make sure that the
assembly containing this type is loaded.
At line:1 char:23
+ [system.drawing.image] <<<< |get-member -static
    + CategoryInfo          : InvalidOperation:
(system.drawing.image:String)
[], RuntimeException
    + FullyQualifiedErrorId : TypeNotFound
```

The solution is to use the [Reflection.Assembly] class to load the required assemblies. One way to do this is with the LoadWithPartialName() method of the Reflection.Assembly class. The syntax is

```
[Reflection.Assembly]::LoadWithPartialName("ClassName")
```

where *ClassName* is the name of the .NET Framework class that completes the requirement. For example, you can use the System.Drawing.Bitmap class to convert a GIF image to JPEG. Because this class requires the assemblies of the System.Windows.Forms class, you must load the related assemblies before you can convert an image.

When you load a reflection assembly, PowerShell confirms this and displays the related output automatically as shown in this example:

```
[Reflection.Assembly]::LoadWithPartialName
("System.Windows.Forms")
```

```
GAC       Version       Location
---       -------       --------
True      v4.0.30319   C:\Windows\assembly\GAC_MSIL\
System.Windows.Forms \v4.0_4.0.0.0__b77a5c561934e089\
System.Windows.For...
```

This output is important. The True value for GAC tells you the assembly loaded successfully. The Version value tells you the specific version of .NET Framework the assembly uses. The location tells you the location in the operating system.

When you call a reflection assembly, I recommend formatting the output as a list as shown in this example:

```
[Reflection.Assembly]::LoadWithPartialName
("System.Windows.Forms") | format-list
```

```
CodeBase :
file:///C:/Windows/assembly/GAC_MSIL/System.Windows.Forms/
4.0_4.0.0.0__b77a5c561934e089/System.Windows.Forms.dll
EntryPoint :
EscapedCodeBase :
file:///C:/Windows/assembly/GAC_MSIL/System.Windows.
Forms/4.0_4.0.0.0__b77a5c561934e089/System.Windows.Forms.dll
FullName   : System.Windows.Forms, Version=4.0.0.0,
Culture=neutral, PublicKeyToken=b77a5c561934e089
GlobalAssemblyCache       : True
HostContext               : 0
ImageFileMachine          :
ImageRuntimeVersion       : v4.0.303139
Location                  :
C:\Windows\assembly\GAC_MSIL\System.Windows.Forms\4.0_4.0.0.0__b
77a5c561934e089\System.Windows.Forms.dll
ManifestModule            : System.Windows.Forms.dll
MetadataToken             :
PortableExecutableKind :
ReflectionOnly            : False
```

This listing gives you important additional details about the assembly you just loaded, including the simple text name, version number, culture identifier, and public key. All of this information is listed as the FullName entry. If you copy the FullName entry exactly, beginning with the simple text name, you have the full load string you need to use the Load() method. Because the Load() method is the preferred way to load assemblies and the LoadWithPartialName() method is deprecated, this will help you prepare for when you can no longer use the LoadWithPartialName() method.

To continue the example, after you've loaded the [System.Windows.Forms] class, you can convert a GIF image in the current directory to JPEG using the following statements:

```
$image = New-Object System.Drawing.Bitmap myimage.gif
$image.Save("mynewimage.jpg","JPEG")
```

Here, you get an image called MyImage.gif in the current directory and then convert the image to JPEG format. You can substitute any GIF image and add an image path as necessary. While you are working with the image, you can view its width, height, and other properties by entering **$image**. You can view methods for working with the image by entering **$image | get-member**.

Performing WMI Queries

Windows Management Instrumentation (WMI) is a management framework that you can use to query a computer to determine its attributes. For example, you can create a WMI query to determine the operating system running on a computer or the amount of available memory. WMI queries by themselves are helpful, especially when used in scripts.

You can use WMI queries to examine settings based on just about any measurable characteristic of a computer, including

- Amount of memory installed
- Available hard disk space
- Processor type or speed
- Network adapter type or speed
- Operating system version, service pack level, or hotfix
- Registry key or key value
- System services that are running

You create WMI queries using the WMI Query Language. The basic syntax is

```
Select * from WMIObjectClass where Condition
```

In this syntax, *WMIObjectClass* is the WMI object class you want to work with, and *Condition* is the condition you want to evaluate. The Select statement returns objects of the specified class. A condition has three parts:

- The name of the object property you are examining
- An operator, such as = for equals, > for greater than, or < for less than
- The value to evaluate

Operators can also be defined by using Is or Like. The Is operator is used to exactly match criteria. The Like condition is used to match a keyword or text string within a value. In the following example, you create a query to look for computers running Windows 8.1 or Windows Server 2012 R2:

```
Select * from Win32_OperatingSystem where Version like "%6.3%"
```

The Win32_OperatingSystem class tracks the overall operating system configuration. The Win32_OperatingSystem class is one of two WMI object classes that you'll use frequently. The other is Win32_ComputerSystem. The Win32_ComputerSystem class tracks the overall computer configuration.

In Windows PowerShell, you can use the Get-WMIObject cmdlet to get a WMI object that you want to work with. The basic syntax is

```
Get-WmiObject -Class WMIClass -Namespace NameSpace
-ComputerName ComputerName
```

where *WMIClass* is the WMI class you want to work with, *NameSpace* sets the namespace to use within WMI, and *ComputerName* sets the name of the computer to work with.

When working with WMI, you should work with the root namespace, as specified by setting the –Namespace parameter to root/cimv2. By using the –Computer parameter, you can specify the computer you want to work with. If you want to work with the local computer, use a dot (.) instead of a computer name. By redirecting the object to Format-List *, you can list all the properties of the object and their values.

Following this, you can examine the Win32_OperatingSystem object and its properties to obtain summary information regarding the operating system configuration of a computer by typing the following command at the Windows PowerShell prompt:

```
Get-WmiObject -Class Win32_OperatingSystem -Namespace root/cimv2
 -ComputerName . | Format-List *
```

To save the output in a file, simply redirect the output to a file. In the following example, you redirect the output to a file in the working directory named os_save.txt:

```
Get-WmiObject -Class Win32_OperatingSystem -Namespace root/cimv2
-ComputerName . | Format-List * > os_save.txt
```

The detailed operating system information tells you a great deal about the operating system running on the computer. The same is true for computer configuration details, which can be obtained by typing the following command at a Windows PowerShell prompt:

```
Get-WmiObject -Class Win32_ComputerSystem -Namespace root/cimv2
-ComputerName . | Format-List *
```

In addition to targeting operating system or computer configuration properties, you might want to target computers based on the amount of disk space and file system type. In the following example, you target computers that have more than 100 megabytes (MB) of available space on the C, D, or G partition:

```
get-wmiobject -query 'Select * from Win32_LogicalDisk where
(Name = "C:" OR Name = "D:"  OR Name = "G:" ) AND DriveType = 3
AND FreeSpace > 104857600 AND FileSystem = "NTFS"'
```

In the preceding example, *DriveType = 3* represents a local disk, and *FreeSpace* units are in bytes (100 MB = 104,857,600 bytes). The partitions must be located on one or more local fixed disks, and they must be running the NTFS file system. Note that while PowerShell understands storage units in MB, KB, or whatever, the WMI query language does not.

In Windows PowerShell, you can examine all the properties of the Win32_LogicalDisk object by typing the following command at the Windows PowerShell prompt:

```
Get-WmiObject -Class Win32_LogicalDisk -Namespace root/cimv2
-ComputerName .  | Format-List *
```

As you'll see, there are many properties you can work with, including Compressed, which indicates whether a disk is compressed. Table 8-3 provides an overview of these and other important WMI object classes.

TABLE 8-3 WMI Classes Commonly Used with Windows PowerShell

WMI CLASS	DESCRIPTIONS
Win32_BaseBoard	Represents the motherboard
Win32_BIOS	Represents the attributes of the computer's firmware
Win32_BootConfiguration	Represents the computer's boot configuration
Win32_CacheMemory	Represents cache memory on the computer
Win32_CDROMDrive	Represents each CD-ROM drive configured on the computer
Win32_ComputerSystem	Represents a computer system in a Windows environment
Win32_Desktop	Represents the common characteristics of a user's desktop
Win32_DesktopMonitor	Represents the type of monitor or display device connected to the computer
Win32_DiskDrive	Represents each physical disk drive on a computer
Win32_DiskPartition	Represents each partitioned area of a physical disk
Win32_DiskQuota	Tracks disk space usage for NTFS volumes

WMI CLASS	DESCRIPTIONS
Win32_Environment	Represents a system environment setting on a computer
Win32_LogicalDisk	Represents each logical disk device used for data storage
Win32_LogonSession	Provides information about the current logon session
Win32_NetworkAdapter	Represents each network adapter on the computer
Win32_NetworkAdapterConfiguration	Represents the configuration of each network adapter on the computer
Win32_NetworkConnection	Represents an active network connection
Win32_OperatingSystem	Represents the working environment for the operating system
Win32_OSRecoveryConfiguration	Represents recovery and dump files
Win32_PageFileUsage	Represents the page file used for handling virtual memory swapping
Win32_PhysicalMemory	Represents each DIMM of physical memory configured on the computer
Win32_PhysicalMemoryArray	Represents the total memory configuration of the computer by capacity and number of memory devices
Win32_Printer	Represents each configured print device on the computer
Win32_PrinterConfiguration	Represents configuration details for print devices

WMI CLASS	DESCRIPTIONS
Win32_PrintJob	Represents active print jobs generated by applications
Win32_Processor	Represents each processor or processor core on the computer
Win32_QuickFixEngineeering	Represents updates that have been applied to the computer
Win32_Registry	Represents the Windows registry
Win32_SCSIController	Represents each SCSI controller on the computer
Win32_Service	Represents each service configured on the computer
Win32_Share	Represents each file share configured on the computer
Win32_SoundDevice	Represents the computer's sound device

Using the techniques I discussed previously, you can examine the properties of any or all of these objects in Windows PowerShell. If you do, you will find that Win32_PhysicalMemoryArray has a MaxCapacity property that tracks the total physical memory in kilobytes. Knowing this, you can easily create a WMI query to look for computers with 256 MB of RAM or more. The WMI query to handle the task is the following:

```
if (get-wmiobject -query "Select * from
Win32_PhysicalMemoryArray where
MaxCapacity > 262000") {write-host $env:computername}

CORPC87
```

I used the value 262000 because there are 262,144 kilobytes in 256 MB, and we want the computer to have at least this capacity. Now if you add this statement to a job running on remote computers as discussed in Chapter 5, "Using Background Jobs and Scheduled Jobs," you can search across the enterprise to find computers that meet your specifications.

To display a complete list of WMI objects, type the following command at the Windows PowerShell prompt:

```
Get-WmiObject -list -Namespace root/cimv2 -ComputerName . |
Format-List name
```

Because the list of available objects is so long, you'll definitely want to redirect the output to a file. In the following example, you redirect the output to a file in the working directory called FullWMIObjectList.txt:

```
Get-WmiObject -list -Namespace root/cimv2 -ComputerName . |
Format-List name > FullWMIObjectList.txt
```

Rather than viewing all WMI classes, you might want to see only the Win32 WMI classes. To view only the Win32 WMI classes, use the following command:

```
Get-WmiObject -list | where {$_.name -like "*Win32_*"}
```

Performing MI Queries in CIM Sessions

Common Information Model (CIM) describes the structure and behavior of managed resources. As discussed in "Establishing CIM Sessions" in Chapter 4, WMI is a CIMOM server service that implements the CIM standard on Windows, and you can use CIM cmdlets to work with MI objects. You typically work with CIM objects on remote computers via CIM sessions.

When managing remote computers, you may find that working with CIM cmdlets is easier than working with WMI cmdlets. A key reason for this is that the CIM cmdlets make it easier to discover and work with Windows resources and components.

Working within CIM sessions is also much more efficient than performing individual MI queries. Why? When you establish a persistent CIM session, you work within the context of this session, and your management computer and the remote computers you are working with don't need to repeatedly establish, provision and remove connections.

How CIM makes Windows resources and components easier to work with is primarily through Get-CimClass, which makes it easy to discover available MI classes. For example, you can enter **Get-CimClass** to list every available MI object.

When you are working with CIM, not only are the WMI classes discussed previously available but so are generalized CIM classes. For example, Win32_OperatingSystem is a WMI class for working with Windows operating systems while CIM_OperatingSystem is a generalized MI class for working with any operating system that supports CIM.

CIM also gives you more options for working with related objects. For example, not only can you work with CIM_OperatingSystem, but you also can work with CIM_InstalledOS.

If you find a specific MI object that you want to work with, such as Win32_DiskDrive or Win32_LogicalDisk, you can use Get-CimClass to examine available methods and properties. In the following example, you work with Win32_LogicalDisk and display its methods and properties:

```
$dd = get-cimclass win32_logicaldisk
$dd.cimclassmethods
$dd.cimclassproperties
```

The methods available include: SetPowerState, Reset, Chkdsk, ScheduleAutoChk, and ExcludeFromAutochk. The properties available include: Caption, Description, InstallDate, Name, Status, Availability, DeviceID, ErrorDescription, LastErrorCode, PowerManagementCapabilities, and more.

> **NOTE**   With CIM cmdlets, the default namespace is root/cimv2.). Thus, unless you specify a different namespace to work with, the root/cimv2 namespace is used.

When you know the methods and properties of an object class, you can then more easily work with related instances of that object class. The cmdlet you use to work with instances of an object class is Get-CimInstance. The basic syntax for Get-CimInstance is:

```
Get-CimInstance -Class ClassName
```

Where ClassName is the name of the MI class you want to examine. In the following example, you store instances of Win32_LogicalDisk in the $dd variable and then list them:

```
$dd = get-ciminstance -class win32_logicaldisk
$dd | fl
```

And the result is output similar to the following:

```
DeviceID     : C:
DriveType    : 3
ProviderName :
FreeSpace    : 196397465600
Size         : 254779846656
VolumeName   : OS

DeviceID     : D:
DriveType    : 3
ProviderName :
FreeSpace    : 8478121984
Size         : 8518627328
VolumeName   : Data
```

Here, note that there are two logical disks on the computer. While the standard properties that are displayed include DeviceID, DriveType, FreeSpace, Size and VolumeName, there are many other available properties that you can work with including: BlockSize, NumberOfBlocks, Compressed, FileSystem, and QuotasDisabled.

You can easily display the value of any property. For example, if you wanted to identify the filesystems used by these logical drives, you would enter:

```
$dd = get-ciminstance -class win32_logicaldisk
$dd.filesystem
```

The resulting output shows the filesystem associated with each logical drive, such as:

```
NTFS
NTFS
```

Rather than working with all instances of an object, you'll often want to examine specific instances of an object, such as only the C drive rather than both the C and D drives. There are several ways you can do this. The first approach is to user a filter and the basic syntax is:

```
Get-CimInstance -Class ClassName -Filter Condition
```

Where *ClassName* is the name of the MI class you want to examine and *Condition* specifies the condition to evaluate and use as a filter. Conditions with Get-CimInstance work the same as discussed previously in "Performing WMI Queries." Consider the following example:

```
$dd = get-ciminstance -class win32_logicaldisk
-filter 'deviceid = "c:"'
```

Here, you use a filter to specify that you only want to examine the logical disk with the DeviceID of C:.

Another way to work with specific instances of an object is to filter using a query and the basic syntax is:

```
Get-CimInstance -Query Query
```

Where *Query* specifies the query string to use as a filter. Query strings with Get-CimInstance work the same as discussed previously in "Performing WMI Queries."

As with WMI, you can use CIM queries to examine settings based on just about any measurable characteristic of a computer. Consider the following example:

```
$dd = get-ciminstance -query 'Select * from
Win32_OperatingSystem where Version like "%6.3%"'
```

Here, you create a query to look for computers running Windows 8.1 or Windows Server 2012 R2.

About the Author

William Stanek (http://www.williamstanek.com/) has more than 20 years of hands-on experience with advanced programming and development. He is a leading technology expert, an award-winning author, and a pretty-darn-good instructional trainer. Over the years, his practical advice has helped millions of programmers, developers, and network engineers all over the world. His current and books include *Windows 8.1 Administration Pocket Consultants*, *Windows Server 2012 R2 Pocket Consultants* and *Windows Server 2012 R2 Inside Outs*.

William has been involved in the commercial Internet community since 1991. His core business and technology experience comes from more than 11 years of military service. He has substantial experience in developing server technology, encryption, and Internet solutions. He has written many technical white papers and training courses on a wide variety of topics. He frequently serves as a subject matter expert and consultant.

William has an MS with distinction in information systems and a BS in computer science, magna cum laude. He is proud to have served in the Persian Gulf War as a combat crewmember on an electronic warfare aircraft. He flew on numerous combat missions into Iraq and was awarded nine medals for his wartime service, including one of the United States of America's highest flying honors, the Air Force Distinguished Flying Cross. Currently, he resides in the Pacific Northwest with his wife and children.

William recently rediscovered his love of the great outdoors. When he's not writing, he can be found hiking, biking, backpacking, traveling, or trekking in search of adventure with his family!

Find William on Twitter at www.twitter.com/WilliamStanek and on Facebook at www.facebook.com/William.Stanek.Author.

CPSIA information can be obtained
at www.ICGtesting.com
Printed in the USA
LVHW06s0612200718
584306LV00009B/23/P